Praise for Tim Hardaway and *Killer Crossover*

"Chicago Hall of Famer Tim Hardaway has done what only a few NBA players have done: he left his permanent mark on the game!"

—Isiah Thomas, NBA Hall of Famer

"Tim Hardaway had great handles, a deadly jump shot and the best crossover dribble in the NBA. He also had the heart of a lion. But he was definitely one of the coolest guys you could ever meet. Absolutely an NBA Great."

—Shawn Kemp, six-time NBA All-Star

"When I was a young assistant coach first in the NBA, Tim Hardaway taught me as much about NBA basketball, in particular pick and roll basketball, as any coach ever did."

—Stan Van Gundy, iconic NBA coach and broadcaster

"Tim Hardaway was an excellent player. He didn't have great length but he made up for it with his solid body and tenacity. He could play the point or the big guard spot. He could guard players bigger than him. On offense, he had great quickness and was always a threat to beat his defender off the dribble. His killer crossover was as good as there ever was. I had the pleasure of coaching him in the 2000 Olympics in Sydney (Australia), where we won gold."

—Rudy Tomjanovich, two-time NBA champion coach

KILLER CROSSOVER

KILLER CROSSOVER

MY LIFE FROM THE CHICAGO STREETS TO BASKETBALL ROYALTY

TIM HARDAWAY

WITH JAKE UITTI

FOREWORD BY CHRIS MULLIN

SPORTS PUBLISHING

Sports Publishing books may be purchased in bulk at special discounts for sales promotion, corporate gifts, fund-raising, or educational purposes. Special editions can also be created to specifications. For details, contact the Special Sales Department, Sports Publishing, 307 West 36th Street, 11th Floor, New York, NY 10018 or sportspubbooks@skyhorsepublishing.com.

Sports Publishing® is a registered trademark of Skyhorse Publishing, Inc.®, a Delaware corporation.

Visit our website at www.sportspubbooks.com.

10 9 8 7 6 5 4 3 2 1

Library of Congress Cataloging-in-Publication Data is available on file.

Cover design by Brian Peterson
Cover photo credit: Getty Images
All insert photographs, unless otherwise noted, are courtesy of the author.

Print ISBN: 978-1-68358-506-0
Ebook ISBN: 978-1-68358-507-7

Printed in the United States of America

I want to dedicate this book, of course, to my parents, Gwendolyn and Donald Hardaway.

I also wish to dedicate it to Minne Eubanks (a.k.a. "Mother, Mother"), my brother Donald Hardaway, my grammar school coach Donald Pittman and my high school coaches Bob Walters and Willie Richie. I'd like to recognize all the faculty at Carver High School, including Miss Hunter, Miss Smith, Mr. and Mrs. Sailes and Mr. Owens, to name a few. I'd also like to dedicate this to all my teammates at Kohn Elementary and Carver High School. As well as my uncles and aunties and my cousins. I'd like to also shout out Kyron, Mike Fuller, Louis Fuller, Kim Fuller, Yvette, Sandra and Jackie. To all my friends like Alonzo Meadows, Mike and Donald Reese, JJ Anderson, Vernado Parker, Buster, Benny Henry—this is for you. And all the people at Eckersaw Park and South Shore park. To my sister-in-law Geraldine (aka Koon and Jerry) and my mother-in-law (God rest her soul) Mrs. Miller. And finally to my lovely wife Yolanda, who without you this never would have been possible, son Tim Jr. and daughters Nia and Nina. Thank you with all my heart.

—Tim

For Sparky and the Boys

—Jake

CONTENTS

FOREWORD

MY first memory of Tim is from his first NBA press conference. I'd never really seen him play before that, so when the Warriors drafted him he came in for his introductory press conference and, almost immediately after, wanted to go play pickup. So some of the guys from the Warriors went to play pickup ball the next day and that's how I first got to know him. I remember he was *overly* confident, boisterous and loud. But he also backed it up with his play.

Tim had that rare combination of a young player coming into the league mixed with incredible confidence—somewhat irrational confidence, to be honest—but still confident. You could just see he loved to play the game, to compete. That's what he wanted to do. To play. You could see that was his main focus in life, like all of us at that point in time. With Tim, you had to watch *and* listen—because he was talking all the time!

As a player, he had the whole package. I think with Tim, we were like, *Man, we haven't seen a guy ball like this before!* He was on the smaller side for a guard, but played in the paint and could finish over anyone, it didn't matter the size. He had a unique combination of skills, both inside and out. He loved to play in the post like a big man (unique at the time for a guy under 6 feet tall), but was dynamic in the pick and roll while also being able to knock down threes and floaters.

When you watched and listened to him, you realized the guy was unique. I think that was what kept him apart from a lot of players in the NBA. Such a special combination of skill and confidence. But his game itself was special. There weren't many guys like him at the time. He had a unique body type, a strong lower body and center of gravity. Balance. And he had this crazy change of direction.

Tim could blow by anybody off the dribble at will. No one could keep him in front of them. If you sent a bigger guy at Tim, he would dribble past them. Or if you sent a smaller guy, Tim could take them into the post. There was no answer for what he brought to the court. You don't even see that kind of thing in today's game. Maybe a few guys, but not many. Maybe they can shoot threes, but they can't go to the post or vice versa. But Tim had it all.

As teammates, we fit together perfectly from day one. That was the greatest thing. First and foremost, it was over basketball. He had that love and desire and passion for practicing, for being in the gym. We did everything from play one-on-one or two-on-two to shooting and working out. That's where our bond first started.

And then, over time, our families became close, which is what you hope for with most teammates. You find out that you have more in common than you have differences. I got to meet his mom and dad over time, and then his kids were born and I got to spend time with the whole family. But our relationship first originated in the gym over basketball and just grew from there.

When it came to Run-TMC, I was the first on the team, obviously, because I was the oldest. Mitch Richmond came second and he was just as great a rookie as Tim—Rookie of the Year,

20 points per game, came in as a polished pro from the jump. But with me and Mitch—he was a two-guard and I was playing small forward at the time—we were missing a point guard. And we were fortunate enough to draft Tim, who was the missing piece.

Not just me and Mitch, but the entire team, the entire organization, the entire Bay Area and our fans became energized. We saw this hope with this young nucleus. Not only did our skills fit perfectly, but our personalities—which are all different—wound up fitting perfectly, too. One of us would be talking, the other would be quiet, the third would be ready to jump in. We each had different leadership styles, and all that fit perfectly on the court.

When Tim came in as a rookie, Don Nelson was an established coach and GM of the Year. He had coached in the league for more than a decade, and worked with some incredible players by the time he'd come to Golden State. He not only knew talent, but he knew what needed to be done to bring a contending team together. So, Tim coming in as the starter was great. We had thirty days of training camp and a lot of that stuff was established in practice. We knew our top eight guys. We had our team.

Today, if I had to think of one moment that sums up Tim Hardaway . . . well, there are really so many. Because Tim had two Hall of Fame careers—one with the Warriors and one with the Heat. He had two incredible careers that were both very different. He wasn't blowing by people as much in Miami, but was still as effective with the three-pointer and being a dynamic playmaker and assist guy.

But there's this clip of Tim when we were together in Golden State and we were playing against the Suns. He gets down the lane and delivers a floater over Charles Barkley, and Barkley fouls him. But when Tim makes the bucket, he goes, "Yeah! In your face!" *Right in Barkley's face!* To me, that's Tim. It could have been Magic or Bird or Gary Payton or Barkley—that's just the way he played. He's as genuine and transparent a person as you'll ever see.

—Chris Mullin
NBA Hall of Famer

PREFACE

YOU can't grow up a fan of the NBA in the '90s and not know the name Tim Hardaway. He was a star in every facet of the game, from his signature crossover and trash talking to his buzzer-beaters and culture-defining teams. Little did I know as a burgeoning basketball fan that I would not only work with the great point guard on his memoir, but also have the opportunity to get to know him as a friend and an excellent storyteller. Tim is easy to talk to, he's both honest and forthcoming. He has a clear perspective on who he is. He's not scared. In short, he's *game*.

Tim's story is essential to the history of basketball, but it's also essential on a human level. He grew up in Chicago and suffered the general abuses of an unforgiving, relentless, and at times violent city. He also suffered the specific hardships of an abusive home. Of course, Tim is not alone in that type of upbringing. But he is one of the few to rise up from such an origin story and find himself—through hard work and determination—at the pinnacle of his craft, being a five-time All-NBA player and at one time the best point guard in the league.

Often talking but never snarling, Tim was a wonder on the court. Thanks to his quick-as-lightning handle, and move known as "The Killer Crossover," he became a household name and, as a result, remains basketball royalty. Standing just shy of six feet, Tim wasn't blessed with imposing height or world-class athleticism. But what he did have was a will to always get better. To take on all challenges and never fear the possibility of failure.

We all fall sometimes, but are not defined by our worst days. I still remember where I was when I heard what Tim said about gay people in 2007, and the feeling of disappointment that a hero could be so close minded. But what is more remarkable is the change Tim has undergone since. It's a statement he regrets and it's one he's done everything to make up for. That is the mark of a champion. We are all fallible, we are all mistaken at times, but few of us change. Yet, admirably, that is what Tim did.

In life, the idea is to keep learning and improving. With hope, this book will show how Tim's childhood, growing up around gangs in Chicago, shaped his basketball ability and how he never stopped improving himself. The father of an NBA player (Tim Hardaway Jr.), Tim has been able to achieve a great deal in his life through the years . . . but he wasn't necessarily meant to, given where he came from.

Tim, to me, is exactly the type of person I want to be when I grow up. Accomplished, charismatic, and striving to always be a better person.

—Jake Uitti

PROLOGUE

I'LL always remember February 14, 2007. It was the day my life changed forever. That morning, I made an appearance on *The Dan Le Batard Show* in Miami. I'd talked with Dan plenty of times and felt comfortable on his show. But it was at the end of our conversation that he asked me one more question. It wasn't a "gotcha" question—it was fair, and I was given the space to answer it however I wanted. As it turned out, I said the wrong thing and not only did I shoot myself in the foot, but I hurt a lot of people in the process—something I'll regret for the rest of my life.

Former NBA player John Amaechi, a 6-foot-10 center who'd played a handful of years in the league, had just come out as gay. So, Dan asked me, "last question before we let you go. How do you deal with a gay teammate?" I could have easily said having a gay teammate didn't bother me—let them live their lives and me live mine. That could have been the end of it. Instead, though, I went on a rant, saying I *hated* gay people. Dan rightly pointed out that my statement was bigoted. When we hung up the phone, I had no idea how badly I'd screwed up.

It has taken me fifteen years to make up for what I said and I will continue to do so for the rest of my life. I will go deeper into what happened after I made those comments on Dan's show later in the book but, suffice to say, while I am not proud at all of what I said or how I thought about homosexuality then, what I am proud of today is the growth I've made. I have learned a lot about the people who I'd previously worked to distance myself from. That's a positive outcome, and I hope those efforts have made other people's lives at least a little bit better, too.

In the following pages, you'll read about my life growing up in Chicago, the gang violence that surrounded me, my abusive childhood, my connection to family, and my basketball career from grammar school to NBA All-Star. You'll read about my journey as a husband and father, a coach and, finally, a Hall of Famer. What I'm proud of most, though, is my ability to grow. It's not easy—that's for sure! But it is necessary. I'm truly sorry for what I said to Dan in 2007, and I know I can't demand forgiveness. I just hope I can show that I've become a better man since then.

INTRODUCTION

IT all started with Magic Johnson. That glitzy and glamorous 6-foot-9 point guard for the Los Angeles Lakers is the one responsible for naming my most famous move. It happened in 1991, when my Run-TMC Golden State Warriors were set to play his Showtime Los Angeles Lakers in the second round of the playoffs. Some reporters were asking Magic about the matchup. So, he went through our roster, listing off which player he was concerned with most.

Mitch Richmond, he said, he's the rock. He's going to come down the court and he's going to bully you. He's going to take you to the hole and score over you. Chris Mullin, Magic continued, he's a shooter. He can shoot from anywhere. He has finesse, he's just real smooth. Then he got to me. Tim Hardaway, he said, *the killer crossover*. If you're not ready for it, he's going to cross you up and make you look *bad* on the court.

With that—and without evening knowing it—Magic gave me my signature moniker. The term, The Killer Crossover, stuck with me my entire career. Stephen Curry, another great Golden State Warrior, has called it the greatest signature move in NBA *history*, while Magic has also said that I was the best crossover dribbler that he's ever seen! But fame for a move wasn't something I ever thought would happen. I have to tip my hat and thank Magic for that one.

Maybe he was trying to get on our good side and make us relax a bit before a big series—Magic always had some idea of how to get an edge. But, looking back, I'm very grateful for what he said. Even after I retired and was inducted into the Naismith Memorial Basketball Hall of Fame in 2022, The Killer Crossover has been a part of my life. From playing in Golden State to Miami, from big wins to horrible losses, it's as much a part of me as the name on my birth certificate.

All my life, I've been shorter than just about everyone I've stepped onto the court with. So I had to invent ways to get open, to work hard for every half-inch. From the streets of Chicago to the NBA, I had to develop moves to get past people that were more physically imposing. Guys try to push or steer you one way, so I had to use that to my advantage. Almost like judo, I learned to get their momentum going one way and then I'd switch it up on them. That way, I could beat my man and score.

Here's how The Killer Crossover works: When I'm coming down the court, I'm looking at my defender's feet to decide which way to go. I see which way they're pointing, and when he checks me, I take him one way, against his feet, dip my shoulder, and boom-*boom*, one dribble-*two dribble*. I'm gone. He's lucky if he's still standing. All of a sudden I'm at the rim, shooting over a guy like Hakeem Olajuwon or David Robinson.

Once I make a move and get past my man, I keep him behind me, using my ass or hips—almost like a stiff arm in football. He's trailing me and he's helpless. If someone came to double-team me, I'd hit the open man—like Chris Mullin, Mitch Richmond, or Alonzo Mourning—and it would be over. My dribble would be so fast and tight—it was "in the box," as we used to say;

between my hips and shoulders—that your eyes couldn't track it. Like a magic trick from Houdini.

I remember one game during the 1990–91 season with Golden State, the team that drafted me. It was a Friday, December 7, against my idol, Isiah Thomas, the reigning two-time champ and future Hall of Fame point guard. He and I both grew up in Chicago, but he was five years older. I used to watch his high school games and pattern myself after him. Well, in Oakland that night, his Detroit Pistons were visiting my Warriors, and I had to give him something.

When I got to the league, Isiah used to let me come to his Detroit home when the Warriors played his Pistons. We would eat penne pasta together. I would say, "I don't expect you to take it easy on me tonight." He would nod and give that famous big, bright smile. So, when his team was in Oakland just a few weeks before Christmas, I gave him a *gift* of my own. During the game, Isiah took a shot from the top of the key and missed it.

Mitch got the rebound and passed me the outlet. I dribbled it up the court and Isiah picked me up. Quickly, I went behind my back and took him to the right side of the floor, near the baseline. Then I dribbled the ball back out close to the three-point arc, waited a moment, then put the ball between my legs with a hard dribble left. Isiah followed me that way, but I put another quick dribble on him that I was by him before he could process.

After I scored over the big Pistons center Bill Laimbeer, I ran back on defense. "He left Isiah just nailed to the floor!" the television announcer shouted. When you're playing against a guy you idolized growing up, who you patterned your game after, and you can give him a move like that, it's real special. Just months later, at the end of the season as we faced the Lakers in the playoffs, Magic blessed me with *The Killer Crossover* name. And the rest is history.

Where I grew up in Chicago, it gets so windy on the outdoor courts that you *have* to develop a good handle. Jump shots weren't always possible in the elements, so you had to be a good one-on-one player and score at the rim when the wind wouldn't let you shoot. In college, people knew I had moves, but they didn't have a name for them. But ever since Magic, folks in El Paso at my alma mater started to take notice and invented their own term: the "UTEP Two-Step."

I remember one especially hard practice at UTEP when we didn't even shoot the ball, we just did defensive drills. But afterward, exhausted, I played one-on-one against a teammate. I don't want to call him out of his name, but he was a long, 6-foot-4 guy who could really defend. In that matchup, I crossed him up so hard and got to the rim, dunking the ball. That's when a custodian on the other side of the gym—we didn't even know he was there—let out a real loud, "Ooooooo! Where did *THAT* come from?"

The seeds were planted then. And I can still see that custodian's face. Shocked and proud of me. But even then, I didn't think a lot about it. It took time to marinate. During my NBA career, I've hit game-winning buzzer-beaters. I've matched up with Michael Jordan. I won an Olympic gold medal. But it's that crossover sums my career up best. It's what I'm remembered for. It shows my will and my killer instinct, all of which were born from how I grew up in Chicago.

But when Magic gave out that scouting report, people paid even closer attention. An All-Star already, he allowed me to grow. And my reputation continued in Miami with guys like Pat

Riley and Alonzo Mourning. But I've had plenty of hard times, too (some even self-inflicted). I've gone through a lot and had to adapt over the course of my life. In that way, the crossover really resonates. This extreme move from one side to the other, that's always been the way for me.

1

DONALD AND GWENDOLYN HARDAWAY

MY father Donald Hardaway was a playground legend in Chicago, the city where I grew up. Every weekend, he'd go from park to park with his guys and outduel whatever challengers they found. Often, I'd go with him, even as a little kid. I'd watch them dismantle the other players. My dad was a six-foot-four center who bested guys much bigger than he was. He could rebound with anyone, score on whomever. My dad, who was known around the courts as "Duck," told me something important early on about the game. "There are no positions on the court," he said. "You want to play with the big guys? You better bust your ass in the paint and play hard."

He might play in three or four games on a single Saturday. It would start at 10:30 a.m. and he'd be done by 5 or 6 p.m. Then he'd go out and hang with friends. As I got older, whenever anyone would talk about him, they'd say, "He's a *bad boy*, Tim," meaning he had immense skill on the court and was feared.

Wherever they thought the best game was, they'd go out there to prove dominance. He and his guys were the best street players in the entire city. It was like that movie *White Men Can't Jump*. They'd play in tournaments, parks, indoors, outdoors, and kick ass. They'd take your money and your spirit. But my dad was feared in other ways, too.

My dad was an alcoholic. He liked vodka best, but would drink it all. And he would beat my ass almost as often as we'd play pickup. When you grow up in a household like that, fear is everywhere. My brother and I feared him, though my mother feared him most. She was a small woman, and he would beat her to the point where she had to call the police. But it was a different time back then. The term "domestic violence" wasn't in anyone's vocabulary. And the cops didn't help. That was how it was in the '60s and '70s—especially in my neighborhood. I remember this one woman from down the street. Her husband would beat on her so bad that she ended up shooting him dead. As they questioned her about it, she said she'd gone to the cops enough times that she had to take matters into her own hands. She couldn't take it anymore. And she got off with no trial.

Life was hard in Chicago back then, for us and for everyone in the neighborhood where we lived. But as long as I can remember, I had basketball to turn to. Born on September 1, 1966, my dad put a ball in my hand back when I was just four months old. All I could do at first was roll it back and forth. I started walking before I turned a year old, and so I'd stand and pass the ball (or roll it) to whomever was around, and they'd pass it back to me over and over.

When my father took me around to the city courts, I'd sit on the ball and watch. During time outs, I'd roll it out there. And if he told me not to, I'd just keep sitting on it and stay on the sidelines. I learned the game by watching him. He told me to play wherever I wanted to, but if I wanted to be a big man, I'd have to do what big men did: rebound. Be nasty. Push, shove down low. Learn how to maneuver among the trees. Learn how to set a pick, learn how to roll. "A center can be a point guard if he wants to," he told me. This was before Magic Johnson hit the league. "If you want to dribble up and down, make good decisions."

Duck was a force. The opposite of flashy. He could dunk on people with either hand. He played down low, was bulky and did the dirty things. His buddies said that no one could budge him. He was the rebound king. Later, when I was in grammar school, my coach would teach me the fundamentals. But I learned about attitude from my dad. And when I got old enough, I would go out onto the courts and work on it by myself. I learned how to be tough with the ball. In pickup games, I learned how to thrive in structure-less basketball and then took those lessons to the structured games later in life. The playground influenced everything I did.

* * *

Dad was a truck driver. My mother, Gwendolyn, worked for the city government. They met way back at a mutual friend's house during a small get-together. Six years after I was born, they had another son, my younger brother, Donald, who I always tried to look out for growing up. Our house was on the southeast side of Chicago, in the South Shore area of the city. It was a normal household, as far as I knew—including the violence. But as I got older, I would leave as often as I could to play around the city, from Hyde Park to Pocket Town (those parks can either build or snatch your confidence). I played at the West Side, North Side, wherever there was a good game.

My dad was hard to deal with because of his alcoholism. He was a tough and brutal man. When he came into the house, we would have to walk on eggshells. He wasn't drunk all the time, but when he got that way, coming back from work or after playing ball with his friends, it was difficult for the rest of the family. You had to be church mouse quiet. Couldn't say nothing. It was like that for as far back as I can remember. When he came through that door, we were scared. Didn't want to ruffle any feathers. We didn't want him to get upset. It was really tough—especially on my mother.

She worked during the day in downtown Chicago for the Board of Education until I was in high school. A secretary, she got a good paycheck. She did what she was supposed to do for the family and then came home and cooked and took care of us kids. She always used to say she wasn't a very good cook, but I disagree. She made spaghetti and meatballs, fried fish, Salisbury steak. I used to love her pot roast and greens. There was a deep love in her food, simple but rich. Though, when things were tight, we had to settle for pork and beans out of a can.

When she and my father met, they were deeply in love. But then things began to break apart. It starts with one slap across the face and snowballs from there. A woman makes a police report. Then the police come back for another. But they don't do shit for you. And after the police come, it only gets worse. He gets upset and takes it out on you. If you left, he'd come find you. It was just like those episodes on television, on the news, in the movies. That stuff is real, and we lived it. So when I see people talk about it on TV nowadays, it makes me cringe. I understand how they feel and what they've been through.

It was hard, worse than any blistering Chicago winter. That behavior can wreck your brain and make you ill—both mentally and physically. Back then there was no one to talk to, nowhere to share your feelings. You just had to deal with it. The toughest was having to watch our mother go through all of it. Dad would pull her hair. She'd run into my room and he'd pull her out. Abusive shit. I wasn't strong enough to do anything about it, either. I tried to get involved, especially as I got older. But he was six-four and I've never been a big person. He outweighed me by 150 pounds. These days, my brother and I never talk about it. Not a word between each other.

We hear stories like ours and just look at each other and keep moving. So far, I haven't sought therapy. I always thought, *What's therapy going to do for me? Keep me safe?* I grew up understanding how to be patient. How to understand people and what they go through. It was as if I got a PhD in sociology. In the streets, at my house. I understood what life could look like from all angles. Books can't prepare you, I don't care how many you've read. It's about what you're going to do in *this* instant, right *here*, right *now*. You have to know when to keep your mouth shut. How and when to diffuse a situation. How to move around a house without being heard. How not to get slapped, how not to get your ass kicked. Because my father wouldn't even wait to get into the house—he'd whoop you in front of the neighbors. When you're an alcoholic, anything can set you off—especially if you need your liquor. To this day, I can walk into any room and immediately tell who is on edge, who should be avoided at all costs. It's a sixth sense that's born and grows quickly. You'd think a childhood like that would've pushed me to never leave my bedroom. To hide or be a wallflower. But I had a spirit that even my upbringing couldn't contain.

I would always get in trouble. One day my dad said not to cross these certain railroad tracks by the house of one of his friends off 126th Street. We'd gone there to spend time with his family. "Don't play with the trains," he said. "You could lose a limb, or worse." But later that day, he saw me out near there messing by those tracks. He came right up to me and slapped me so hard in front of people. Then I had to sit in time out while the other kids played. He was right to be angry, but that hit really smarted. It was his way of trying to teach me a lesson and I had to learn the hard way (no pun intended).

Another time he beat my ass at my friend's house and told me to stand in the corner for the rest of the day while everyone else was out playing. If he caught me in a lie, he'd whoop me. In the summers, he'd tell me not to let any of my friends in the house. But one day when I was in sixth grade, I tested him. As a kid, you always think you can outsmart your parents but, on this occasion, I was wrong. I'd invited a friend over, thinking Dad wouldn't be home for a while, but he came home early from work and found us. He waited until that night, but made sure I felt my mistake. "I'm going to beat your butt *nekked*," he told me. "You're going to beat me *nekked*?" I repeated. "Yes," he said. And he did just that. He made me take all my clothes off and he beat me. From then on, I never went against his word. It's not like I was a bad kid—I wasn't setting things on fire or hurting anyone. It's just how it was with him. It's hard for me to even talk about it now. Today, my parents are still alive and this isn't information I've volunteered often. I fear if someone reads this, they may look at them differently and they'll feel ashamed.

Understand, I'm only saying this to show that I didn't come from a place of ease. And for those out there like me, it's *okay*. It's not your fault and you can make a different life for yourself. Like I did in the NBA, putting all my efforts into the game of basketball. I don't want my parents to feel embarrassed for this. Because I know they already do. But I also can't help that this is my story. That this is my brother's story. This was what we saw as kids and how we got introduced to the world. Thankfully, over time, things changed (Dad has been sober since 1996). But it didn't happen all at once, and it certainly wasn't easy.

* * *

My father's father wasn't an alcoholic—though he used to run moonshine from Chicago to Mississippi. He used to give us little presents like new headphones back in the day, too. My father's mother, Julia Hardaway, who passed away just a few years ago, also never drank. Neither did Dad's two sisters. His mother would wonder where my father got it from. His anger, his drinking. It was unexplained. My father would get pulled over for DUIs but, like domestic violence, they weren't given the same credence they are today. I mean, it wasn't even until 1973 that the Supreme Court ruled women had the right to abortion (though the same court has since nullified that). It wasn't only my mother who was terrified. Women were scared. There was nowhere to turn.

I mean, I guess it could have been worse. There were even more awful eras in American history. Times when entire families were slaughtered. But knowing that doesn't make our situation any easier. There was another time when I left the house as a twelve-year-old. Dad told me to be back before the lights in the house came on. I was a mile or two from home, hooping. And, of course, I forgot about the time. So, when I got back, he asked, "Do you want to be on punishment, or get a butt whooping?" The first would be easier but last longer. So I told him just to beat my ass.

The next day, I went to Rosenblum Park and he told me to be home before dark. We were having a good run. I was going against grown men, not kids my age. They were in their twenties, thirties, forties. And I was out there holding my own. But I got home late and got another butt kicking. He said, "Where were you!" And I told him the truth, but I guess he didn't believe me. He thought I was out causing trouble, being reckless. The next day, I went to the courts at the park again. About an hour into the game, I saw my dad's truck pull up. *Oh lord*, I whispered to myself. The guys heard me and asked what was wrong. I started *shaking*. "That's my dad up there," I said. "He's going to beat my ass."

But the guys just looked around as if they couldn't see him. "Who?" one said. "Duck?" That confused me. "I don't know no Duck," I said. But then they pointed to my father. "Him?" I nodded, "Yeah, that's my dad." They were surprised to find out my dad was one of the local legends. "That's Duck!" My father called me over to his truck. "Tim," he shouted. "Come 'ere!" So, I went over, scared. "You can ask them," I said. "I've been here the past two days hooping. You can ask them!" The guys spoke up for me. "Yeah, Duck. He's been here the whole time! You might have something there. *He's* good!" Dad looked at the group. "For real?"

The guys vouched for me. Then my old man looked down at me in my eyes and said, "I'm sorry." That was the first time he'd ever said those two words to me. "I owe you," he said. Suddenly, he felt a moment of shame for having kicked my ass so bad those two times, just for playing ball and losing track of the time. It's hard to look back and think about those moments, hard to talk about them. But that's how I got my tough skin. I'm not grateful for it. That would be sick. But I can see the cause and effect. To this day, it surprises me that he apologized that afternoon. It must have been during a moment of sobriety.

Apologizing is hard. It means you messed up, but also that you may have messed up dozens of times before. I can forgive a man for wronging me, even my father. But I won't ever forget it. I grew up in what felt like a warzone at times thanks to him and the gangs in Chicago. Violence was everywhere. It wasn't just gangs, though. Even my own cousins tried to pick on me. I'm not saying this to engender sympathy. I don't need that. I'm just telling it like it is. My cousins were bigger and we'd wrestle. They'd give me frogs on my arm. Sometimes they'd take to tickling me until I was in tears (that's why I'm not ticklish today).

I wanted to be big like them, but I was always smaller. I had to learn to get them on the sly. Before they got me. I'd have to slap them on the head and run out of the house in a rare chance at freedom. But they'd get me back, push me up against the wall in the house and sometimes punch me in the stomach. They'd say, "Don't cry! You better not cry or I'll give you another one!" The adults would be upstairs, but I couldn't go to them to tell on my cousins. So I kept my mouth closed. That's how I toughened myself up. How I got stronger, for better or worse. That was just the way it was. You always had to be on the lookout.

* * *

That mentality made it to the playground, too. As I grew up from a kid and entered grammar school, it was all about toughness. When I was young, I would play all types of sports. Football, baseball, soccer, volleyball. I was short (in grammar school, I was about 5-foot-3 at a time when some of my peers were 6-foot-6 or even 6-foot-9 by the eighth grade!), so I'd play running back or sometimes even quarterback on the football field. I could throw the ball and run fast. Despite my size, I've always been athletic. We never had shoulder pads when playing in the neighborhood. Just your sneakers and a ball. Sometimes you'd go for a long pass or go across the middle and, if you did, you'd better watch yourself. Some kids left the game unable to walk. You'd hit your head on rocks, run into poles, you name it.

Charles Darwin would have been proud of us—only the strong survived. On the diamond, I liked to pitch and was good at it. But I found the outfield boring, so I stopped playing. I also liked playing volleyball. We had volleyball tournaments in grammar school, playing different classes around the city. And my coach would tell me that I wasn't supposed to step in front of my teammates and take their shots but, he added, when the game was on the line, it would be good for me to do so. I had to give them confidence during the game but, if we needed a point, I could take things into my own hands. Together, we won the seventh grade tournament.

Growing up how I did, I became observant. Alert. I was smart, even though I hardly ever did my homework. When I played basketball, even as a youngin, I knew how to lead by example, how to direct people. "Set a pick for him, get that guy open!" I'd say to a teammate dribbling the ball at the top of the key. "Move, cut! Set a back screen!" Some older guys would ask me how I knew how to play this way. I'd just say, "Look and learn." I knew how to pay attention to details. It was all right there on television when we watched the game. It was like the game slowed down when I watched it. I could see every move.

There were so many legends from Chicago—Isiah Thomas, Doc Rivers, Cazzie Russell, Terry Cummings, Mo Cheeks, Rickey Green, Mitchell J. J. Anderson, and more. I'd just take stuff from their game and incorporate it into my own. Whether on TV or in a high school gym, I watched what they did and made it my own. I was on a team with Rickey Green, who was drafted by the Golden State Warriors in 1977 and was an All-Star with the Utah Jazz in 1984, and just by watching him play twice a week I found myself ahead of the game. Rickey would even ask *me* how I handled the ball so well, and I would ask him how he got it up the court so quickly. We gave each other tips, even though he'd already been in the league for a decade. That's how you get better: never stop learning.

Being so close to current and future pros like that would give me the confidence to play better. It's not only the physical tricks we traded but knowing that I was accepted by big names like that made me feel good about my game. Like I belonged. You know it when you belong with the big guys—they pick you for their team, give you high-fives or say things like "You hoppin' now, boy!" Indeed, brains-plus-trauma is a potent combination. If I had talented guys on my team, we'd be unstoppable. If I had a weaker squad, I'd do everything I could to instill energy and strengthen them. I did the same thing when I played soccer. At day camps during little tournaments, my teams would always do well. My secret? I tried hard and was never scared to fail.

My camp counselors would ask me, "How do you know how to play soccer?" And I'd tell them I saw it on TV. I was coordinated and observant. Those were the keys for me. Those traits alone could keep me going. They got me through the days of getting picked on. When you're short, you get picked on. That's a fact—especially if you want to be a basketball player. For me, it started in sixth grade. The other kids would say, "You can't play!" or "You're too small!" But it just drove me harder. If you can handle it, things like that just make you stronger as a person. It turns your mind into metal, and iron sharpens iron. It makes you pay attention to detail. It makes you understand that if you want to be the type of player you dream about, then you have to deal with naysayers and shit talkers. Most people, all they do is talk. Those who can't do something just talk about it. The trick is to be someone that can do it. So, you just work on your game. Alone. In the cold. In the snow. Everything is about being the best. You realize that it's death to stick around lower levels. That's the benefit of being picked on. That's the benefit of your peers choosing other people ahead of you. You tell yourself, *Okay, they think HE'S better? Time to show 'em he's not.* You get relentless.

Today, I am 5-foot-11 and three-quarters of an inch tall. And while that's not short for the average man, it is for an NBA player (who average around 6-foot-6!). Growing up, my parents thought I might not even get as tall as I am now. My dad was always saying, "When you going to grow, boy?" But I could still play. In sixth grade, I tried out for the class team and did well. The coach told me to come back and try out for the seventh-grade team. So I did that and did well there. Then he said,

"Come out for eighth grade tryouts." But even if I was good enough to play on that team, he cautioned, I wouldn't because of my height. But I played so well in the tryouts that I made the squad.

The first uniform Coach gave me fit like a dress. My mother had to alter it. At some point in grammar school I got a little growth spurt, but that was it for me. Thankfully, I have long arms.

And while I didn't have long legs, I've always had quick hands and quick feet. You have to lean on your attributes, not your shortcomings. I did what I had to do. When I was young, I dribbled the ball everywhere. I'd dribble it to pick up milk from the corner store or when my dad asked me to buy him cigarettes or pop. I knew by the time I hit sixth grade that basketball, more than anything else, was what I wanted to do. What I wanted to be best at.

My grammar school coach was a man named Donald Pittman. He taught me my foundation, teaching me how to be effective from anywhere on the court. I'd seen my dad do it in real life and now I wanted to learn how—to be just like him. So Coach Pittman taught me from square one. He showed me how to post up. How to drop-step. How to shoot with my left *and* right hands. How to take jump-hooks. How to go to the hoop fearlessly. How to work hard. How to take a hit and give one back and still make the shot. He taught me how to run a team and be a captain. He taught me how to be a leader.

One afternoon, he took me out of school to go on a drive. It was in 1977, if I remember correctly. I was in sixth grade and eleven years old, and we went to the city's International Amphitheatre. He wanted to show me a star guard who was playing for St. Joseph's in the Chicago high school semifinals. Coach Pittman said, "I want you to check this little guy out. He's No. 11." So I didn't take my eyes off him. He was killing everybody. Dribbling, shooting, scoring, defending. "That's how *you* play," Coach Pittman said. "ME?" I replied. "Yes," he said. "That's how you play. You make your team better. You give your team confidence like he does."

Coach gave *me* confidence that day. As we sat there watching the future NBA Hall of Famer from St. Joseph's, I began to think about my future as a hooper. I wanted to play the game the way it was supposed to be played. I wasn't thinking about the pros or even college. I just wanted to prepare my team to win and get better. "I don't play like him!" I said. Then, without missing a beat Coach Pittman said—and I'll never forget it—"Believe me, yes you do." That's when I started patterning my game after the great Isiah Thomas. Still, though, despite what Coach said, I didn't see stars in my eyes. When your life is so hard as a young person, you don't get an ego too quickly. At least, I didn't.

* * *

My mom and dad separated when I was in the sixth grade. You never want something like that to happen, but I was glad it did for my safety and that of my family. Still, it was hard to get over. My mother wasn't taking his shit anymore. She left him in 1978, but even then it took him some time to figure it all out, to understand what he needed to do to get sober. We had to stay away from him for two years. He didn't want to let my mother have the house. To get away, mom took us to a friend's house and we stayed there until she figured her next move. He knew he couldn't bother her there because the woman she was staying with was the ex-wife of one of his friends. That man wasn't going to let my father mess with his ex and their kids. Wasn't going to let him bang on their door at all hours, not with his children there sleeping. Dad knew he'd have to answer to the guy if he acted up. So he had to leave it alone. All he could cling to was spite. It was a smart move by my mother. After they formally divorced, which was around the time I graduated grammar school, he was out of the family house for good and we could move back in. My parents never got back together, and it took me the better part of a year to be willing to see him again. I still loved him, but I knew I had to have space.

A little later, mom got herself a new job. She knew she was going to have to take care of herself, so she got a gig as a postal worker delivering mail. Good benefits and a pension. She walked neighborhoods putting letters and packages into people's mail slots in hot summers and snowy winters. She did it all for me and my brother—her boys. She always talked about *her boys.* She sacrificed for us, and did an incredible job raising us, too. She would take days off from work without pay so that she could show me the bus routes I needed to take in order to get to school every day.

She always wanted to make sure I was safe and that she knew where I would be during the week. Mom was selfless. As far as her new postal job, she didn't like it *one bit.* But she worked it diligently, day in and day out, until I finished college and made the NBA. Once I made the pros, she said she was done with working altogether! "You're in the NBA now," she said. "You can take care of me now." And that was just fine by me. I could take care of her for a little while then. It was my turn to carry the load for her in that way. And I was proud to do it. I wanted to get her everything her heart desired.

* * *

As a kid, I either wore Chuck Taylor's or PRO-Keds. I used to like the all-white ones. My mother would tell me, "You can only have one leather pair of shoes for the year." So I would get them right before my first basketball game of the season. And I took care of them bad boys like they were my babies. All year long, I felt so lucky to even have one pair. Every day after school I'd come home and clean them up. If they needed white-out, I'd paint them. I would scrub them with a toothbrush and soap, too. These shoes were *mine*, so I had to take care of them. I rarely ever got something I wanted, so when I did, I had to dote over them daily.

Of course, quietly, I wanted more than I got. Growing up, we weren't poor, but we didn't have money to throw around. Not with how hard my dad drank when I was a kid. If I ever asked my parents for something, I was always ready to hear *no*. If you ask a question, you should always be ready for that. If I didn't *need* a new pair of shoes, I knew I wouldn't get one. To this day and all through my NBA career, when someone told me no, I understood. Today, I often hear kids ask their parents, "Why not?" And I think, *wow*. If you asked my parents "Why not?" in the '70s, you'd get your ass handed to you. And if you said it the wrong way, you might have been knocked out on the spot.

Back then, you learned how to keep your mouth shut. Maybe that's why I talked so much trash on the court—I was making up for lost time. Yes, you had to keep your mouth shut around your parents back then. They worked too hard for you to talk back. At worst you could give a face and walk away, but even that was risky. Patience is an important virtue. You've got to be patient. That doesn't mean you shouldn't work hard. It just means that not everything comes to you right away. Sometimes you have to create your own future with your own two hands.

* * *

As a boy, some of my favorite memories involved creativity. I had a good group of friends, and we used to make stuff all the time. We made our own basketball rims to put up around the house. We also rode bikes around the city and made our own fun. We used to shag balls for golfers and make a little bit of money. That's what I miss most when I think back on my life. Hanging around the neighborhood with my buddies. I miss those days in grammar school. The way we could find joy in the littlest things. We went from park to park, basking in the camaraderie between friends. Playing football, fighting each other on the playground in good fun. Just learning about the world as kids do. On weekends, someone would come over to your house and just sit on the porch waiting for you. Maybe as early as seven or eight in the morning. They'd knock on your door and before you knew it there would be half-a-dozen guys hanging around. You'd talk for an hour and then someone would suggest getting the bikes. Then you'd throw some decent clothes on and be out all day. That's freedom, and something many kids this generation have no clue about. It was definitely a different time, but it was a special time.

The best food in the neighborhood was at this place called Italian Fiesta. They had the greatest pizza. Thin crust. And

Harold's Chicken, which is still there—don't get me started on their bird. There was Leon's Barbeque, too. There, you could get a plate of French fries smothered in BBQ sauce for 75 cents. That would fill you up all day, enough to play basketball until the night set in. The fries would be so hot that they'd burn the roof of your mouth. Your hands would be sticky and your tongue would be on fire. Sometimes four of us chowed down on one of those big plates. It was great. A group of boys just getting out into the world.

You need friends like that in your life when you're coming up. Like my buddy Alonzo Meadows, who lived two doors down. We're still friends to this day. Ever since 1977. We'd run around the city together, testing each other, having each other's backs. Then when you came home at night, if no one was watching the TV, you'd sit yourself down and put on *Hawaii Five-0, Happy Days, Kung Fu, Lost in Space.* We'd watch Godzilla and King Kong movies. We only had the three network channels and WFLD on channel 32 where the cheap horror movies would come on. Those scary ones where you couldn't look away.

* * *

Sometimes, when kids know they're good at sports, they start to think about Division-I schools or the pros. For me, it wasn't about that. The only thing I started thinking about was the pro-am at Chicago State University. I wanted to be a good high school player, and I wanted to play in that game. When I was a kid, I'd get there at 5 p.m. for a seven o'clock game because they were so packed. That's where I saw Isiah Thomas, Terry Cummings, Rickey Green, Rod Higgins, Mo Cheeks, Reggie

Theus, Mark Aguirre, J. J. Anderson, and even Michael Jordan come through and lace 'em up. To me, that was *making it.* The best to come through Chicago were welcome there. That was the badge of honor I dreamed of. If I played there, it meant I was one of the best in town.

To get there, during the summers, I played on a team based in a community center near my house. Those were the best organized runs available when I was in grammar school. There were no AAU or traveling teams. Back then, we played outside. What that taught me most of all was how to fall. You didn't want to bust your ass on concrete and get those strawberry scrapes on your knees or the palms of your hands. Didn't want cuts on your elbows or forearms. You learned how to keep your balance. Today, most kids only play in indoor gyms. They don't know the dangers of asphalt. But that's how you got better.

Little did I know, though, that should have been the same mentality I had for my schoolwork. There were dangers everywhere in Chicago, including being lazy in school. Sadly, I succumbed to that. I struggled in the classroom—not because I was dumb or couldn't handle the work, but because I didn't focus. And I paid for it. It's embarrassing to say, but I flunked and had to repeat the eighth grade. If people were ridiculing me before because I was short, now they had even more ammunition. I wasn't slow or stupid, but I sure made myself look it by failing. It didn't help that my home life was a mess or that my parents' marriage was falling apart before my eyes.

What was worse? Until I got my grades up that second go-round, I couldn't play on the team. My mother was not happy at all. In fact, she actually thought my coach held me back so that we could win another grade school championship with me back again in eighth grade. We'd already won a bunch my first eighth grade year, but I told her that wasn't the case. I'd messed up all on my own, not doing my work. I'd just been going to school, occupying blank space. I only cared about basketball and the local tournaments and the games against other schools. For those not from the area, Chicago really cares about its grammar school and high school basketball leagues.

But when I repeated the year, all the coaches would let me do were drills and calisthenics, like running the stairs and wind sprints. I wasn't allowed to play in any of the scrimmages or the games. In the end, it was a wakeup call—one I sorely needed and one that was good for me to experience at such a young age. Thankfully, I managed to turn my situation around. I passed grammar school and was able to move on into high school. That wasn't anything easy, either. In the warzone of inner-city Chicago, it's never just one thing out to get you. There are always landmines.

2

CARVER HIGH

THE older I got in Chicago, the more gangs and fighting through them seemed to be part of my life. Today, as I write this, there are still gangs doing horrible stuff in the city, and it breaks my heart. As I approached high school, it was especially bad. The gangs were constantly trying to recruit me and my buddies to join their ranks. I had to run from them more times than I could count. Down alleys, hiding under cars. Sometimes I had to pull snow in front of me as I hid underneath automobiles so that the gangs couldn't find me. Once I got to high school, you couldn't go in certain bathrooms because that's where gangs like the Disciples or the Vice Lords hung out. You couldn't wear your hat brim a certain way without offending some of them. You'd have to use an out-of-the-way bathroom upstairs and be late to class just to avoid them. Where I lived, the main gang was the Vice Lords. Today, there is an estimated thirty-five thousand members in that gang alone, spanning dozens of cities around Illinois and Michigan. Founded in 1957, they're one of the oldest street and prison gangs in Chicago. Sometimes four or five of them would chase me. You can't fight four or five motherfuckers at a time every day. It's impossible. So I had to plan long, circuitous routes home to avoid them. While I never wanted to be in one, their members were everywhere.

When I took the bus back and forth from school, which took an hour and a half each way and included several transfers (that's how dedicated I was to attend the right school for my sports career), I'd have to travel through three different gang territories. It got to the point where I had to keep my head on a swivel so that I wouldn't get knocked out. Somebody might punch you in the dome for no reason, just because they could. My father told me to always be on alert and aware where I was at all times. "You better know what's going on around you," he said. It's strange how that skill transferred to the basketball court later in my life. At the parks, you had to know which gangs were there. The city was just overflowing with drugs and violence, and it was easier to get pulled in then to stay out.

I never wanted to be part of it. I wanted to get out of Chicago, not die on the streets. I recall hearing a story about Isiah Thomas's mother. She used to sit on her front porch on the west side to keep the gangbangers away from her house. She'd tell them that her children were off limits. Back then, if you gave members an inch, they might literally take over your house. It sounds crazy, but even with your parents right there, they'd come in and start taking over the place as if it was theirs. If you showed weakness, they'd come for you and get you. It got to the point where you had to have people have your back. Thankfully, Dad knew guys who helped with that.

* * *

When I'd finished grammar school and I was getting ready to go to high school, my mother and I visited Fenger High School, which also required a two-bus trek from my house. The place, which opened in 1893, is one of the worst schools in the entire country. Back then, there was a lottery for kids and, depending on where you were chosen, that's just where you went. Lottery makes it sound good, though, and Fenger was far from that. I'd heard it was bad, but when my mother and I visited, I found out just how awful it was. If you've ever seen the Morgan Freeman movie *Lean on Me*, it was like that. When we got there, we walked through the hallways and saw it was entirely fucked up.

You might think I'm lying, but I remember we got just halfway down the hall and saw drugs, gangs, and broken furniture everywhere. There was no control. We got just a few steps and my mother, who'd named me after a biblical figure, said out loud, "Oh *HELL* no!" We turned around and walked out and back to the bus stop. When we got home, she called the school district, the principal of my grammar school, and my coach, and said, "Tim is NOT going to that school. Y'all figure out what y'all got to do. But he is NOT going there. There is no damn way!" Her plan worked, and I was sent to Carver Area High School.

Today, I hear that Fenger is still terrible. Who knows what would have happened to me if I had been forced to go there. I'm damn sure I wouldn't have become what I did. So, thank God I got out of it. Carver, though, was no barrel of laughs, either. Not only was it tough at first, but it took me ninety minutes just to get there and another ninety to get home. I thought I must have had the longest commute in the city, but I found out people were taking the bus from the west side of the city out to Carver, which was more than two hours. I had to get up at five thirty in the morning and make the 6:25 bus to get there on time.

When I got to high school, I thought I was going to start on the varsity team and be an instant star. But I had another rude awakening. Being a freshman is tough. For me, as a basketball player, I knew I was better than a lot of the guys on the team. The Chicago city courts and parks taught me that. But you have to wait your turn because of seniority. I wasn't crying about it, but you'd hear some guys yapping about how good they are when you know they're weak. Hearing them fueled me to bust their asses in practice and get better so that I could have my day. I wanted to be better than them and show them I was.

Though now in high school, I still wasn't tall, but my handle with the ball was excellent and I could shoot pretty well from outside. I was quick and knew how to lead a team, even as a freshman. But as hard as I worked on the court, I tried to stay humble. As I went through high school, I was lucky to have a lot of people in my corner. One teacher in particular, Ms. Hunter, would say, "Let me get my safety pin out and make sure your head isn't getting too big, Tim!" She was our gym teacher and one of my favorites.

Freshman year was tough. I was terrified to go to high school at first. New beginnings. New territory. New atmosphere. New people to meet and figure out. There were older people in school whose lives you had no connection to, no experience with. You didn't know where they came from or what they might do. I had to be alert all over again and keep my head on a swivel. The lives these new people had to go through each and every day—how would they impact yours? I didn't know who to trust, so I had to rely on the people skills I'd learned in grammar school to get my bearings. What made it harder was that the basketball coach put me on varsity right away. While it was what I wanted, in theory, I'm not sure it was what was best for me.

It might have been better if I had played a year on junior varsity for a season to ramp up. The older kids on the team took offense to me being promoted so quickly. They saw me as a threat, even though I was shorter than most of them. So some of them treated me badly, picking fights and promising more. Some just talked to me like I was a dog. I was out there by myself, too. No older brother or sister to teach me the ropes. No one to vouch for me. I was the oldest in the family, so I had to figure it all out quickly. Plus, with the school being far from home, I didn't have any of my buddies with me to help. As far as the team went, I played in the games, but my minutes were often yanked around. One game I'd start and then the next I wouldn't play at all.

It's like the coach, Bob Walters, couldn't make up his mind—he had a lot of players in his ear telling him how he should or shouldn't be playing me. I didn't want to upset the team or make anyone dislike me, so I knew I had to keep quiet and just wait my turn. In the end, the whole year was pretty disappointing. I'm not sure what I was expecting, but it just didn't go how I'd thought it would. How I dreamed high school could be. But that's life. There were a lot of disgruntled feelings. But all I wanted to do was play. What made it worse was my dad was coming to games all drunk and shitty. I had to ignore it, but he was loud, pointing at people and yelling.

I had to shake it off and just push ahead. There was no time to waste. There was a lot of talent on the team but, then again, there was a lot of talent in Chicago. I mean, every high school was stacked. We played Mendel Catholic High School, a local powerhouse, during a Thanksgiving game my freshman year and got our asses whooped. We lost to them by about 50 points. That was another growing experience. I knew some of the guys on their team and that summer, they wouldn't let me live it down. "Yeah, we blew y'all motherfuckers out!" Mendel had guys who were six-nine, six-ten, and seven-feet tall on their front line.

Their guards were six-four or six-five, and I was still just five-ten. It was definitely a learning experience, to say the least. In that year's state playoffs we lost early, but I knew we'd be back next year, better and ready. Outside of basketball, I didn't do much of anything. I made friends here and there but I never went on any dates with girls. I just went to school, practice, home, did homework, and went to sleep. I tried to survive. In the summer after my freshman year, I played in tournaments like the John B. McClendon league on the west side, near the University of Chicago, trying to improve. And if I ever lost a game, it stuck with me for days until I could get a win.

Other than that, I mostly stayed around my house and worked on getting better. I played against grown men at South Shore High School near my house. I spent some of the days riding my bike around with my friends, eating fries with barbecue sauce and playing ball at nearby parks. It was all about basketball and all about improving. So when my sophomore year came around, I was ready to take more control of the team. To start making a name for myself. My mind was growing, as was my maturity. In one game late in the year, I blocked another guy's shot, pinning his stuff on the backboard. We went down the other way and I scored a layup.

After the game, I was with my dad and some guys he hung out with, and we were headed out to get something to eat. I turned to one of them and said, "Yeah, man, you see me pin that shot on the glass?" But the old guy stopped me. His name was Moe, and was one of my dad's best friends. Moe said, "Look, you little bitty motherfucker. You don't write your story. You let other people write it. Don't brag on yourself." That was his way of saying, "Do you want me to get the safety pin?" From then on, I shut up. I didn't talk about myself or build myself up to other people. That always stuck with me. I'd let anyone but me do it.

We had a good year my sophomore season but I thought we could have been better and advanced in the playoffs if we had more seasoning. So I had a talk with Coach Walters. The team was better, but I knew we had a lot of work to do if we wanted to compete against the city's top schools. I wanted to prove that anyone I played against simply wasn't in my league. I told him that if we didn't start to play better teams in my junior year that I'd leave Carver. I told him that I wanted to show what I could do, and the only way I could do that was if we played in marquee matchups. My old grammar school coach was now the varsity coach at South Shore, and I knew I could transfer there.

I wanted to play Roberson High School, King High School, and Crane High School. Places that everyone knew were great. People thought their point guards were better than me, but I knew they weren't. Even if we lost, it would make the team better and I could showcase my talent. To his credit, Coach Walters made it happen. Things were looking up. After my sophomore year, even the gangs started to leave me alone. They knew I had talent and that gang life wasn't for me. "He's going somewhere," they'd say. They actually made sure to keep me safe. It was a huge turnaround from even months before.

Maybe that gave me confidence because, around this time, I told my dad to stop attending my games if he was going to keep coming drunk. "Dad, I love you," I said, "but you're embarrassing me. I'd rather you just not come to the game if you're going to be fucked up." That was rough on him. I could see it in his eyes. But it wasn't something he could fight. My mother had already left him and now he was hearing it from me, that I couldn't stand to be around him. Dad knew I was good and now he knew he was messing with my future. That wasn't an easy pill for him to swallow. But he stopped coming by for a while. If he wanted to see his boys, he knew he'd have to change.

* * *

Going into my junior year, Coach Walters set up a good slate of opponents for us. He did the right thing by me. He set up games at neutral sites, as well as at our gym and theirs. I knew what I could do against the city's top talent but, what's more, it helped my teammates grow and realize their skill levels. They tested themselves, and it opened up their games, too. My leadership paid off again in that way. All I wanted to do was get better and prove what we could do. In the playoffs that year, we went a little further than in the previous seasons, despite harder competition.

While we still lost in the second round, the following season looked bright. It was also looking good for me on a personal level. In February 1984, near the end of my junior year, I met the woman who'd one day become my wife. Throughout high school, I spent time with a few girls here and there, but nothing serious. That was until I met Yolanda. She was going to another school, and one night I met her by the gym when I was out there scouting another player. My dad, sober, drove me to the game and when we arrived snow flurries were falling. But when he and I walked out after, it was coming down like a blizzard.

Shit, I thought, *now I have to get it all off the car*. It was a tedious process and one I had to do often in the winter. It wasn't especially cold, but there was maybe a foot of snow on the car. As I was getting ready to get it off, that's when I saw her. I did a double take and looked again. "Dad," I said, brashly, "why don't you go ahead and get this snow off the car. I'll be right back. I need to go talk to this girl and get her number." I surprised even myself. You didn't tell your father back then to clean the snow off himself—especially my dad. But I knew I had to talk to this girl. I saw her and just said, *"Damn!"*

She was tall and slender, about 5-foot-8 and light-skinned. When you see somebody like that, everything in your mind screams that they're the one for you. There is an irrepressible urge to go over and talk to them. That's the way it is, and that's the way it was on that snowy night. Of course, I didn't know she was going to be the woman I'd marry and she didn't know either, but the spark of something good was there. I knew if I didn't go over and get her number, I might regret it for the rest of my life. It wasn't exactly the most convenient time with the snow coming down, but *fuck it*.

I walked up to her, all smooth and shit, and asked her name. "Yolanda Adkins," she said. I found out she was a year older than me and about to graduate from high school. I told her what I was doing, how I was there with my dad scouting, how I was a ball player. "I just wanted to ask you for your number so I can give you a call," I said sweetly. When she gave me her digits, I was so hyped! I walked back to the car—you know that strutting pimp walk with all the swagger? That was me. I was cheesing from ear to ear. *Yeah, I got that number!* But then I got back to the car and the snow was still covering the car. My dad hadn't lifted a finger. There went my big head!

But dad was smiling, like, *Yeah, that's my son.* At least he'd put the key in the ignition and warmed the car up. Dad was still the same short-tempered guy, but by now he wasn't drinking. He wasn't loud, acting a fool for the time being, pointing at people like you do when you're drunk. He'd gotten sober after my mother had left him. He took it all hard, but managed to stay clean for a while. Maybe he'd slip up here and there, maybe for a few weeks. But he realized he didn't like himself all fucked up. So he worked hard to stop for long stretches.

He finally realized he wasn't okay with his head hurting, with his money gone, with losing his family. Wasn't cool with the dark road he was walking down. His sobriety would last until I was out of college. After that, he went through another relapse. In the meantime, to stop, he went to treatment centers (he's still in AA today!). He thought he could beat his addiction, but sometimes it takes multiple efforts. Addiction is a life-long disease and one that people struggle with every day or even every hour. I'm proud of all the times he tried to help himself, and while I don't forget all the issues we had, I know how to forgive them.

* * *

My path to the NBA wasn't yet clear while I was in high school. In fact, in my junior year, I wasn't getting a single college recruitment letter. Not one. Nobody wanted me. No one came to see me, no schools called. Except UTEP and the team's graduate assistant, Rus Bradburd, who was also from the Chicago area (and is now an excellent author), near Lincoln Park. He'd heard about me after a UTEP assistant, Tim Floyd, went to a Nike camp where people were talking me up, even though I wasn't at the camp (probably because people thought I was too small). On Floyd's advice, Bradburd tracked me down. He first saw me at playing at South Shore Park.

Rus later said that it looked as if I had eyes in the back of my head and that I was hitting every jumper, despite the wind. He asked around about me and found out I was the city's best-kept secret. So, late in my junior year season, he met me and told me about Texas at El Paso. As I started researching the place, I saw that Hall of Famer Nate "Tiny" Archibald went there when the school was called Texas Western. I also saw that the school was the first all-Black team to win an NCAA championship. UTEP was also the first school in the south to integrate its sports programs. Coach Walters pushed me to sign early, in part, because of that fact.

The basketball team had beaten the all-white University of Kentucky team, coached by Adolph Rupp, in 1966 (the year I was born). That UTEP squad had Willie Cager and Bobby Joe Hill, and was coached by Don Haskins, who was still there when Rus talked to me about the place. It had a history of small guards like Archibald, Hill, and Luster Goodwin. Nolan Richardson went there, too. It all seemed so perfect, a good fit in every sense of the word. So, early in my senior year, after Don Haskins came up to see me play later in the process, I told Rus that I'd sign with UTEP, and I put my name on the dotted line that fall.

I also liked the team's schedule, too. In the WAC, I knew I'd see the country. Maybe I could've waited, even given my word to

UTEP and strung them along to see if some other school would recruit me after a great senior year. But I wasn't like that. They'd shown me love and loyalty when no other school did, and I wanted to do the same. I was grateful to have a chance to play Division-I, as that's all I'd ever hoped for. All you need is one opportunity, and that's what Rus Bradburd and Don Haskins did. They took a chance on a smaller guard and gave me a place to make my mark at the next level. They said I'd play as a freshman, too, and that I wouldn't need to "redshirt" or sit out a year.

* * *

Going into my senior season at Carver, everyone knew where I was headed next. Between my junior and senior season, despite not getting any recruitment letters, I was finally invited to a Nike All-American basketball camp. This was a major stepping-stone. It was also at this camp where I changed my jump shot. Those who saw me in the pros likely noticed that, when I shot, I almost curled the ball over my head and let it fly. But as a younger player, my shot started lower, on the side of my head by my right ear with my left hand in front of my forehead. This made my shot easy to block, and I couldn't have that at the next level.

It wasn't a problem in lower levels of the game because I was always quick and could get past guys, but when I went to the All-American camp at Princeton University, I knew I had to make an adjustment. The person who helped was Craig Robinson. Back then, Craig was just a ball player I knew from Chicago. But people today know him now as the former men's basketball coach at Oregon State University and the brother of Michelle Obama. But at the Nike camp, he was just one of the counselors.

He came up to me one day when I was shooting around and pulled me aside. "Tim," he said. "I think you should change your jumper. It would be good for you." I said, "Let me see what you got," and Craig showed me how to shoot from above my head. "Shoot like this for about twenty minutes and see how it feels." Well, I did just that . . . and I never went back. I got comfortable almost immediately and knew it was the change I needed to take my game to the next level (both literally and metaphorically). Later, when I got to UTEP to play for the Miners, I would perfect my shot thanks to a great deal of repetition. But I'd set the foundation then and there at that Nike camp. It's funny how small the world can be. Little did I know that the man who helped me change my jumper would be the same person whose sister would be the first Black First Lady of the United States.

* * *

My senior year in 1984–85 was my breakout. Even so, I worked hard to stay humble. Whether it was the safety pin jokes or my friends, I kept my feet on the ground and my eyes looking forward. I never wanted "yes men" around me and so that's how it went. Ever since staying back as an eighth grader, I wanted to be held accountable for everything. Not to mess up. A good teacher can help with that. That was Carver's assistant principal, Mr. Richie. He lived about 10 minutes away from me in Chicago and would drop me off at home after practice when he could. At times he'd also pick me up and give me a ride to school in the morning.

Mr. Richie passed away from cancer when I got to the NBA, and I miss him dearly. Another favorite teacher was Mr. Sailes. He was the school accountant, and also did the books for a local church.

He was always a warm, kind-hearted person who treated me like an adult. But my favorite teacher was Ms. Hunter. She was a gym teacher, cheerleading coach, and women's basketball team coach. And one of her players when I was at Carver was the future WNBA MVP, Yolanda Griffith. When Carver retired my number in 2022, Ms. Hunter was there. She came up to me during the ceremony and laughed, "I still got my safety pin, Tim!" I smiled. "I bet you do!"

As far as the basketball team my senior year, we were ready to go far. The difficult part of the season, though, was that Coach Walters was dealing with cancer. Born and raised in Arkansas, there were seven boys and three girls in his family, and cancer took all of the men. As he coached us that season, he had to wear a colostomy bag. The cancer was eating at his intestines. It was brutal. In the city playoffs, we had a good seed and ended up playing South Shore, led by my former grammar school coach, Mr. Pittman, whose team I'd almost jumped to.

He'd followed me to Carver when I enrolled as a freshman and coached junior varsity. Then he became the varsity coach at South Shore, which was walking distance from where I lived. But since Coach Walters got our schedule straight, I stuck around. Coach Pittman was worried that if I'd left Carver for his program, people would have been upset. "They're going to kill me if you come here," he told me. He thought the refs wouldn't give his teams another call. But it was all moot in the end. When we matched up against his team in the playoffs, Coach Walters advised me not to stay home in the neighborhood the night before the game. "Everyone knows you live around there," he said. "They won't let you rest." He didn't want folks calling my house all night, didn't want them messing with me. "You can't stay home," he said. But I told him, "Coach, that ain't nothing.

That's just another day for me. People talking shit. If anything, that makes me MORE ready!" But he wouldn't take no for an answer and took me to his house, where I spent the night. His wife served me breakfast in the morning and then I went to school. That night in the quarterfinal game against South Shore, I scored 45 points. "Told you," Coach Walters said. But I knew I would have had that no matter where I slept before the game.

The playoffs went well for us. We were supposed to play King next, but they were upset in the semifinals by Simeon, a team that we'd played twice a year in our conference and were familiar with. When the cards are in your favor, you go with 'em! We made it all the way to the 1985 Chicago public league championship and would face off against Simeon. Heading into the finals, I came in averaging 23 points. Simeon had future NBA star Nick Anderson, too. He was one of the great talents in the city. But not everyone makes it like we eventually did. Take Simeon, which was without its 6-foot-8 star Ben Wilson, who'd been a top recruit but was murdered the same day the team's season was to begin. Another victim of the city. (Anderson actually wore Wilson's No. 25 jersey during his collegiate and NBA career to honor his fallen teammate.)

My team had good players like Jerry Smith, Caleb Davis, Wade Jenkins, and Rodrick Hudson. Simeon had guys like David Knight, Eric David, Erving Small, Allen Gordon, and Deion Butler. They were coached by Bob Hambric, who'd never had a losing season. Wearing my No. 10 jersey, I opened the championship game with an assist from about half court to Wade. Then I scored the second bucket for our team. I was directing traffic from the jump, and we were going back and forth with the highly favored Simeon. The game's TV announcers called me one of the best guards in the city. "When you're short, you've got to be smart," they said of me. "And this kid is smart."

The fresh-faced Nick Anderson, a future star for the Orlando Magic, came off the bench for Simeon. He was a junior and one of the team's top scorers, their extra punch. Much of the game was played inside and the rail-thin, 6-foot-5 Anderson could rebound with the best. After the first quarter we led 13–12, but then Simeon went on a run and we fell behind, 29–17. Then 33–23. They just kept adding a point here and a point there to their lead. With seven minutes left in the fourth quarter, they were up by ten, 50–40. They were double- and triple-teaming me, trying to take the ball from my hand after I passed halfcourt.

We cut the score to 50–45 with 4:37 left after I got us a bucket, but Nick answered to increase their lead to 52–45. I got a layup on the other end to make it 52–47 with four minutes left. "He's taking over the ballgame!" the announcer said. Nick hit two free throws, and I responded with an assist to my teammate Wade Jenkins. The score was 53–49 with 3:30 left. Simeon got a bucket and then I answered again, scoring my 20th point of the game. It was 55–51. Simeon got the lead to 57–51 with 2:18 left and then we cut it to 58–53 with 1:40 to go. I got a steal and took it down the court but missed a layup. With a minute left, Simeon was up six and we couldn't get any closer.

* * *

It was disappointing to lose the city championship, but making the game was an honor. I'd averaged 20-plus points as a senior, and now I had the rest of my career in front of me. But first came a rite of passage. Up until this time, I'd never dunked. I was feeling good about myself and, in the gym one day, I thought, *You know what? Let me try and dunk this damn ball.* I was playing pickup, but during a break I set my sights on the rim. I decided I would try it like Spud Webb in the NBA's Slam Dunk Contest. So I bounced the ball up off the court and it went high in the air. Then I leapt up and got it and as I came back down toward the rim, I slammed the thing home.

The other guys in the gym said, "Man, we never seen you dunk before!" It was actually the first time I'd ever tried it. Turns out I could have been doing it long before! I was checking boxes left and right, but before I went to UTEP, I got to experience my biggest dream. I couldn't play in the Chicago State pro-am until after high school, that was the rule. But after I graduated, I made sure to sign up. The pro-am began around July 1 and I couldn't wait. My first team in the pro-am boasted NBA shooting guard Eddie Johnson, a 20-point scorer who was from the city. But he wasn't the only guy there from the league. Doc Rivers and Mo Cheeks came, too.

Eddie was a scorer, so it was maybe for that reason that our coach in the pro-am made the team all about him. "Get the ball to Eddie," he told me over and over. *To Eddie?* I thought. *Shit, I want to work on MY game, too!* Eddie was going to get his shots, but I wasn't there to be his sidekick! Some coaches just can't get out of their players' way. What they should be doing is seeing who needs help. But if a guy can ball, let him do it. Oh well, I'd do what I needed to do. That first game in the pro-am came against Darren Brickman, a skilled high school player who never made the pros.

People called him "Ali Baba" because he was such a thief on the court. Darren could just snatch the ball right from you. He would pick you up in the backcourt, 94 feet from the basket.

You had to shake him. I'd played him before in many hot gyms in pickup games that sometimes went to 150 points. Played him in places like Robichaux, Fernwood, LeClaire, and other spots. As I brought the ball up on the Chicago State court, at first I didn't get past the free-throw line before he picked me up and stripped the ball. *Damn!* The crowd *oohed* and *aahed.* They were always up for a show. *Okay, then!*

When I got it back, he picked me up at full court again. But without a pick from a teammate, I shook him and went the distance and scored a basket of my own, drawing a foul. The crowd went wild again—this time for me. That's when I knew I belonged. The rest of the season went well despite my coach always telling me to "Get Eddie the ball." And while I played in the pro-am in later years, I didn't suit up for that coach again. I knew everything that I did had to be about getting better. I had a career ahead of me and if I played my cards right, it could last several decades. After the pro-am finished, it was time to head down to UTEP.

Memory Lane: Rus Bradburd

Tim Hardaway arrived in El Paso in 1985 with an already-impressive skill set: polished dribbling, imagination when leading a fast break, and uncanny anticipation on defense. What would separate Tim from the more highly recruited—and what powered his dramatic rise—was his determination to keep improving. Through sheer sweat, smarts, and humility, Tim made himself into an accurate three-point shooter, someone who could slow down to direct Coach Don Haskins's half-court offense and also grow into a shrewd man-to-man defender. This humility and eagerness to improve has carried over into every area of his life.

I think a lot about the first time I saw Tim play—outdoors, in the wind, at South Shore Park, in a 3-on-3 half-court setting. In a funny way, what stood out to me was what he did *not* do that day. Coach Haskins insisted on rabid and relentless effort, and that day Tim hardly broke a sweat. What got my attention, though, was his vision—it was like everyone else was on beginners level Pac Man, level one, and Tim was an expert, toying with them as they plodded around as though playing in galoshes in the Chicago snow.

Years later, after he exploded onto the NBA scene, captivating fans, media, and Spike Lee, I started to think about a stark contrast in Tim's life. Yes, he revolutionized the game, due to his cutting edge crossover dribble and breathtaking ball skills. He popularized dribbling wizardry, spawned a generation of copycats, and brought the game into the modern era. Yet, in many ways, Tim has always been "old school," a throwback to a bygone era—and not just in his dedication to practice, his work ethic.

Carver High School wasn't close to his home, but he traveled there most days with his grade school coach, Don Pittman, who'd gone to Carver when Tim did. Yet, when Pittman left for his own head job—at nearby South Shore High School—Tim was true to his school and he stayed behind. At UTEP, after starting on a Top 20 team as a sophomore, he had chances to transfer, go to bigger conference. Instead, he remained loyal to the crusty and gruff Haskins. To this day, he's still married to his high school sweetheart. That's Tim Hardaway, to me: he's the old school revolutionary.

3

GROWING UP AT UTEP

EL Paso is a long way from Chicago—around 1,500 miles. I officially enrolled in 1985. To play my position well, I'd always studied the mannerisms of my opponents like I studied those of the people around me growing up in Chicago. When you come from a tough place, it becomes a sixth sense. You watch how a person moves. On the court, you watch how they play. What their dribble looks like, where they like to shoot. I'm a people person, but that works both ways. When it's good, I have chemistry. When it's bad, I'm a detective.

Part of my investigations included my handle with the ball. You can guide your defenders based on your dribbling. And it was a skill I'd perfected—even before shooting and passing—when I was young. I went outside in the Chicago cold by myself to work on it. That's all there was when the gyms were closed from the blizzards. Or if there was too much snow or rain I'd go down into my family's unfinished basement. There were two seven-foot beams holding up the ceiling five feet apart. The walls were about eight feet apart. So I would practice by dribbling around those beams. In and out, crossovers. I'd use them like picks. I'd make bounce passes to the walls. For hours.

My imagination was my defender. Other times I'd be in a group of my friends on the sidewalk. Grass would be on either side and we called that space out of bounds. There would be four or five kids and they'd all be trying to steal the ball from me. And I'd dribble on the concrete with nowhere to go, just fending them off. Holding one kid back with my arm, switching hands, dribbling between my legs. That was the game we played. Sometimes we didn't have anything else to do because our parents would tell us not to step off the block and we didn't want to play Atari or read anymore. "Can't go off the block today, Tim," Mom would tell me. I'd ask why and she'd say, "What I tell you?"

It was the same on an outdoor court. I'd put my own nets up on the hoops (if you left yours there, they'd get stolen). Without a net, if a ball went through without hitting the rim, it could bounce 100 yards before you could chase it down. I pretended Isiah Thomas was guarding me and I'd go at him. I didn't need a coach, cones, or anything else. If you want to get better, you can get better with next to nothing. That's the beauty of basketball. I'd do stutter-steps, jump stops. I'd run up and down full court, full speed, stop and pop. Left hand, right hand. I'd switch on a dime, shoot. Run fast breaks. All I wanted to do was be like Isiah.

From the moment my coach said I played like him, it's all I could think about. I wanted to emulate him. I wanted to push myself to be *better* than him. I studied his moves from college to the pros, how he finger-rolled his layups just over the rim, how he shot the ball off the glass, how tough he could be on defense.

I even studied his feet, how he positioned himself against an offense player. I never told anyone that's what I was doing, but I even started moving my feet like him. Like a young musician covering songs from a master, I worked to be just like Isiah. More than anything, I loved how he gave his teammates confidence. You could see it in their eyes.

This is what prepared me, sharpened me. I wanted to be *that* motherfucker. So when I got to UTEP, going through the coach's drills wasn't an issue. They made me better. I'm so proud that I signed with UTEP. After my senior year and the Chicago pro-ams, people were trying to get me to transfer to other schools. But I told them to kiss my ass. I'm loyal to the people who are loyal to me. So for those guys who didn't believe in me at first to ask me to diss those who were, that was some ignorant shit. My thought was, *You didn't want me then, why should I want you now*? I saw them look past me, rather than at me. But now I was a D-I player.

* * *

After Yolanda and I had met that snowy day my junior year, we began to date. We talked on the phone often and went out on dates around Chicago. Since she was a year older than me, during my senior season at Carver, she was already in her first year at Olive-Harvey Community College on the south side of the city. Yolanda lived in the Golden Gates neighborhood of the city, which was close to the Altgeld Gardens homes and Carver. It was an exciting time for me as a senior in high school. Love was in the air. As such, when we'd hang out, we'd have to take the bus and meet each other in different spots around the city.

Neither of us owned a car. Our first date was dinner and a movie, though for the life of me I can't remember which movie it was (though she probably does). Everything flowed well with her. We had immediate chemistry and our communication was fluid, the conversations fun and engaging. A few months into the summer of 1984, after we'd met and started dating, she asked me, "So what do you do all day?" I told her I played basketball. "It's impossible to play basketball *all* day," she said. "No, it's not," I told her. She wanted to come see me. The issue was that there's an unwritten rule in the city: no bringing your girl to the courts.

They can come see a school game, but they can't be there during pickup runs. But she kept pushing. "I want to see you play!" If you get into a heated game, guys can start talking major trash. They can talk shit about you in front of your girl or even pick her out and start clowning on her. I wanted to avoid that, but she insisted. So I relented, and she came with me to one of my summer runs. We met at one of the bus stops by the courts and she sat to watch as I began to play. It was a good game for me that day, I must have won four or five in a row. In between, I'd go over and talk to her. But the guys started to call me out.

One guy said, "What the hell is this? You know there's a rule, don't bring your girl to hoop!" I told him to chill, that I was trying to make a good impression. And that he couldn't guard me anyway! But he wouldn't stop. Yolanda couldn't understand it, the territorial feelings of the other guys. "This is unbelievable!" she said. But I told her, "Yeah, this is how it is. This is what I do. I said I play ball all day!" After a few hours, she got bored and realized I didn't have time to chat. So, during a break, I walked her back to the bus stop and she went home. I'd felt bad that she'd been sitting all alone, but I had to keep my workout going.

She made it home and wasn't upset with me. The situation proved, however, that it was hard to mix a relationship with what I had to do to keep getting better. So, later, when I went to UTEP and she transferred into the school, I wasn't sure how it was going to work out. It was nice of the university to help us out and accept her enrollment out of community college along with mine. And I was hopeful, but it was rocky. When you don't grow up with a blueprint for a romantic relationship, it can be hard to find your way on your own. We tried to make it work despite my coaches warning me it would be difficult.

* * *

Heading into college, I knew there was a lot I had to do to improve my game, but I believed in myself that I could do it. The hardest part was clearing my head. The city of El Paso is one of the best-kept secrets in the entire US. It's a slow-moving place right on the border of Texas and Juarez, Mexico, and as a result it has a lot of history. You can hike up the Franklin Mountains and learn about the original settlers in the region. You can feel culture in the air. It was a big change from Chicago. The people in El Paso are genuine and kind and welcomed me with open arms. Living in that city gave me a chance to think about my future and what I wanted for my life.

Thank God for UTEP. To this day, I still have friends in El Paso, and I always enjoy going back there to visit and eat at spots like Luby's with its Texas-sized dinner entrees or Grandy's with its breakfast menu. UTEP, which was founded in 1913, was originally a mining college where students learned how to find and identify metals. The school has the motto, "Knowledge and Refinement." And that was exactly my strategy when I arrived. I wanted to learn more and get better at everything. But life doesn't always go as planned. What's the saying, again? *Man plans, God laughs.* I learned that well at the university.

* * *

Coach Don Haskins made history in basketball by the time he was thirty-six years old. A former player at Oklahoma A&M, he got the job at UTEP in 1961 and held it until 1999. And in 1966, during an era in which many thought Blacks were inferior as people and athletes, he beat the all-white University of Kentucky team with his all-Black starting lineup (UTEP was then known as Texas Western) to win the NCAA championship. That went a long way to throw cold water on racial segregation in college hoops. Haskins, who served as an assistant during the 1972 Munich Summer Olympics, also recruited Tiny Archibald, who was an assistant at UTEP when I attended.

Haskins was a mentor to future NBA coach Tim Floyd, who is now the head man at UTEP. His career casts a long shadow. When I showed up on campus, people warned me about him. Don't be scared, they said, but he looks just like a bear. That was his nickname, "The Bear." I was like, *How can a man look like a bear?* But when I was first introduced to him, I thought to myself, *Damn, this dude looks EXACTLY like a bear!* It was uncanny. During practices he would resemble a snarling grizzly. But he was great to me. I didn't get a chance to really know him until I left school. He kept his kinder, fatherly side separate from his rigid coaching side.

Coach Haskins was always looking out for us, making sure we made class every day. A future Hall of Famer, he was tough. He made sure you were paying attention in practice, reminding you why you were there in the first place. He also wanted all his players to graduate. He was very detail-oriented and taught me that being early was on time and on time was late. He encouraged us to ask questions, which I really appreciated. Plus, coming in as a freshman, I knew I had to learn the ropes and pay my dues. I came off the bench my first season. Of course, I thought I was ready for college competition, but there were other guys there with more experience.

Haskins was loyal to his upperclassmen—especially the ones who had goals to play at the next level. He knew they'd earned their status. At the same time, he didn't give them free passes. Coach Haskins wasn't afraid to single people out in practice—that's where he did most of his talking—or should I say yelling. There were many occasions where people left the gym mad or even in tears, including myself once or twice. But you learned from that. From his . . . well . . . "constructive criticism." There was always a message in his words, no matter how loudly he delivered them. Over my UTEP career, I'd guess that I left a practice heated four or five times.

Even so, I never quit. Though Coach would kill you in front of everybody and totally embarrass you, at the end he'd come over to you and give you some praise, a "Good job, kid." Whenever he yelled, I would try to listen to the message, not the delivery. I didn't pay attention to the screaming as much as the idea within it. I knew it was all meant to make me a better person and basketball player, and that's what I was at UTEP to do. Coach needed to be comfortable with me in the game, and I needed to be comfortable with myself. Iron sharpens iron. Greatness isn't always smooth or pretty.

* * *

As a freshman, I knew it wasn't yet my turn to dominate. For now, I had to play my role. When I got in the game, my responsibility was to control the tempo and pick up my man on defense, to move my feet and play smart in a limited role. I wasn't looking to score—that wasn't what the team needed. If the other team pressed, it was my job to dribble through them, to advance the ball. I remember one game in particular, when Georgetown visited us. Coached by big John Thompson, they had five future NBA players on the roster, including Reggie Williams, David Wingate, and Charles Smith. They were loaded and ranked high that season.

But they were in for a surprise when they came to see us on December 27 at the aptly named Don Haskins Center. I remember zig-zagging through their defense. And while I didn't look to shoot my jumper often, I was able to set up my teammates. We gave the undefeated Hoyas their first loss of the year, 78–64. That was big for us.

My freshman year, I played about 15 minutes per game, scoring 4.1 points with just under a steal and two assists per game. I wasn't mad about coming off the bench. I was patient. Coach only had five losing seasons in his career—he knew what he was doing.

By the end of the season, we were 27–5 after beating Wyoming in the WAC championship. We landed a No. 10 seed in the NCAA's West Regional in Ogden, Utah. We matched up against No. 7 Bradley, which boasted future NBA pro Hersey Hawkins, who averaged 18.7 points per game that year. But we fell to the Braves, 83–65. Though I only played 10 minutes (notching two assists), it was good just to make the tourney. When we went back to campus, it was time to get back to work in class and on the court. Though I hadn't quite decided yet, I was working toward becoming a Criminal Justice major. I wanted to be a probation officer and help people.

On the court, between classes, I worked on my jumper. I'd hardly been able to use it during my freshman season, instead concentrating on layups and floaters. But I wanted to prove to Coach that my shot was reliable and could be a weapon for us next year. So I worked with Billy Barron, who ran the intramural leagues on campus. He said he could help me with my shot. "You need to shoot 500 jumpers per day," he said. "You're fine shooting off the dribble but, here in college, teams play a lot of zone. So you have to get your catch-and-shoot game up." He was right, and I agreed to take his help. I knew I needed all the pointers I could get, especially since I'd just fundamentally changed my shooting style. I needed reps and coaching to keep improving and be my most effective on the court.

We met five days a week and he brought two basketballs. "It's going to be tough for me until you get used to it," he said. "I'm going to be chasing your rebounds all over the gym! But it will be worth it." Bill had worked with a number of other UTEP players this way over the years, including guards Luster Goodwin and Jeep Jackson. "The first week you're going to be shooting bricks," he said. "But after the first two or three days, you'll get accustomed to it." He had me shoot 25 shots in a row, always moving in between. Run to one spot, catch and shoot. Rebound. Run to the next, catch and shoot. Rebound.

Sometimes my misses would roll to the other side of the gym or hit nothing but the backboard. But I learned how to further hone my shot and have a consistent motion every time, whether I was on the move or in place. I concentrated on repetition. I shot in blocks of 25, taking a total of 500 each day. When my legs began to fade, my arms took over. When my arms went out, I'd have to compensate with both legs *and* arms. Slowly, I started to perfect it. When the school year ended in late May, I'd worked with Bill for two months straight and made real progress. I was sinking 300–325 per 500 rack. When I went home to play in summer leagues, I was lights out.

* * *

Sophomore year, I was in the starting backcourt with senior Jeep Jackson. As an underclassman, my job was still to set up the juniors and seniors on the team. But, at the same time, I had the freedom to look for my own shot. As a result, my scoring jumped from four points per game as a freshman to ten as a sophomore. My minutes doubled and my assists went up from two to about five per game. I also averaged 2.2 steals per game, compared to just under one the previous season. That's how I got most of my offense, off steals—picking pockets or jumping in passing lanes and quickly going the other way.

Defense leads to offense. That was my mindset. It was the kind of mentality that helped me gain more national recognition. I even won the MVP Awards for the 1987 Sun Bowl Invitational Tournament. In practice, I showed Coach that I'd worked on my jumper and, slowly, he gave me more rope during games. The other development that year was the new freshman that Coach Haskins brought in to the team, future NBA All-Star Antonio Davis, a big power forward who could rebound and score with anyone in the country. When he arrived, you could tell he was inexperienced, but had a lot of potential. He was like a baby deer about to turn into a buck.

In the pros, Antonio was an important part of the Indiana Pacers, but with us, he was still a youngin. Over the course of the season, he and I worked to develop chemistry. A point guard needs a good big man, and the 6-foot-9 forward was just that. While he only got about nine minutes per game as a freshman, I was excited about what the future held.

That year, I helped lead UTEP to a 25–7 record, finishing with an eight-game winning streak before losing in the conference tournament to Wyoming. Even so, we made the NCAA tournament. A No. 7 seed, we matched up against No. 10 Arizona in the first round . . . except the game was played in Tucson. On *their campus.*

That Arizona team was stacked. It boasted future pros Sean Elliott (a 20-point scorer in college), Tom Tolbert, Anthony Cook, and Jud Buechler, along with my Chicago pal and future MLB All-Star, Kenny Lofton. The NCAA knew it was a conflict of interest, and it ended up being the last time a team played a home game in the tourney like that.

But that didn't help us then. Arizona had endured injuries to Elliott and other players that season and, despite their lower seed, were favored to win. But they didn't know UTEP had come to play! Nobody knew Coach Haskins was getting us ready for war.

In the locker room, Coach said no one should play as hard as we play. We'd put in so much time and hard work beating each other up, he said, that now it was time to go out there and beat them up on their home floor. "Go out there and work HARDER than them," he said. "With more ENERGY than them! If you let them out-energy you or outdo your effort, you're hurting YOURSELVES!" He was right. As we were warming up before the game, we knew Arizona had more pressure on them than we did. Every time we went down and got a stop or came back on offense to score, we could feel their shoulders getting heavier.

The game was nip-and-tuck. We were up four, then they went up. But by the end of the second half, you could tell they were exhausted. The pressure had gotten to them. At the end of regulation, our guard Chris Blocker made a shot, but the refs said his toe was on the line and what we thought was a three turned out to be a two, which sent the game to overtime tied at 79. Seeing them gassed, we put things into another gear and completely outplayed them in the extra period, outscoring them 19–12 and taking the victory, 98–91. Nobody had given us a chance—Arizona was thought to make their own run in the tournament. But then UTEP came along. I notched six assists, and it was one of the highlights of my college career.

In the next round, however, we weren't so lucky. We went up against the No. 2 University of Iowa, led by B. J. Armstrong and other pros like Kevin Gamble and Brad Lohaus. It was a close one, but we lost in the end, 84–82. I had 11 points and six more assists, but it just wasn't enough. While we'd made it further than the year prior, and we'd lost to an Iowa team with seven future pros that later made the Elite Eight, the loss still stung. For the future, we had two future pros and one was Davis, who barely played as a freshman. Still, there's always next season! So I went back to campus and continued to work on my game. One of the ways I did that was hooping with the locals around the city.

In El Paso, there are a lot of Mexican people since the city is on the border with our southern neighbor. And I used to play tons of pickup games in the university's intramural gym with them. That gym would get so sweltering hot. You'd get so sweaty you had to sit in the shade before you got in the car. The guys would come in after work and just play. Their average height was maybe six-feet, so guys like the rebounding machine Antonio Davis wouldn't have gotten anything out of a game like that, but it helped me. Those guys challenged my ball handling skills. It was a fun battle. They brought the best out of me every time.

* * *

Sadly, that same year, our UTEP team experienced tragedy. On May 2, 1987, weeks after the NCAA tournament, our guard Jeep Jackson died of cardiac arrest. He was just twenty-three years old. And as far as we knew, Jeep didn't have any history of heart trouble. We were shocked—especially Coach Haskins. After playing a few minutes in an exhibition game, Jeep collapsed in the gym while sitting on the bench, passing out mid-conversation with Kyle Stewart. When the ambulance arrived, he was already dead. The California-born Jackson was a criminal justice major and had just been named to the All-Western Athletic Conference first team. It was a tragedy for us all.

Adding to the hard times, Yolanda and I were splitting up, too. That connection we had, it was no longer smoldering. Instead, it was fading. I still loved her, but I knew I needed to spread my wings on my own. It wasn't that I wanted to chase after girls, but I had to know what it was like to be an independent person in El Paso. When she'd enrolled at UTEP as a student with me my first year, leaving Olive-Henry, my coaches had warned me that having a steady girlfriend was going to wear thin. They weren't being cruel, it was just that being a student-athlete was two full-time jobs. I had my dorm and she had an apartment, but we were often together. I had to always think about her, if she was okay, what she was doing at home, if she was occupied. It was too much for me. They warned it would be a distraction—and it was.

I couldn't keep my mind on what I needed to do. If I wanted to make it to the next level, I had to focus on myself. It hurt to tell her this, and I know it hurt her to hear it. It hurt to see her leave, but it had to happen. If it was meant to be, I told myself, we would reconnect. It's hard to fall in love with your high school sweetheart. There is so much life to live. But when Yolanda went back to Chicago, I was able to have more time to reflect on the work at hand and building a bond with my teammates, while freeing up my mind and keeping my eyes looking straight ahead. When I came back to the city to visit in the summers, we still hung out. We'd still talk on the phone some nights—we kept lines of communication open. We'd see movies and eat dinner together. We remained friends and even acted a little closer than that at times, but she understood that I had to concentrate on my career at UTEP. After the summer, I prepared for my junior season. This was going to be my biggest test to date. I was no longer an up-and-comer. I had to be a team leader. It was going to be a challenge—one I was more than ready to attack head-on.

After my sophomore year, I faced a big decision. I'd just come off a season starting in 30 of our 31 games, averaging 10 points, 4.8 assists and 2.2 steals. But there was a problem: my knee was killing me. Growing up in Chicago, I played on too much concrete. The result was that, in the summer after my sophomore year, I found out I had a cyst on my right knee. The thing hurt so badly that I knew I needed surgery. The question was when to get it? I thought about waiting to go under the knife the summer after my junior campaign, but I just couldn't take the pain. My knee felt like it was on fire.

My doctor, knowing I was in pain, asked if I could wait, as there may be new technology in the works that could help. But, in the end, it was just too much, and I elected for surgery. Months after I got the procedure, he said that if I had been able to hold off, I could have had arthroscopic surgery, which would have meant he wouldn't have had to remove any cartilage—but my body was telling me that I needed to act immediately, so it is what it is. Today, though, I still walk with a bit of a limp. Not because I'm hurting, but just because that's how my leg moves now. I knew it'd be something I would have to deal with for the rest of my life. But, luckily, when I made the pros, I was able to find medicine that has helped me ever since.

* * *

Junior year, now living off campus as an upper-classman, I returned to UTEP ready for a bigger challenge. One of the people there who helped me was Tiny Archibald, the 6-foot-1 former NBA scoring champ, six-time All-Star, champion, and future Hall of Famer. Now an assistant with our team, he'd given me tips during my sophomore year about scoring angles, footwork, and how to bait defenders on offense. But when I came back for my junior year, he noticed something new in me. "Damn, what happened?" he asked. I told him I had worked all summer, playing with pros like Mo Cheeks in the Chicago pro-ams. "You've elevated, Tim," he said. "You're going to the NBA." I grinned from ear to ear. Getting that type of praise from such a great baller meant a lot to me, showing my hard work was paying off.

He was a huge supporter for me and Antonio Davis. The plan for both of us was always to make it to the NBA, but we knew it would take baby steps every year in college. We had to work at it, day and night. First it was to get better, then it was to wait our turns for the upperclassmen to move on. Then it was to prove ourselves in the game. Then it was to lead our team. I'd shot all those shots with Billy Barron and improved. And I knew what it took to make the pros since I'd been around NBA guys in Chicago my whole life. I understood their language. But when Coach Archibald told me I had a shot to make the league, well . . . that's all I needed to hear.

"You've got a good head on your shoulders," he said. "You know how to run a team and how to take over a game. You just have to do it night in and night out now and be consistent. You can't have a bad game for the next two years." I nodded and said, "Okay! I can do that." He told Antonio to keep rebounding and blocking shots and that everything else would come. "Your forte is the dirty work," Nate said. "Taking charges, playing good defense. That's how you're going to change games." In the end, every word Nate said was correct. Sometimes you just need someone to give you the blueprint.

To kick off that season, I earned my second MVP of the Sun Bowl Invitational Tournament. I finished the year as our team's second-leading scorer and first in assists, steals, and minutes played. At times, I thought about Jeep and all he'd taught me about running a team. When to get your own points and when to get others involved. Playing point guard is an art form. That season, I scored nearly 14 points per game to go along with 2.4 steals and 5.7 assists while controlling the pace of the game and being the team liaison between us and Coach Haskins. Just as Jeep had shown me, I helped teach guys like freshman Prince Stewart on what needed to be done.

UTEP was now my team. It took on my character—rugged, quick, and fun. We were unafraid, and ranked as high as #18 during the season. I was the captain, and Coach Haskins trusted me. Patience is a virtue, and I earned his faith over the years. I brought us belief because I was confident. Writers predicted us to have a down season since so many upperclassmen had left, but I led us to a 23–10 record and earned a spot on second-team All-WAC. One of our biggest wins came on January 8 against the No. 5 team in the country, Wyoming. They had a big 6-foot-11 center and future first-round pick in Eric Leckner, who everyone thought would eat us up. But Antonio kept him in check.

Already on a five-game winning streak, we were up 43–35 in the second half . . . but they wouldn't go away. It was 65–62 with just a few minutes left in the game, and though it was a hard-fought game, we managed to hold on, winning in an upset, 68–62. Though they beat us a month later in Wyoming and edged us out by four in the WAC Final, we still made our third-straight NCAA tournament. We were a No. 9 seed, and would face No. 8 Seton Hall, which had future pros in Mark Bryant and John Morton. We knew it was going to be tough. Too tough, in the end. Though only down four after the first half, P. J. Carlesimo's squad outscored us by 12 in the second, giving them an 80–64 win.

While it was far from the way we'd hoped the tourney would go, we'd still had a strong season and I knew my senior year would be one to remember. To start, we got another infusion of talent. Future pro Greg Foster transferred to UTEP from UCLA. Growing up in Oakland, Greg had played with another great point guard in Gary Payton. Then, after two years at UCLA, he came over to UTEP for his junior and senior campaigns. We were happy to have him—he was a highly touted guy and could hoop. He averaged 11.1 points per game his first season with us. But that year, my offense exploded. Still, there was no thought of me leaving after my junior year for the pros. The NBA scouts just weren't checking for me in that way yet. I felt I was NBA-ready, but I was maybe the only one who did at the time. So I dedicated myself to my final year at UTEP.

Knowing the importance of showing out for my senior year, I was the team's leading scorer, averaging 22 points and shooting over 50 percent, adding 5.4 assists, and 2.8 steals per game. I made first team All-WAC, and my output had me finishing as UTEP's all-time leading scorer (though that was later eclipsed by Antoine Gillespie in 1995). But, no matter what, I knew I was one of the best point guards in the country. I also had a great backcourt mate in Prince Stewart. He matched my intensity, and we pushed each other every day after practice, working on moves and shooting. Antonio was great, too, notching 14.3 points and eight boards. We had size and skill. Senior year was the most fun I'd ever had playing basketball. But it didn't start out that way.

A basketball team has to feel like a family if it's going to work. And in my senior year, for whatever reason, our UTEP team didn't gel in that way—not until the WAC Tournament. From there, we just took off. I remember one halftime speech in the first game of the tournament—I addressed the team like a wartime general. I don't know why exactly, maybe it was the pressure of the postseason, but everyone got in line and on my back after that. It was a galvanizing moment, and led to a terrific end to my final college year.

We went 26–7 on the season, and during our last home game, my mom and Yolanda came down to celebrate me for senior night. Endings and transitions can be hard—even when you're looking forward to your future. The whole thing was emotional. My final regular-season game was at home against San Diego State, and we killed them, 93–69. The fans showed me a lot of love, knowing it was my last game at the Don Haskins Center. We used that victory to springboard into the WAC Tournament, which we won, beating Wyoming, our foes from the previous season, in double-overtime, followed by victories against New Mexico and Colorado State. Those wins propelled us into the NCAA tournament for my fourth year in a row.

A No. 7 seed, we matched up against brilliant guard Mahmoud Abdul-Rauf (then Chris Jackson) and No. 10 LSU. If I needed a breakout on the national stage, this was it. I knew people would be tuning in to see a matchup of two NBA prospects. Mahmoud had averaged 30.2 points as a freshman (he went to the NBA following his sophomore season), but in our game, my team was able to get the better of his. He scored 33 points on a bunch of pull-up jumpers, and I added 31 on threes and layups. I also had three steals and nine assists. Antonio had 13 points and nine rebounds, and Greg added four points and nine boards.

Playing as a team, we won the game handily, 85–74. Mahmoud and I didn't guard one another much. We both wanted to check each other, as if we were at the playground, testing offensives against defenses, but our coaches wanted us to save our energy. It was my first time playing against a guard who was so skilled. He could shoot from anywhere and score with the best. But during this game, I showed the world how quick I was. I used spin dribbles and my tight crossover. I pushed the ball, handling it with deftness. I knifed through defenses, scored with a smoothness, and was the consummate floor general, fitting passes into tight spaces and directing traffic.

Getting our first tourney win since my sophomore year, we faced the No. 2 seed Indiana in the second round, coached by Haskins's fishing buddy, the always-irritated Bob Knight. Though we went in with high hopes, we lost that one badly, 92–69. But while Indiana looked poised for more, it was the University of Michigan that went on to win the 1989 title against Seton Hall. That Final Four also included Duke and Illinois. I had a lot of friends on the Illinois team, which fell to Michigan. Sharpshooting guard Glen Rice was on a heater that year. Nobody could stop him and my future Miami Heat teammate Terry Mills. That duo went on to beat Seton Hall to make Michigan history and win the whole thing.

For me, my college career was over. In my final season, I'd shown my mettle. I'd led the WAC in both steals and assists, and was at the top in scoring. For that I was named WAC Player of the Year and won the Frances Pomeroy Naismith Award for best 6-foot-and-under player in the country—all after getting no scholarship offers for much of my high school career. Add two more trophies to the case! My stock grew throughout the year, and I began to have a real following. Thousands of fans and a slew of media people were wondering what my next move would be. Many appreciated what I could do with the ball, but more began to speculate on where I might be drafted in the NBA.

With the season complete, and doing my best to shut out all the noise, it was time for some personal reflection. It had been a wild ride over my four years in El Paso, one I'd never forget. I'd made the tourney in each of my four years and left as the school leader in points and steals (which I still hold). The city taught me good values and the people embraced me. Before I left campus, I said goodbye to my teammates—that was hard. College had made me into a better player and a better man, thanks to everyone who helped. But after graduation and saying my final goodbyes, I left on a personal road trip. I wanted some space to think about the next steps. I knew, though, that it was time for me to go on to the next level, my college degree (in criminal justice) in hand.

4

WITH THE FOURTEENTH PICK . . .

THE NBA had never been my dream as a kid. But now that I had a chance to make it, I couldn't stop thinking about it. After all the work I'd put in at UTEP, I knew I could succeed at the next level. Once you enter the draft, there are about a billion hoops you have to jump through before you can hear your name called (if you're even lucky enough to get that opportunity). One of the first things I had to do was play in the annual senior game in Seattle, Washington, which would be seen by tons of scouts. One of my teammates during the senior game was Michael Smith. He played at BYU, a team I was familiar with from the WAC, and was drafted that summer by the Boston Celtics.

He was supposed to be the next big thing behind Larry Bird. Like Bird, he had this unorthodox shot. But in the senior game, he was a good wingman for me. We played well together, and I ended up winning MVP honors. After the game, I flew back to El Paso with my trophy. My next trip would be to Portsmouth, Virginia, for another tournament.

Like the senior game in Seattle, I took home the MVP at the Portsmouth Invitational. In fact, I was the last person ever to get the award despite my team not winning the championship. We lost in double-overtime, but I still got the MVP nod—that's the type of show I put on—scoring, assisting, and running the break on all those NBA hopefuls. I was making a name for myself among the attending NBA scouts. If they didn't know my name before, they sure as hell knew it now. The final tournament I played was in Orlando, Florida. That was a big invite for me, even with all I had already accomplished that summer. I was looking forward to seeing some big-name guards on the court. My last opportunity before (hopefully) stepping onto the NBA hardwood.

I wanted to match up against Syracuse's Sherman Douglas, UCLA's Pooh Richardson, Iowa's B. J. Armstrong, Florida State's George McCloud, and Oakland's Mookie Blaylock. I took every matchup personally. Unfortunately, aside from Richardson, the other guys didn't end up playing in Orlando. Sherman, Mookie, and George bowed out (I don't think McCloud even came), and B. J. broke his hand. I was mad at those guys for missing the game. I really wanted to go against them and show that this 6-foot guy from UTEP was the best point guard prospect in the country. But I made the second All-Tournament team and, again, increased my stock in the process.

Next, it was time to visit individual teams for workouts. A bunch of them wanted to take a look at me, but the two that showed the most interest were the Indiana Pacers and expansion Minnesota Timberwolves. Team executives had already seen what I could do in a college game. Now, they wanted to see me shoot and whether or not I could dunk. They wanted to see how quick I was and what my lateral movement was like. They'd all heard about my skills, but now wanted to see them up close. The word was that my jumper was flat, without any rotation, but that it always went in. So I just had to prove that I could make the shots when they counted.

The more jumpers I made, the higher my stock rose. In the interviews, teams wanted to know about my motor. "Why do you always play so hard?" they asked. I told them that my drive came from always being doubted and underestimated. I said I liked to turn a negative into a positive. Rumor had it Doug Collins liked me for the Bulls, but the team ended up picking center Stacey King with the No. 6 pick. Then they got B. J. Armstrong later at No. 18. He was probably a better fit to put around Michael Jordan in the team's offense anyway.

The day of the draft, I still didn't know where I would land. The day before Tuesday's draft, the Golden State Warriors wanted me to fly from Chicago to Oakland to do one last-minute practice. I tried to get on a plane, but there was a problem: a typhoon had arrived in Chicago and all flights were cancelled.

After waiting for hours in the hopes that I'd still be able to get out of Chicago, I went home at two in the morning, as no flights were leaving O'Hare.

Indiana, which had the No. 7 pick, and their coach Dick Versace liked me, as did Minnesota and Bill Musselman, which had the No. 10 pick. I'd destroyed my workouts with both teams, opening eyeball after eyeball. The day of the draft, I was invited to New York to be on site, since everyone knew I would get picked in the first round. There was a big buzz around me. But when I fell to Golden State at No. 14, I was surprised, especially since I hadn't made it out to Oakland that night because of the typhoon. It wasn't that I was mad that I "fell" in the draft—I'm a confident guy, but I also take nothing for granted. That I made the NBA at all was a gift. I just didn't know the Warriors wanted me like that.

What I came to find out was that the Warriors coach Don Nelson put out word to whomever would listen that I had bad knees. Apparently he wanted me that bad! When I found that out, I was pissed. Years later, I talked to Bill Musselman's son, Eric, who told me even decades later Bill was *still* mad at Nellie for that. Another team that passed on me was the Celtics. When I'd heard about their interest ahead of the draft, I was intrigued. My dad had long been a Celtics fan. He liked Larry Bird and the way the Celtics moved the ball. But they passed me by, too, in favor of Smith. Later, when I played against Boston, Bird told me he was upset with their GM, Red Auerbach.

Larry said he went into Red's office and cussed him out. "Man, we needed Tim Hardaway, what were you thinking?" he told me he said to Red. But sometimes fate works in your favor, even when you think it won't. In the end, I found the right home in Oakland with Nellie. The 1989 draft, which was the first to be broadcast live by the NBA, and was definitely a momentous occasion for everyone involved—especially those of us who got drafted. It was an additional honor to be just the third player from UTEP ever taken in the first round. And while I was happy to be going to Oakland, I knew Nellie had messed up my money since later lottery picks make less than those taken in the top spots. But I'd soon find that Golden State was the best in the world for me to go. It was a run-and-gun team with a great deal of upside.

* * *

If I had gone to the Timberwolves, I could have been the expansion team's first star. If I had gone to the Pacers, I could have played with sharp-shooter Reggie Miller. But instead, I went to a team with fourth-year wing Chris Mullin and second-year guard Mitch Richmond, as well as a slew of other interesting players, including 7-foot-7 center, Manute Bol. It was a squad coached by run-and-gunner Don Nelson, a former signal caller with the Milwaukee Bucks in the 1970s and 1980s. He'd recently come down from the general manager's office in Golden State after letting go of previous head coach, George Karl, to take on the role himself for the upcoming season.

Nellie's style was all about pace and scoring, which was great for me. When I got to meet him, one of the first things he told me was, "You know I lied to everybody to get you." He said it almost matter-of-factly, but there was a little smirk. "I told everybody you had bum knees." I just shook my head. "And I know I took a lot of money out of your pocket, but you're going to benefit from coming here. You're going to be alright." I believed him, too. I knew Nellie was a great coach and I was excited to learn.

The day of my introductory press conference, when I signed my rookie contract, I was itching to play basketball so bad that I asked Chris Mullin, Mitch Richmond, and Rod Higgins if they wanted to play pickup. Mully had the key to the gym where Jason Kidd went to high school—St. Joseph Notre Dame in Alameda—and so we went over there and got a run in. We must have played for three or four hours, and I clicked with them right away. Chris was an unbelievable player in college at St. John's. Mitch was coming off winning Rookie of the Year honors and could do it all. And Rod Higgins, who I knew from the Chicago pro-ams, was a terrific big man. He was Mr. Fundamental even before Tim Duncan.

I was already getting geeked for the year. Being a rookie is intimidating. But in my back pocket I had a vote of confidence from one of the greats. Going into my senior year at UTEP, I was playing in a Chicago pro-am at Illinois Institute Tech with guys like Nick Anderson, Byron Irvin (who played for Portland), and a few other standouts. That's when a friend turned to me and said, "MJ is coming to play today." I said, "MJ *who*?" And he said, "MJ, fool. Michael Jordan!" I replied, "Yeah, well, y'all still going to get your asses whooped!" The other team also had Terry Cummings and Craig Hodges, along with Mike. They were trying to stack their squad against us.

But I wasn't backing down. The game was heated, back and forth. But the other team ended up winning (despite my trash talking) in double-overtime. MJ fouled out, but since it was summer league, no one enforced the rule. Once he'd arrived, it was standing room only in the gym, a fire hazard (but no one cared about that). People sat on top of whatever they could find. No one was about to kick him out of the game. In the end, it was a great battle. He had 65 points and I had 62. And after it was done, Mike turned to me and said, "Good game." Then he looked up and said, "You got a chance."

I knew exactly what he meant. This was 1988, when he was already *Jordan*. He was a four-time All-Star, two-time scoring champion, and an MVP. What he said carried big weight. And he'd just told me, a rising college senior, that I had a real chance at the pros. He gave me an inch and I took a damn mile. Every game I played after that, I knew I was worthy. I didn't tell anyone that story back then, not even my mother. I just kept it to myself and used it as fuel. But when I finally made it to the league, while I knew I had a lot to learn and get better at, I never thought I didn't belong.

* * *

Aside from basketball, though, there is a ton that rookies need to understand about the NBA. First and foremost are finances. It can be hard when you see the checks coming in fast and furious. I know it sounds like one of them good problems, but a lot of NBA players don't have financial sense—especially back then. It's a lot of fucking money coming in every two weeks. It can burn a hole in your pocket if you're not careful. My rookie year, I made about $500,000, but I knew how to save most of it. My mother had always taught me that I didn't owe anybody anything. So I remembered that.

She and my father told me "no" so often when I was younger that I didn't mind saying that to anyone trying to glom onto me. The only thing I knew was that I wanted to take care of my mother and let her quit her job at the post office. She'd taught me how to pay my bills, which helped me know where all my money was going. Even so, I wanted to make a splash, and my first big purchase was a red Jeep Cherokee with special gold rims and gray interior. When I took that ride home, I thought I was the *shit*! While I would have played the game for free if I'd had to, it was nice knowing that I could take care of myself and my mother now. We had a safety net.

If I did well, my contracts would only get bigger and all I had to do was hold onto my dough. In fact, one of the first things Nellie talked to me about was money. "I want you to understand this," he said one day. "This shit goes by very quick. The next thing you know, you're retired. Ten years—*boom*. Whatever money you make, make sure you take care of it." Those two things stuck with me my whole career. Thankfully, I also had a good agent who worked with me. A guy my high school coach had known for years. He was a lawyer in Chicago, Henry Thomas. And he'd become essential to me.

He'd played point guard at Harlan High School in Chicago, which was a basketball powerhouse. They'd won the city tournament when Henry was a junior and senior while I was still in diapers. After high school he attended Bradley University, where he was a starter on the team. He'd always wanted to be a sports agent after that and saw me as his way in. One summer, Henry served as my high school coach and really pushed me hard. He said he only wanted me to go to the hoop with my left hand, to make it stronger. If I went right, he took me out. I thought, *Man, what's wrong with this guy*? In the end it was the best thing for me. He must have taken me out of games six times before I got it through my head.

While in high school, Henry would give me tickets to go see the Bulls play at Chicago Stadium. And while it was a really nice gesture, the seats were so high up on the third balcony that we could touch the arena's ceiling. It didn't matter, though, because we were *there* able to see NBA games live and in person. While at UTEP, he took me aside one day during my sophomore year and said, "Tim, I don't know if you're going to make the NBA, I don't know if you're talented enough. But by the time you get out of college, I want to be your agent. We can try to make it together." At the time, nobody believed in me that much.

And here was Henry saying he was going to do whatever he could for me, and I never forgot that support. Even after I'd graduated, no one offered to represent me. Some agents had reached out for conversations, but in doing so they also tried to badmouth Henry and that was enough for me to close the door on them. But once I showed out in Seattle, Portsmouth, and Orlando, they came running to "help." By then it was too late for them. "Y'all had your chance, and you blew it!" I trusted Henry, we started our careers together in the NBA, and he ended up representing me for the entirety of my career. Later he would have clients like Dwayne Wadde and Chris Bosh. Today, I'm the Godfather to his kids. We were like family until the day he died in January of 2018.

* * *

Growing up, there were a lot of players better than me from Chicago who didn't make the NBA. For some reason, though, I did. I guess I never let the streets break me. I never let giant expectations ruin my head. One of the reasons was that I was patient. I never thought I needed to hit any check points by any certain age. I just knew I had to keep working to get better and avoid any distractions or dangerous elements. People always want to rush to the next thing. But if you're patient, you will win the day. It might take longer than you want, but if you go through the right steps, you'll be good. You'll make the mountain top and stay there.

That was my mentality when entering rookie camp. When I was drafted, twenty-two of the top twenty-five players picked were seniors. The other two were juniors and one was Shawn Kemp, who didn't go to college and was only a year removed from high school (but he was Shawn Kemp, so enough said). Even Michael Jordan was a junior when he left UNC in 1984. I was twenty-three when we began Warriors rookie training camp in July, just weeks after the draft. It was held at New Hampshire College, where Coach Nelson and his old Celtic pal Satch Sanders ran pre-season workouts. The other big rookie there was Lithuanian Šarūnas Marčiulionis, who'd been drafted in 1987, but wasn't able to come to the pros until 1989 after playing in the USSR.

We had a good group of guys. Phil Handy, the future Lakers assistant, was there, too, though he didn't make the team. Camp was tough, especially the first few days. There was a lot of verbiage to learn, like V-Back (which is a name for boxing out a certain man), different plays, rotation assignments, you name it. I knew some of the nuances of the game, but the slang was hard to pick up at first. Some of the rules were different in the NBA, too, like illegal defense. To avoid it, you're taught that, if you step in the lane as a defender, you have 2.9 seconds to get out unless you're double-teaming someone. That was different from college. We had to think quickly.

It took us rooks a few days before they even let us play five-on-five. Coach was on my ass about everything. He was on Šarūnas, too. He loved beating up on rookies. Coach was running two-a-day practices. We'd have the first one in the morning for several hours from nine to noon, then we'd go back to the team hotel, rest, get treatment, and then come back around 6 p.m. and run more until 8:30. It was like that every day—mornings for drills and learning the playbook and nights for practicing offensive strategy. But after about a week, I started to get the hang of things. The repetition helped. I tried to learn everything as fast as possible, absorbing it all so I wouldn't get my butt handed to me by Nellie. By the tenth day of the two-week camp, my offense started to come around. Before that, I'd just been embarrassing myself.

I kept turning the ball over, couldn't make shots. I was befuddled. But near the end of rookie camp, I finally began to put it all together. Mitch Richmond, who was entering his second year after earning Rookie of the Year honors, came to practice for a few days, but he didn't have to do any of the hard stuff. He was just there to see the new crop of youngins. Chris Mullin hadn't yet shown his face, nor had Manute Bol or my former pro-am friend Rod Higgins. After camp, the Warriors sent us home and I rested for several weeks. It was late September when the team called us back for full training camp with the entire roster. Two more fun weeks before preseason games in October and then the start of the regular season.

The Warriors held team camp at the College of Alameda, which was about 10 minutes outside of Oakland. Back then, most teams—other than Detroit and Chicago—didn't have their own practice facility. After some grueling practices where I got to know guys like Mitch and Mully, we began the short exhibition preseason.

Prior to training camp, I thought I would be a third- or fourth-year player before I was an NBA starter. But it had all happened so quickly. In my eyes, I was coming in as a backup to the incumbent Winston Garland (father of future NBA All-Star Darius Garland). I was going to learn from him and, in a few years, take the reins. But Nellie put my name up on the chalkboard as the starter. Also, to my surprise, it was something Garland—who'd been a double-digit scorer and finished second in Rookie of the Year voting two seasons prior—handled with class. We had zero bad blood. He was never visibly pissed at Nellie's decision though, I knew I would have been if I was in his shoes.

I got a gift with Nellie, lucky he believed in me. He saw something in me, and I'll always be grateful for that.

At that time, each team played three exhibition games (not five, like today) before the regular season began. The first game would see the starters play a lot, maybe 40 minutes. In the second game, starters only played about 10 minutes so the coach could get a look at the fringe guys to see who he wanted to keep. The third game was the last warmup.

In our first game, just by coincidence, we played in a familiar locale for me—El Paso! When I'd told Greg, Prince, and Antonio that I'd see them again on campus, I never would've guessed it would have been that fall with my new NBA team. That's fate. When the game began, my teammates played a little joke on me. "Tim, you lead us out," they told me. So I ran out and never turned around until I got out to halfcourt. When I looked back, I realized I was all by myself and the rest of the team was back in the tunnel laughing. Thankfully, I was out there in front of the UTEP crowd—*my* crowd. The one I played in front of for four years.

Taking it all in, I just put my arms up and they gave me a standing ovation. All the Jazz players were laughing, too. But it all worked out! The arena buzzed. In a way, it was the best of what could have happened—they actually did me a favor. I had my own little moment pregame, celebrating my "making it" with the El

Paso faithful. In the huddle moments later, Mullin, Mitch, and Rod Higgins snickered and said only I could've gotten away with that. When the game finally started, I was lined up against John Stockton. Already an All-Star, he'd led the league in assists and steals the previous season. That night, I learned a lot about the NBA. I was thrown into the fire and burned a few times by one of the greatest point guards to ever play the game. Whenever you play John, you pick things up. The guy is one of the savviest players in NBA history. He went out every night and played the same way each time. He controlled the situation, engaged his teammates, and was always ready to try and whoop your butt. The other thing was, he never talked on the court. It was eerie and awe-inspiring.

* * *

The first time I stepped into an actual NBA locker room—not for practice, not for preseason, but before an actual game—it was a *holy shit* moment. I just stopped when I walked through the door and said to myself, *I'm in a fucking NBA locker room.* That's exactly how it was. I was in awe. Preseason is cool, rookie camp is cool, training camp is cool. But it feels *real* when the season starts and you're there for the first of 82 games. You're working hard in practice, but you can never mimic game speed until tipoff. And so when I got to the locker room before that first game, my mind sizzled with excitement.

When you're the point guard of a team, you're like the quarterback. You're telling people where to go and what to do, relaying the coach's message to your teammates. You need to know what everyone is doing and where everyone should be. It somehow never felt too much for me to handle—I was born for the job.

With all that in the back of my mind, I walked into the locker room ahead of my game one, and there are the established pros going through their already established pregame routines. Mitch Richmond, for example, would get so focused and so quiet on the bus that we just knew the guy guarding him on a given night was done for. Chris Mullin, a three-time MVP of the Big East in college and NBA All-Star, was always prepared, from his conditioning to his technique coming off screens. People were scared of these guys on the court—and they were on my side!

Then there was big Manute Bol, who talked trash all the time, God rest his soul. We had veteran forward Terry Teagle, a perennial double-digit scorer. Rod Higgins was another big-time bucket-getter. But the best part about it was there was no bullshit in the room. No one out for individual stats and star power. Everyone on that team wanted to win. It made me realize that I'd gone to the right team because all I wanted to do was win, too. It wasn't a collection of guys who were hating on you, trying to push you down for their benefit. Or guys who thought you were out for their job. It was all about victories.

And so began our quest.

* * *

As I mentioned, Coach Nelson inserted me as the starting point guard from day one. After I got the starting gig, my confidence went to another level. Indeed, as soon as I stepped onto the floor, I was ready to ball and make a name for myself in the best basketball league on the planet.

I wanted to bust people's asses on the court. I immediately became more assertive. Nellie just told me, "Do what you're supposed to do out there and you'll be fine." After all, it was just basketball!

Well, in my first game, it took some time. I was 0–7 from the floor and finished with zero points in 23 minutes—with five fouls! We lost that one to Phoenix, 136–106. Our next game against Houston at home—my first time in front of the Warriors crowd—and I had just six points, to go along with five turnovers, in another loss. It wasn't until my fourth game (the team's seventh) that I scored double digits. (I'd missed a few games prior, sick with strep throat.) We had a rough start to the year, going 4–14. But then the wins came. We won 12 out of the next 15, including two six-game winning streaks. I averaged 12 points and nine assists in that stretch. I'd arrived.

* * *

Let me take a moment here to tell a quick story here about my man Manute Bol. The 7-foot-7 center from South Sudan remains one of the most unique players in NBA history. He'd been taken in the 1983 draft by the Washington Bullets (leading to some famous photos with 5-foot-3 guard Muggsy Bogues). After four seasons in DC, he'd come to Golden State. The 1989–90 season was his second with the Warriors and, when I got there, he was wearing my signature No. 10—the number I'd worn all my life. As a rookie, though, I found out sometimes guys will sell you their number if the price is right.

I thought that was cool, so I asked Manute about it. I didn't know what he might say—$10,000, $20,000—but maybe my teammates were setting me up. I thought it would be a hard negotiation, but I said. "Nutey, can I ask you something?" He said, "Yes." I said, "How much is it going to cost me to get my number back?" He said, "You really want the number?" I said, "Yeah, yeah!" He looked at me and said, "$500,000!" At this time, Manute was making about $400,000 a season. I said, "What?"

He repeated the number, but that was my paycheck for the entire season. He said, "If it's worth it to you, you'll pay $500,000, your whole paycheck. And I will give it to you." So I went to the uniform guy and said, "I'll take No. 5, please!" But the little secret is that, after all that, Manute got traded the following season to the 76ers (for a first-round draft pick, which we later used to select Chris Gatling). I don't want to say he got dealt just so I could get my No. 10, but basically that was why. Nellie had my back there! He told me, "You got your number now!" That kind of thing still happens today, too. I heard someone from the Houston Rockets was just dealt because he wore Kevin Durant's number and wouldn't give it up. After that, I wore No. 10 for the rest of my career until my last season in Indiana, where I wore No. 14.

But other than that silly exchange, Manute was by far one of my favorite teammates. He's a legendary guy. He used to say he hunted lions in Africa. Today, South Sudan has a proud basketball tradition, but it largely started with him. The tall, lanky guy was one of the coolest people in the world and one of the coolest to put on a basketball uniform, too. On the court, he was all about winning and teamwork. He was also kind and respectful. He did his job, which was primarily to block shots. He was so tall that he damn near blocked out the sun—and definitely the basket!

But after every game, Manute liked to have a 12-pack of Heineken. He'd suck them down! I'd say, "How can you drink all of them fucking beers!?" He'd just smile. Back in those days, it was normal to have beer in the locker room or on the bus after a game. Nellie used to leave the postgame press conference for the bus with two beers in each coat pocket and two in each inside pocket of his suit, along with one in each hand. That was the Don Nelson six-pack.

Everything was about team unity. Everyone had to be a good teammate. Don Nelson set a good role for that, and Manute, for a while anyway, personified it.

* * *

Back in Oakland, it felt strange to be in a new city. I'd gone from growing up in Chicago to making a home in El Paso to now living in the Bay Area. Though I'd had some good people teach me important lessons along the way, I was essentially alone. A few tips I'd learned from teammates included, "If you're going to drink, make sure you keep your glass with you" and "If you're going to smoke weed, know where it comes from" and "If you don't want to do something, walk away" and "You don't need an Adidas tracksuit." Oakland had a reputation back then for being dangerous, but I was used to it coming from Chicago. Old heads like to give advice, and I was happy to hear what they had to say.

But, more than that, what I needed was Yolanda.

When I went out to Oakland in the fall, we began discussing the idea. "Why don't you come out here?" I offered. We thought it would be a good idea to try one last time to see if we could make our relationship work. While we split up after my first year at UTEP, we'd kept in touch and stayed close enough. Now in Oakland, I needed a familiar face, someone I could trust and talk to. So we gave it a shot. We'd never actually lived together before, and this was our chance to go for it. She liked the idea, so she left her restaurant job in Chicago and flew out to the Bay to meet me. When she did, she brought damn near everything she owned! Everything but the actual kitchen sink. When I picked her up at the airport, I said, "Wow, did you have to bring *everything*?" She said, "Well, I don't plan on going back." I retorted, coyly, "You plan on staying, huh?" She nodded.

By now we were in a better place, more mature than when we'd first gotten together. What also helped was that we could start a new life from scratch out in Oakland. Not only as individual adults, but as a couple, working together to forge a future our way. Being far from Chicago and all our friends was actually a benefit to our relationship. Not because either was bad, but because they just distracted us from moving forward. So, from that moment at the airport thirty-six years ago, we've been together. Trust me, it hasn't all been bliss—there has been plenty of arguing. Yet it's what we both wanted and needed.

We've always loved one another, but we also had things we needed to work out first. We talked through a lot of issues. We wanted the relationship to work, but we had to learn to empathize with one another. She was the partner of an NBA player, and I was someone who had a pressure-packed job with lots of travel that was only just starting. I'm proud to say that we have *never* gotten into any physical altercations. After seeing my parents do that, I swore that wouldn't ever be my path. But there were definitely nights I had to sleep on the couch! We had to learn what we needed and what the other couldn't give. We had to grow up and find out what a true partnership was.

* * *

While I'd graduated from UTEP ahead of the NBA draft, I was still the youngest player on the Warriors roster. Because of that, and with being a role player on both my high school and college teams, I didn't think I'd be entering the year as a starter . . . but Nellie had other ideas. From the first game of the season, he immediately put me in the starting lineup, though on a trial basis. I hadn't started my first year in high school or in college, but I did in the NBA. To keep the gig, I did whatever Coach told me. I wanted to have fun, but I wanted to play good defense and keep my teammates involved. I knew I had to learn to communicate rotations on the court and encourage my guys. I tried to keep things lively, and Nellie liked my charisma, confidence, and sense of competition.

I wasn't afraid to talk back to him occasionally, too, but he knew I would always listen to his direction. Coach was an accomplished player from the 1960s and 1970s Boston Celtics. He knew what it took to win—he had five rings. And while he never tried to turn me into anyone from those teams, I knew what he said was scripture, stuff learned from Bill Russell and Red Auerbach. Most of all, Nellie liked to get the ball out and run. Get a rebound and *go*. It was all about racing up the court and getting reps together as a team. The main goal my rookie year was to build chemistry with Mitch and Mully. And by the end of the season, we were clicking.

The idea was to score fast and often. Nellie thought outside the box and wasn't afraid to let us guards and forwards run the break. Soon, we'd define an area with the concept. Nellie wanted us to move constantly. Motion offense—that was the name of the game. Mully would run ahead and I'd throw long passes to him for easy layups. Or me and Mitch would run give-and-gos and get people on their back heels. It was the precursor to the seven-seconds-or-less Phoenix Suns some twenty years later. We were young, talented, and could run. We were a Big-3, but not in the design of the Boston Celtics trees with their giant front-court. We were racecars.

The trouble for me that season was less on the court than it was off. For much of the season, I'd played with a bad case of strep throat and didn't even really know it. When I finally got to the doctor, he gave me the diagnosis. He told me I could kick it quickly if I got a giant shot in my ass. Now, I hate needles. *Hate them.* And when he showed me what he was talking about, it was this giant syringe that looked to be six feet long. What made it worse was that I had to stay relaxed to get it; for some reason you can't tense up. By the time the ordeal was done, the entire hospital bed was drenched with sweat. "Wow, you *really* don't like needles!" Yolanda noted.

But that aside, everything came together by the final game of the season. It had an up and down year, and we entered the game with a record of 36–45. Our final opponent of the season, on April 22, would be the Seattle SuperSonics. They were trying to make the playoffs and, if they beat us, would be one game better than the Houston Rockets and make the postseason as the eighth seed. Though we were already out of it, we wanted to play the role of spoils—so we came out firing. After a high-scoring first quarter, in which we were tied at 34, Dale Ellis, Xavier McDaniel, and the Sonics kept pushing and had an eight-point lead at the half. That meant nothing to us, as we were just getting warmed up. We came out the locker room ready to turn things up, and cut the lead to four by the end of the third. The fourth was all ours. While they had scored at least 30 points in each of the first three quarters, he held them to 26 and, when the buzzer sounded, we won by two, 124–122.

I scored 28 points that game (which was tied for my season high, which I'd done ten days before against the Mavericks) to go along with three steals, six assists, and eight rebounds. Only Ellis scored more points with 33. After that win, we knew we had something special and would be able to build off that for next year.

In my rookie season, I'd started in 78 games and averaged 14.7 points, 8.7 assists, and 3.9 rebounds. I'd held my own in the league and only got my butt whooped a couple times by guys like Kevin Johnson and Mark Price. Those dudes were so fast—you can study the NBA game all you want, look at all the film you can, but until you get used to the speed of some players, you're done for.

Even so, I had a rookie year that put me in the same conversations as some of the all-time greats. Being a distributor was my main focus, and one of my highlights was having a 19/19/10 game against the Nuggets in January—the first triple-double of my career. We obviously won the game, 139–122. For the season, my 689 assists were the third-most by a rookie in NBA history, only behind Mark Jackson and Oscar Robertson. I also had 34 games with 10 or more assists which was, at the time, the third most for a rookie (again, behind Jackson and O).

As a team, we finished the season first in pace, and I led all rookies in assists and steals and Top 10 in the league in both. (I thought I could have won Rookie of the Year, but David

Robinson won the award unanimously.) After the season, I went back to Chicago and worked on my body, played more basketball, and cleared my mind. Then in the fall, I returned to Oakland early for training camp. I had one goal: be a terror. I wanted to scare opposing guards and lead my team to the playoffs. Yolanda and I were still going strong and making a home in the Bay. Life was good—hard, but good. With luck, things would continue in that direction. With luck.

Memory Lane: Rod Higgins

The first time I met Tim was an interesting moment. He had just gotten drafted by the Warriors and Coach Don Nelson asked if I, along with Mitch Richmond, would go to the hotel and hang out with him, go to dinner, what have you. Just connect with him. So, we ended up going to the old Oakland Hilton to pick Tim up. When we get over there, we ask Tim, "What do you want to do? You want to get something to eat? Go to the mall?" And Tim says, his answer to both of us, was, "No, I want to go to the gym and bust y'all's ass."

That was my initial meeting with him. We were like, "Oooohhhhh, okay!" So we went to Alameda, to the high school where Jason Kidd went because Mitch had the keys to the gym. We get there and start playing one-on-one. That was typical Tim—knowing him now, having played with him and been around him all these years, I saw what a great player he was, and that is indicative of that first meeting. You can just hear his voice saying it, too, because he has this unmistakable voice.

I didn't know him when I played in the Chicago pro-ams, as I was a few years older. So when I was playing in those games in the Chicago summer league, that was in the early 1980s and Tim was probably in high school. And there weren't any high school players at that point playing in the pro-am. But, obviously, Tim's reputation started to come out of the city that he was a player. And he took the long road from his neighborhood to UTEP to Golden State and Miami and the Hall of Fame.

In Golden State—Tim and I laugh about this all the time—he and I used to always play HORSE. Before shootarounds, we'd go to the side basket to play. At the old Oakland Coliseum, there were the two main baskets, and we had this side basket. We'd say, "We're going to go play in the ghetto." When you're from Chicago, there are a lot of ghettos. And we joked with one another that the side basket was the ghetto there. So we'd go over and play HORSE in the ghetto.

Manute used to come over and try to come into the game and we told him he wasn't good enough! He'd talk trash to us. But Tim and I became tight like that by shooting together. After shootaround was over—it was normally from 11 a.m. to noon back in those days—he and I would stay in the gym and shoot halfcourt shots for the next hour. We'd play $50 a make, and we'd have two pay periods during the year: the All-Star break and at the end of the season.

But this is one of the moments I tease him about, because I used to always kick his ass and take his money. You can ask him! It's one of my favorite things because of Tim's bravado. You beat him and he's still talking trash to you! But I was getting the money on that one. In the end, though, Tim helped me a lot. I was a limited offensive player, predominately a catch and shoot guy. So I needed a dominant point guard like him, like Tim, who cannot just create for himself but gets guys like me shots as well.

He was able to get me in places where I didn't have to do anything besides lay it up or shoot it. Tim was that good. Not only that, but the evolution of him as a man has been really impressive. Everyone has a journey, but given the highs and lows of his career, to still be able to be part of the game is great. And to see him and his wife Yolanda spend a lot of time with their son in the game, that's incredible. All of that has helped Tim become the person he is today. Even the controversy that he went through—to bounce back from that and to be a better person is just amazing.

5

RUN-TMC

THE New York City–born trio, Run-DMC, was the first rap group to garner a gold record. They were skilled, fun, and complementary. In other words, they were to hip-hop what my Warriors team wanted to be for basketball. A style for the new generation. While a basketball team is (obviously) more than three players, our Warriors core at the time was Chris Mullin, Mitch Richmond, and myself. Chris and Mitch were like the rappers, Joseph "Run" Simmons and Darryl "DM" McDaniels. And I was the guy who set them up, like DJ Jason "Jam Master Jay" Mizell. And, ahead of the 1990–91 season, Coach Nelson made that very dynamic known.

On the first day of training camp—which is the day Nellie also passed out the playbooks (and if you didn't give them back at the end of the year, it was a $50,000 fine)—he got the whole team together and pointed at me. "This is my *captain*," he said. "I'm giving him the keys to the car." Nellie brought me front and center—I thought he was playing a joke at first. "Whatever Tim says," Nellie continued, in earnest, "it's coming from me.

And if you don't like it, don't like what he says, then you and I have a problem." Coach hadn't told me he was going to do this. I was as stunned as anyone.

While I'd essentially started the entire year as a rookie, that season felt more like a trial period. Truth be told, I thought I'd come in as a first-year player and sit behind Winston Garland, who'd been the team's starter for the previous two seasons before I'd arrived. He averaged about 13 points a game and finished second to Mark Jackson in Rookie of the Year voting in 1987–88. But Nellie put me in from the jump. Now, though, he was consecrating it. Blessing it. Putting his stamp on it and, despite all the talent on the team, was making me its preeminent leader. He was letting that decision be known to the rest of the team—if anyone had an issue with me being the man, they could take it up with him. But there weren't any issues—that's just how much of a family our Warriors team was. After he announced it, I went up to Nellie and said, "Are you sure? What about Chris and Mitch?"

"Don't worry about it," he said. "I've got confidence in you and those guys love you. They'll follow your lead. Just go out there and do what you do. Be Tim Hardaway. You're a unique player—you actually don't even know how good you can be yet."

From that moment, we were on a mission to make the playoffs, and I was the new lead dog. We'd finished 10th in the Western Conference the year prior with a 37–45 record. But it was a new season. The playoffs were our goal. If we made the postseason, everything else would fall into line. Nellie had bestowed on me a big honor, and I wasn't going to let him down—or anyone else for that matter.

From that first practice, we really began clicking as a team—better than any squad I'd ever been on. Most of us had already played a full season together, so with the time off to reflect and hone our skills, we all stepped back onto the floor with the same mindset and goal. We hummed through drills, didn't miss a beat on offense. Run-TMC (T for Tim, M for Mitch, and C for Chris) may have been conceived late in my rookie year, but it was officially born during that first practice.

We were lucky that Nellie was an offensive genius. The NBA is still using his "Nellie Ball" ideas today—like the stretch big. (But Nellie could be tough, too. One time he cut a guy, Mike Smrek, because he refused to foul someone in a game. "Everyone say goodbye to Mike, this is his last day," Nellie announced in a practice. I'd never seen that before.)

While Nellie had given many of us the green light to shoot from three, it wasn't like today's game where everyone shoots from deep—especially the big men. In fact, Nellie encouraged it! It wasn't like he demanded we shoot 40 threes per game but, if we were open, we could let it fly. All Nellie said was to make sure we didn't have a "foot foul," which meant no long two-pointers with your foot on the three-point line. Nellie liked the long ball, and was definitely ahead of the curve in that aspect—even going back to his time coaching the Bucks in the mid-'80s. For instance, in Manute Bol's three seasons in Washington, he had attempted a total of three treys. Yet in his first season with Nellie in 1988–89, he attempted 91, and another 48 the following year. Our backup 7-footer Paul Mokeski could also shoot. Tom Tolbert was another one of our bigs who got the green light to shoot from anywhere. Tom was also the team cut-up, keeping the guys loose. He would say something off the wall and we'd all just bust up laughing.

My role, though, was the team trash talker. I was the guy who gave the boys confidence. If someone was trying to talk down to one of my guys, I'd build him back up. "Oh, he thinks this is going to be easy?" I might say to Tom after a guy like Gary Payton wouldn't shut up about him. "Let's go kick his ass!" One time, Kevin Willis was talking smack to us. "Tim can't guard you," he said to one of his guards. But one of my teammates looked at Kevin, "You shouldn't have done that!" We busted him up that night and whooped his team. After the game, Kevin came over to me and said, "You're right, I shouldn't have done that!"

We weren't scared of anybody. We knew Run-TMC could play with any team in the NBA. We were the real deal. Chris, Mitch (who we also called "Rock"), and everyone else followed my lead. I was the engine for the whole group. I'd even go at people talking smack in the stands. When we were on the road, we heard it all, from shouts to racial epithets.

Thing is, people didn't know how bad it was back then because there were no cell phones to record it. But it was rough. Still, growing up on the streets of Chicago, I had thick skin. Joke was on them! It was like water off a duck's back. With me, Mitch, and Chris, we just dominated. (In fact, we were just the second trio in Warriors history to have three players average 20 PPG for a season: Mully (25.7), Mitch (23.9), me (22.9).) Teams could try to stop two of us, but they could never take all three of us out of the game. We always had an answer. Mitch and Chris were two of the best shooters in the NBA—their shots never seemed to hit the rim, *nothing but net.* With me leading the break, we had all we needed to score. It wasn't as if we were taking anyone by surprise, either. Our chemistry was on display the season prior, even if our record didn't show it. In fact we averaged 116.6 point per game!

Wearing my No. 10 jersey with Manute gone now, I was all set. We came out of camp as one, and were ready to take on all comers . . . and that's just what we did. We wanted to send a message to the league that we were for real, and in our first game of the season made that point clear. On November 2, 1990, we faced off against the Denver Nuggets, and showed what our offense could do. After four quarters, we came out on top in a 162–158 victory, which remains the highest-scoring NBA game ever in regulation. Mully had 38, I had 32, and Mitch had 29.

When we ran the break, I could sense their footsteps on my right and left, running with me as I pushed the ball. We'd come down the court on a fast break and I knew just where to get it to them. If one was curling off a screen or if the other was popping out for a jumper, I would wait and get them the ball in the perfect place, right in their shooting pocket, so they could let it fly. I knew exactly how hard or soft to throw it, how to lay a bounce pass so it would hit them in the hands. The ball would find them in their chest or their waist, and they'd catch and shoot. With big Rod Higgins trailing, I had options all around me. That's what you develop when you play as a group. But even with the success of my rookie year and how our team began to gel, I knew I still needed to improve. To get better. And who better to learn from than my TMC boys! If I'd be sitting down during practice, I'd watch Mully and Mitch run the floor, studying them. It not only helped add tricks to my offensive game, but allowed me a different view of them running the floor so that I could better get them the rock for a bucket. I'd also find just where they wanted the ball. We worked on bad passes to see what would happen if I gave them the ball to the right or left of where they wanted. How they'd adjust. We focused on all scenarios. Those guys worked incredibly hard on every detail.

Mitch, Mully, and I practiced together often to sharpen our chemistry. We often played three-on-three full-court against the likes of Šarūnas, Rod Higgins, and Mario Ellie. We'd work on timing, passing the ball to the perfect spot when one of us came off a pick, going at a defender at the free-throw line. It was all about movement, movement, movement.

On offense, I prided myself on getting to the basket. My penetration was elite, and I played with a ton of energy. Swagger was perhaps my biggest attribute. I wanted to breathe life into my team and snatch life from our opponents with every crossover, jump shot, assist, and steal. I knew I still had things to improve upon, including my jumper, but I was still young and had the desire . . . plus it helped to be able to play with such stars like Mitch and Mully. It was like we were made in a basketball laboratory for one another. I was the tip of the spear, and they were flying right along with me.

We had a set playbook, but on any given night Nellie would let us throw it out and just run our stuff. He'd say in the locker room, ahead of games some nights, "I'm not going to call a single play. As long as you're sharing the basketball, be yourselves." The only rule the guys gave me was that, even though I was so good at breaking my man down, I couldn't do it immediately. I had to save it like a well-earned punchline to use at the perfect time. After all, why show your best move off in the first quarter when you might need to break it out in the fourth? We also were lucky to have such a strong fanbase that showed us love, though I'm sure they also appreciate that, if we scored enough points, our fans got free pizza—so you *know* they were into it! Our goal each night was to get to 120 points, and we were confident that if we hit that mark, we'd win in the game (and were 22–4 when scoring 120!). Who needed defense?

Mullin, who'd been in Golden State since 1985, averaged 25.1 points per game in my rookie season and 25.7 in my second. In his first three years he'd averaged less than 17. Mitch, who'd won Rookie of the Year the season before I joined, averaged 23.9 points in my second year (his third), his best to that point. Together we averaged more than 72 points per game. And today, all three of us are in the Hall of Fame.

But you don't make the Hall without work, and I was lucky to have a front-row seat on the time and effort they put in to honing their craft. I still remember watching Chris—he'd work alone for an hour in practice, shooting over and over (where, I swear, he never missed), and then he'd run with the team for another 90 minutes.

The former *three-time* Big East Player of the Year would be perfect for two and a half hours. When I tell people that, they think I'm exaggerating. But I swear to God, it's true. I watched him hit every single shot for two and a half hours. Layups, threes, midrange jumpers. He was always in a groove. He must have made 100 in a row! He was one of the most focused players I've ever been around. Chris wasn't an especially athletic guy, so he had to work harder than most to succeed. That pushed me to stay in the gym longer. Like Nikola Jokić or Luka Dončić, Chris wasn't a fast player. But at 6-foot-7, he used his height and pace to his advantage—and he knew how important that was to our offense. If everyone else is playing fast—fast twitch, fast first-step—well, if you play slow, they won't know how to adjust. With Chris, everything was slow, so he threw other teams off rhythm. Playing against him, guys would *just* miss blocking his shot or *just* miss tipping the ball away. They'd be *just* a half second off time with everything. He knew how to use picks—no one could keep up with his pace. That's how Joker and Luka play today. If Joker does something, people often just race right past him, not used to his pace. They wonder, *How did I miss that?* But it's because he's so slow. Talented, but a glacier.

And Mitch? Well, he was just a bully on the court. The 6-foot-5 guard played hard and physical and could do it all. He was like a wrecking ball with Stephen Curry's jump shot. We needed that because ball in the early 1990s was *physical.* We were tough. I grew up with the mentality of, "if you're not bleeding, it's not a foul." In the NBA at that time, if you got hit, you kept going. You'd take the hit and get right back up. As a point guard, if I passed the ball and then came through the lane, I was prepared to get smacked, elbowed, or even punched. That was just the norm. You'd better cover your chest or stomach because something was coming.

And not sometimes—*every time.* If we were playing Utah, for example, I knew big Mark Eaton or Karl Malone were going to rough me up in the paint. I had to be strong enough not to get hurt, but I knew I was going to feel it (these days I laugh at some of the "flagrant fouls" NBA refs call in the games compared to what we dealt with on a nightly basis). We had to learn how to deal with it all, or even use it to our advantage.

As I've said before, practice is key. You can throw a bunch of All-Stars on the court, but if they've never played together then it's just every man for themself. However, if you match them up with a "team" that has worked together, then it doesn't matter if they have no "stars." Odds are they'll take the W. And that's how we approached things. Whether after a win or a loss, we continued to practice, honing our game. We knew that communication was key, and were always talking. We'd figure out what to do if a defender was playing us a certain way. We'd develop signals about going backdoor on a cut to the basket. We'd know just when to throw a pass by someone's ear to brush them off, almost like a baseball player. I learned that from the wily John Stockton.

We'd talk about how to defend someone, how to steer him one way so a teammate would be in help position for a steal. Everything we did was part of a plan—and it paid off. While Mitch didn't make it (though he was top 10 in scoring at the break), Chris and I made the 1990–91 All-Star team. For Chris, it was his third in a row. For me, it was my first. (Mitch would make six All-Star teams later in his career.) Nellie came into practice one day and announced the news. "Tim Hardaway," he said, "you're an All-Star. Chris Mullin, you're an All-Star." I couldn't believe it. It was a *wow* moment.

It was fantastic news, especially coming from Nellie. He had already taught me so much in such a short time. It was the little stuff, the details—like how to position your hands or feet to defend a guy a certain way. Or how to move without the ball. He drilled into me what he called "baseline drift." When your teammate is driving baseline and you're at the top of the key, you have to bust your butt to the weak-side corner to give him an outlet. It's something Stephen Curry and Klay Thompson perfected most recently. But Nellie was having us do it decades before. There were other things, too. Like how to set up a lob pass for a dunk or when to do a spin move. Nellie was ahead of the game.

After I got the news that I was an All-Star, I couldn't wait to get home to tell Yolanda and call my parents. We had a game that night, too, and while I don't remember who we played, I know the Oakland crowd gave me a standing ovation when the PA announcer introduced me as "All-Star Tim Hardaway!" I couldn't help but smile from ear to ear. That was the hardest part—you'd have to go from smiling and enjoying yourself to playing hard in the game. From being on Cloud-9 to *let's play basketball* against a good team. But that's alright. It was all worth it, of course. I was scoring well and top five in assists.

* * *

That entire season, I wore the initials "MEE" on my shoes to honor my maternal grandmother, Minnie E. Eubanks, who we called, "Mother, Mother." She'd passed away in the summer of 1990 after my first full year in the league. That was rough. She died too soon. I'd taken my mother, brother, and Yolanda to Disney World because my mom had never been. But when we got back from Orlando, all my family members were already at our house. Instantly, I knew something was wrong. She'd drank herself to death. It was a sad ending to a great life, and so I dedicated the rest of my career to her.

My grandma had given me the confidence that I later instilled in all of my teammates. She taught me how to persevere. She taught me to be the best person that I could be. She told me that if I was going to do anything, that I should work to become the best at it. She told me to never let anyone take my confidence from me. Never. She put that in my head, and I never forgot it. Born in Mound Bayou, Mississippi, she'd moved to Chicago with her sisters and brothers. But as an adult, she always had a problem with alcohol—ironic, given my mother's decision to be with my father, who was also an alcoholic.

Minnie and my great grandmother lived with us when I was in high school. She worked as a hair stylist in Chicago. She lived with us for part of her life, and owned her own beauty parlor that she ran with a friend. They did hair every day, Tuesday through Saturday. My father's mother Julia also lived in Chicago. I would visit her after school some days and she always made sure I did my homework. She was always telling me to get my mind together, that repetition in anything I did would help me better accomplish my goals. That helped me become a responsible adult later in life. Both women had big impacts on me, and even though they're no longer with us, they'll stay with me for the rest of my life.

It hurt to lose my grandmother when I did, but I used her memory as fuel. And by the All-Star break that season, my Golden State Warriors were looking good. We were sitting at 26–20, fourth in the Pacific Division (which was better than the 24–25 record we had at the break the previous season). After my cyst surgery in college, it wasn't a sure thing that my right knee would hold up. But I was doing okay thanks to a guy I called "Doc Hollywood." During my rookie season, someone on the Warriors noticed that I was flatfooted. So they sent me to a doctor in San Francisco to get some orthotics for my shoes. While I was there, this guy, Doc Hollywood, suggested I take some medicine for my knee.

He gave me these giant horse pills that he said would improve blood flow to my right knee. He said they would help the knee not get stuck and maybe even help some cartilage to reform.

"Alright, cool," I said. He told me I had to take three giant horse pills per day, but I was willing to do whatever it took. Today, I still use that medication, called Glucosamine Chondrotin. And, thank God, my knees don't hurt like they could. I'm still walking without pain. My joints are still able to work. Before I started taking the stuff, I could feel when the weather changed. If it got cold, my knee would get stuff. Modern medicine, man, it's wild stuff.

* * *

The All-Star Game was in Charlotte that year, home of the expansion Hornets, which had only been in the league for a couple seasons. My friend, the 5-foot-3 Muggsy Bogues, was their point guard. They also had Rex Chapman, Earl Cureton, Dell Curry, Kendall Gill, and J. R. Reid. But now wasn't the time to think about other teams. I was there to enjoy myself for the big weekend. For the East, the starters included my buddy Isiah Thomas, Michael Jordan, Larry Bird, Charles Barkley, and Patrick Ewing, along with Dominique Wilkins, Bernard King, and a few others. (Isiah and Bird were both announced staters, but due to injury didn't play.)

For my side in the West, we had Magic Johnson, Kevin Johnson, Karl Malone, David Robinson, and my guy Mully as the starters. Coming off the bench were me, James Worthy, Clyde Drexler, and John Stockton, along with others. In a hard-fought battle, the East ended up beating us by just two points, 116–114. We almost won the game, but a Kevin Johnson three-pointer was waived off after a basket interference call on Malone. That same weekend, I also took part in the three-point competition. Shooting along with me were Craig Hodges, Terry Porter, Dennis "3D" Scott, Danny Ainge, Hersey Hawkins, Glen Rice, and Drexler.

In the first round of the contest, me and Porter tied with scores of 15, but he beat me in a 30-second tiebreaker and my day was done. Truthfully, I never really liked the three-point contest, even though I participated in a couple of them. When you're shooting the ball, there's this camera hanging above you. When we practiced, it wasn't there. But during the event, there it was. It's close enough that it distracted me, taking my concentration away from the rim. I always hated that thing. That year, Hodges won the competition (hitting 19-straight shots at one point), his second of three in a row.

There are a lot of events during All-Star weekend. In the morning on Saturday, there was the Jam Session event that began at 8 a.m. All these kids from different local schools would come and fill up the arena in the morning, which was great. We'd meet and talk with them and shoot around, too. And from there, we'd have practice for the game a few hours later. But the problem was, if you went out the night before, you were groggy. That weekend, I think I only got a couple of hours of sleep. In fact, there was one night when I went out and got a taste of what it meant to be a star.

Me and some friends of mine found a club in Charlotte one night. We were rolling *deep*—there were about forty of us! The club in downtown Charlotte had this long line in front. My buddy said to me, "Go up there and tell them you're Tim Hardaway." But I said, "Man, they're not going to let all of us in there!" But my friend assured me—after all, I was an NBA All-Star. He got me to go up to the door. I talked to the doorman.

"Hey," I said, "I'm Tim Hardaway and I have some friends with me." And the guy extended his hand and said, "Hey, Tim! Congratulations! How many are you?"

I told him we were forty but he just said, "Go on in. Just tell me when to stop." My jaw dropped. He was going to let whoever I wanted inside. I just had to tell him where the end of our line was! I'd never had anything like that happen before. So we all went inside and immediately realized that there weren't even that many people there. It was just like the club owner was waiting for a big group like mine. They just kept the line of people outside, making it look like it would be all jam packed. So we all stretched out and had a good time. That was the life, I have to say. It didn't even matter I had just five points in 12 minutes in the actual game!

For the players, the weekend is as much about being in a room with the twenty-four best guys in the league as it is about anything else. You're in awe when you walk into that locker room before tip-off. You see Magic Johnson, John Stockton, Kevin Johnson, Clyde Drexler. And you just start joking, like, "Hey, Clyde! I can't believe you dunked it like that on so-and-so last week!" He'd say, "Man, he shouldn't have been there!" You make plans for what events or parties you want to go to later. You take pictures, sign autographs, ask about each other's families. That's how it's been for me, from my first appearance to my fifth.

* * *

When the playoffs came that season, we were seventh in the West with a record of 44–38. We'd improved our record by seven games and officially made the postseason. We didn't care who we played, whether it was Portland, Utah, or San Antonio—all of which were top seeds. They were jockeying for position while we were solid at the seventh spot. We just believed we were unstoppable on offense. On the same token, our "small ball" lineup had to make up for our lack of size on defense with quickness. Every team was going to be bigger than us, but they'd also be slower. Our job was to make sure our biggest advantage wasn't also our downfall. We'd flown commercial airplanes all season, but once we made the playoffs, our owner Jim Fitzgerald sprung for private flights. Only a few teams used private planes at this time—the Detroit Pistons were the first, and it greatly benefited them in the late 1980s. After a five-game winning streak to end the season, we were matched up against the No. 2 seeded San Antonio Spurs. Flying to Texas from Oakland, we thought we could get used to this private air travel.

We had a great team that season with our Run-TMC trio and bench guys like Lithuanian legend Šarūnas Marciulionis, rookie Tyrone Hill, and newly signed Mario Elie, to name a few. But in the first game in San Antonio against the Spurs, we struggled. The Spurs were ready for us—ready for war. Though we had a small lead after the first quarter, they outscored us by 27 in the second and third, and were up by more than 20 heading into the fourth. Their star center David Robinson scored 30 points and grabbed 13 rebounds. Their New York City–born point guard Rod Strickland added another 30 with 13 assists, and their shooting guard Willie Anderson had the game of his life, scoring 38. Despite Mully and Mitch each dropping 29 to go along with my 19 points and eight assists, we lost by nine, 130–121.

But Nellie wasn't fazed. He just said, "Don't worry fellas, we're going to win this series." I was shocked to hear him say that so directly. He didn't yell or scream or even put us through our paces in practice. Instead, we just watched a little film and had a 30–45-minute shootaround. He told me and Mitch to stop turning the ball over so much and that was basically it—nothing major, just a few tweaks. After practice, though, eight of us decided to play four-on-four full court, and that's when things clicked—if for no other reason than the confidence Nellie instilled in us. Nellie went upstairs to look over a few things as we stayed on the court and ran. It was me, Chris, Mitch, and Rod Higgins against Mario, Vincent Askew, Šarūnas, and Tyrone. We went up and down hard for about an hour.

Then Nellie came back down and said he wanted to play HORSE with his assistant coaches, so they kicked us off the court and put all the basketballs away. "Y'all just get out of here," he said. "Get some rest and get ready for tomorrow." And in the next game in San Antonio, we were a different team. We had a different walk, a different charisma. It continued at shootaround that morning, and we carried that confidence into the game, crushing the Spurs, 111–98. I had 20 points with nine assists, Mully had 27 with six assists and seven rebounds, and Mitch had 16 and six. Lead by Šarūnas's 16, our bench outscored theirs, 37–16. It was, through and through, a team effort.

We knew a key to beating them was taking Robinson out of his element (though he still put up 28 points and 15 rebounds). He couldn't guard the rim under the basket because we had our sharp-shooting big men step outside, which left the lane wide open for me to drive the ball. Tom Tolbert and Rod Higgins kept him out of the paint. It's the kind of stuff teams run today, but we were doing it thirty years ago. Plus, we knew that if we were able to keep them under 100 points a game (as they had averaged more than 107 on the season), we could win the series.

We went back to Oakland for Game Three and, while it was close, we pulled it out, 109–106. All five of their starters scored in double digits, including my old college foe Sean Elliott. But Run-TMC combined for 71 points, and I added 11 assists and eight rebounds. Two days later we finished off the No. 2 seed Spurs, 110–97. We kept them under 100 points for the second time in the series and were finally able to hold David Robinson under 20 points. Though I only hit three of ten three-pointers, I finished with a game highs in points (32) and assists (9).

The history of Warriors basketball goes way back to guys like Wilt Chamberlain, Al Attles, Rick Barry, and numerous others. The fans are knowledgeable, and they always bring it when they come to the arena. As a result, during the playoffs, they are loud. If you're playing the right way, they'll give you all the love in the world. That's how the people of Oakland are. But if you're not putting in your all or doing what you're supposed to be doing, they'll let you know. I loved the fans in Golden State and especially so during the postseason. We brought it and it got *loud*.

From one good team to the next, we headed to LA to face off against Magic (who had gifted me my killer crossover title) and the third-seeded Lakers in the Western Conference Semis. Mitch, he said, was the guy who could kill you all types of ways, Chris was the dead-eye shooter. I had the move that would break your ankles. Maybe he was buttering us up—Magic always had an angle. Either way, the playoffs began on their floor at the Great Western Forum in Inglewood, California, on May 5, 1991. We weren't scared, but knew they had a lot of basketball history on their side. By now, though, Showtime had changed. No more

Kareem Abdul-Jabbar, no more Michael Cooper. Instead, they had Vlade Divac and Sam Perkins.

In Game One, LA came out to a quick 10-point lead in the first quarter, 35–25. And while we kept the game pretty even from that point on, we could never get a run to cut their lead, and they took the opening game by that same 10 points, 126–116. I had a team-high 33 points with nine assists, but what hurt us was that Mullin didn't play. He'd injured his knee in practice and was out for a game. Magic took advantage and notched a triple-double, with 21 points, 17 assists, and 10 rebounds. Byron Scott had 27 and James Worthy scored 25.

But just like the previous series, Game Two was a different story. We landed the first blow, going up three points in the first quarter on the road. But the Lakers landed a haymaker in the second quarter to go up by nine. It was a tough matchup.

We came out after halftime all guns a blazing, outscoring them 41–30 in the third. During the break, we collected ourselves and reminded each other to make Magic a scorer, not a passer. That was the key to beating LA. By the time the final buzzer sounded, we'd won by a single point, 125–124. Mullin was back for that game and scored 41 points—he was a wizard out there, hitting everything. I got 28 with 14 assists and a whopping eight steals. Mitch added 22, though he fouled out late. We were undersized, so we had to scramble some on defense and Mitch had to use his fouls on bigger guys. We were always in some sort of defense rotation, trying to make up for our lack of height. Magic scored 44 for his team, while Worthy added 23 and Perkins scored 24.

But after the game, Magic told reporters that if he had to keep scoring like that, his Lakers were going to lose. He still had nine assists and 12 rebounds, but was taxed. He wanted a more free-flowing game. To get people open and see them score. We had them where we wanted them . . . or so we thought.

With Game Three back on our home court, we made a big miscalculation. The Warriors wanted to make a big deal of our matchup against the glitzy Lakers. So, before the game, they flew in Run-DMC and had them introduce us to the crowd. It was a marketer's dream, but only served to anger Magic and the crew.

After that, we saw why Magic and the Lakers were the real deal, why they'd won five NBA championships. He just killed us, mentally and physically. We'd taken Game Two and then rubbed salt in the wound with Run-DMC. As the "It's Tricky" rappers were hyping us up, I looked over to the Laker bench and saw Magic huddling his guys up. He told me afterward what he said to them, "See! They think they can kick our ass! They're treating this like one of my Summer Groove games. But this is REAL. This is the playoffs!" He worked us, putting up 15 points and 15 rebounds, while Worthy dropped 36 and Byron added 23 with seven steals. Me and Mitch scored 24 and Mullin had 11 assists, but we lost by three, 115–112. They killed us in Game Four, 123–107, and finished us off in LA in Game Five, 124–119, to win the series. Though I had 27 points and 20 assists and Chris and Mitch each scored 26, it just wasn't enough. It was a tough way to go out. But, in another way, our Run-TMC team was ahead of schedule. We'd done well in the playoffs after finishing 44–38 on the season. For my part, I'd scored 22.9 points per game along with 2.6 steals, 9.7 assists, and four rebounds. I'd also shot 38.5 percent from three (looks like all those shooting reps had paid off).

But in the NBA, things can change quickly. One mistake can mean a decade of sorrow. A single trade, an injury, or some other miscue can spell doom for a franchise. Little did I know that was exactly what was right around the corner for the Golden State Warriors. Little did I know our hope of building a contending team in Oakland was about to come to a screeching halt. But that's what can happen in a league where draft picks and players can be dealt from one team to another in an instant. Indeed, in the 1990s there was no such thing as the player empowerment era—and Run-TMC was about to be a casualty of that.

Memory Lane: Paul Mokeski

Timmy was one of the most competitive guys I've met, and I've met some competitive dudes. I played against Michael Jordan, Larry Bird, Magic Johnson, Moses Malone, and a lot of other greats. On the floor, Tim would rip your throat out. He's like me. When people saw me play, they thought I was mean and tough and a jerk. They'd ask my wife, "Is he an asshole?" But off the floor, I'm like a big teddy bear. Kids love me, animals love me! In a different way, Tim is similar to that. On the floor, no one wanted to mess with him, but off the floor, on the plane, at practice, he was one of the most easygoing, funniest guys out there.

That's a switch you have to turn on to be able to perform at the level he did. And he's Mr. Crossover. People might forget that. Allen Iverson? Timmy was doing that, embarrassing people way before him. If ESPN was like it is today back then, there would be highlights of him every night crossing people up like Magic Johnson, whoever. I played 12 years in the NBA on some great teams with some great guys, though I don't know if I ever had as much fun with a group than I did with

Run-TMC, with Mitch and Mully and Šarūnas—just all those guys. We just loved playing together.

I don't want to speak out of turn or out of school, so to speak, but the toughness when it came to Timmy Hardaway was immediately evident to me. We were teammates during the 1990–91 season, but I also was working with Dallas when he was with the Mavericks later in his career. One stretch, we played, like, five games in eight nights on the road. But we had to get to a gym in the middle of it to get some shots up, maybe go through some stuff and scrimmage a little bit—nothing crazy so no one got hurt. Just a light practice. Well, there was a rookie on the team. A big dude, 6-foot-8, a rebounder. The other thing with Tim Hardaway, he could talk trash with the best of them.

People talk about Michael Jordan and Larry Bird and, yes, they were great. But Tim was one of the best. Him and Chris Mullin. Timmy was great at trash talking. So the scrimmage that day at practice got a little more heated than it should have. The rookie thought he should start talking to Tim. It got a little intense. And push came to shove, and I remember looking over there and Timmy saying to this dude, who is way bigger than him, "Don't you walk up on me. Don't walk up on me." The next thing I know, the big dude is on the floor and Timmy was saying, "I told you don't walk up on me. I'm from Chicago. I said don't do it!"

6

BREAKING UP THE BAND

WHEN I found out about the trade, I was devastated. On the court, I was a pit bull. I didn't back down and could get by anyone at all times. But off the court, hearing about the deal to send Mitch away, bothered me. It seemed impossible that the three of us—me, Chris, and Mitch—would only get to play together for two seasons. It seemed to us that our fast-paced style was about to take the league by storm. We were the highest-scoring team during the 1989–90 season and second in 1990–91. We had great fans and had sold out every home game my second year, too, along with just about every road game. What more could anyone want? We could have really done something special.

After we'd lost to the Lakers in the semifinals, though, Nellie said he got pressure from the owners to add size and defense, though I felt there was no reason Mitch had to be dealt for that. In the end, that became Golden State's "Original Sin." You don't destroy your core for the fringes. Together, Chris, Mitch, and I were one of the highest scoring trios in NBA *history*, with three guys who all scored above 20 points per game. Second only to Denver's Alex English, Kiki Vandeweghe, and Dan Issel in 1982–83 (more recently, Kevin Durant, Klay Thompson, and Stephen Curry surpassed us). We even had one of the best nicknames in basketball. Run-TMC.

At first, we were known as the "Big Three" but then there was an event to rename us. The *San Francisco Examiner* sponsored a "Name the Warriors" contest, and they received more than 1,500 entries in their ballot box over two weeks. Then we got on TV before a game to pick the best. The paper put all the entries in one of those lottery balls you spin to mix them all up. There were so many that Chris Mullin told the cameras to cut for a second and he took two big handfuls out. Some of the other names included "The Marks Brothers," "Three Amigos," "Joint Chiefs of Stats," "Blood Thirsty Gym Rats from Hell," "Heat, Meat and Sweet" and "Three-Mendous." But we liked Run-TMC best, so we kept that one.

What made the whole thing worse was that the three of us got along so well—even off the court. Mitch, Mully, and I would hang out—often with Rod Higgins—going out to dinner after games. We'd also have BBQs at each other's houses, go to our kids' birthday parties. We played HORSE all the time. Chris and Mitch won most of the games, but I'd occasionally get one off them. Mully liked to take shots from behind the halfcourt line or out of bounds on the sideline. Mitch liked the off-the-glass shots from the top of the key. I had to learn how to keep up! My knockout shot, which is something my son practices, was to put my feet on the corner where the baseline meets the sideline and shoot from there. The hard part about that one is shooting the ball across your body. But I learned to make that one and if you can do that well, you can win a lot of games. All that is to say we had good times together, challenging each other, making the other better. Not only did we have talent and drive on the floor, but we had chemistry. You can't buy or fake that in the NBA. It's one of those things that happens on its own and is a rare thing. As rare as a good nickname.

Basketball players often want to be musicians and vice versa. And with our name, we blended the two. The official winner of the contest was a musician named Peter Elman, but I don't know what he got for his efforts. But as a trio, we were so good together. At a time when the NBA was rugged and physical and teams were scoring in the 70s or 80s, we were an inferno. Don Nelson, our team's head coach and head exec, should have known it, but somehow he and the organization lost sight of all that. In return for Mitch, we got Billy Owens, a versatile, 6-foot-9 rookie from Syracuse University who Sacramento had taken with the third overall pick in the 1991 draft.

Billy was supposed to give us a versatile presence. He brought different dimensions to the game that Nellie liked. Someone who could grab a rebound and take it up court, like a Scottie Pippen. While we already had Tyrone Hill, he was more of an inside player like Stacey King. But when Mitch left, I lost more than just a teammate. I lost a good friend. Seeing him go left a void. When he was dealt, Chris and I were in the same room together with Nellie. He alerted us to the deal and said it was "going to be good for us." But Chris and I were speechless. Today, I can only wonder what if Mitch had stayed. I know Nellie regrets it, too. He recently said that he'd "never make that trade again." While we had a good season during Mitch's first year away, the team soon tumbled, and then crumbled. Nothing was the same.

Mitch said he got a call from Nellie twenty minutes before we were set to get on a bus on our way to the first game of the season. He said he walked into Nellie's hotel room and said, "I know you're trading me but as long as it's not to the Sacramento Kings, it will be okay." Nellie just hung his head. Mitch just walked out, knowing his fate. Nellie called me and Mully into the room to let us know. All we could muster in a response was, "What? Why?" He said we had to get bigger and better. We looked at him, like, "Okay." But we knew it was one of the worst ideas in NBA history. Mitch's departure was the beginning of the end. Mully later said Run-TMC was the most fun he'd ever had hooping.

The media is still talking about us to this day, and Stephen Curry wore one of our hats during his championship parade! But the night of the trade, as crazy as it sounds, we had a game to play. Officially, the deal was made on November 1, 1991, and it was Mitch, Les Jepsen, and a 1995 second-round pick for Owens. That night, we had to play the Denver Nuggets on the road, in our first game of the season. Though we were still reeling from the news, we won the game, 108–105. I led us with 25 points and four other guys, including Mully, scored in double digits. What's even more wild is that the next night, we had another game, a back-to-back. This time it was at home against, guess who? The Sacramento Kings. How's that for fate?

A few hours before tipoff, Mitch came into the arena and walked into our locker room. We were all happy to see him. But after we said our hellos, we realized Mitch had simply walked into the wrong room by mistake. "Oh, damn, that's right," he said, shaking off his confusion. He walked out with his head down. We were all still disgusted with the deal, especially him.

That night, he walked out of the locker room and out of the arena entirely. He just left the building, like Elvis. He told the Kings that he needed a couple more days to process the deal. I think it took him a week to finally report to Sacramento. That night against the Kings, and without Mitch in their lineup, we won by 62 points.

It was a good thing Mitch wasn't there to experience that ass kicking. He would have been so mad. But I know that once he reported, he didn't mope, didn't cry about the situation. He was a consummate professional. He played his ass off for Sacramento and, truth be told, put the team on the map for the first time in a real way. Michael Jordan even called him "one of the best players in the game."

Mitch went on to be a six-time All-Star for the Kings. He gave them an identity that stuck. It was a great trade for them, but not so much for us. Nothing bad on Billy Owens, but the trade killed our chemistry. While Owens fit in well, averaging 14.3 points and eight rebounds and finishing third in Rookie of the Year voting that year behind Larry Johnson and Dikembe Mutombo, it just wasn't the same. Billy wasn't a great shooter and, as time went on, he and Nellie butted heads. Coach wanted to help him with his game, suggesting he shoot his free throws underhand or one-handed, but Billy didn't want to listen. Some even questioned his work ethic.

Though he had skills, Billy didn't want to do what it took to improve. The whole thing was just too bad. Thankfully for us, Šarūnas made a big leap that season. He went from averaging 10.9 points to 18.9 and finished second in the Sixth Man of the Year Award voting. Šarūnas was a tough-minded guy and a legend in Europe. He knew how to play and at times even took over games. Today, everyone says Manu Ginóbili brought the wily Eurostep to the NBA. But no, sorry, it was Šarūnas a decade before. He also had a lightning-quick behind-the-back move that helped him get to the basket with ease.

During the season, Chris and I averaged 49 points per game combined and the Warriors led the NBA in scoring again. That, despite once shooting 0–17 in a game against the Timberwolves on December 27—some nights you can't buy a bucket. Let me just tell this story real quick: A few nights before this game, I was giving Mitch Richmond some shit. He'd just gone 0–13 in a game with Sacramento, and two nights later I set the record and went 0–17. Minnesota had these canary yellow locker rooms. They were supposed to relax you or something. Maybe make you lackadaisical for the game. I always got my pregame shots up in the morning and, before the game, I'd look at film or just relax.

I felt good in warmups and, during the course of the game, I made plays. I was just barely missing shots. It all came to a head when I got a steal at midcourt. I remember dribbling to the hoop and saying to myself, "Oh shit, I'm going to miss this layup all by myself!" I hadn't even gotten to the free-throw line and I was already psyching myself out.

The game went to overtime. Thankfully, we won. I only scored two points, but still dished out 13 assists. After the game, all the reporters sprinted to me. "What are y'all here for?" I asked. "I didn't do nothing tonight!"

"Oh, yes you did!" they said. "You set the record!"

Man, I still have the record today. The worst single-game shooting performance in NBA history. Nellie didn't care about it, especially since we won. I wasn't worried either. And just so everyone knows, I had 30 points against the Lakers in LA the next night. We won that one, too!

A few weeks later, Mully and I were both named to the All-Star team, this time both as starters, and Don Nelson was named coach of the team. But I didn't get a chance to start the contest because I gave my spot up to Magic Johnson. The guy who invented the term "killer crossover" had experienced one of the most shocking summers in the history of basketball. Ahead of the 1991–92 season, just months after playing in the NBA Finals against Michael Jordan and the Bulls, Magic had been diagnosed with HIV. After a few attempts to keep playing, he retired.

But the fans still loved Magic, and he was voted into the starting point guard spot. At first, there were questions about whether he would, could, or should play. People asked, "If Magic comes back, are you going to give him your spot?" My buddy tried to tell me I should keep it. But my thought was that if they said he could play, it was only the right thing to do to let him start the game. Especially if that's what the fans wanted. Besides, I thought, if he was still in the league, he would have easily been named the starter anyway. So, I said, let him have my spot and go out with a bang. Little did I know he would take home the MVP Award!

The East was coached by Phil Jackson of the Bulls and their starters were Isiah Thomas, Michael Jordan, Larry Bird, Charles Barkley, and Patrick Ewing (though Bird sat out the game with an injury). The East had Mark Price, Dennis Rodman, Dominique Wilkins, and a bunch of other greats. The West featured Magic, Clyde Drexler, Mully, Karl Malone, and David Robinson in the starting five, along with myself, Dan Majerle, Hakeem Olajuwon, John Stockton, James Worthy, and a few others. While I scored

14 points and had seven assists, and Jordan dropped 18 with five assists, the story of the game was Magic.

Because HIV was so new to mainstream culture, some had been worried about playing against him. People were scared because nobody really understood the disease. All we knew was that it was killing people left and right. But once the NBA doctors said we couldn't catch it through sweat or by playing against him, we breathed a little easier. Of course, some still spoke out about it, including guys like Karl Malone. But the 1992 All-Star game in Orlando became the Magic Johnson show. Hanging out with him in the locker room before the game—it was his first NBA appearance in months—was great. It was a lot of fun to have his smiling face back in the locker room.

You could see Magic was taking it all in. Nobody knew if this would be his last time in an NBA locker room. If so, he was all smiles, joking with us. In the game, the East challenged him. Dennis Rodman, who said he didn't care about his HIV diagnosis, took it as a personal challenge. Scottie Pippen, too. They wanted to see where he was at with his game, where his skills were. Could Magic still play? Would he be rusty or fatigued? But he wasn't either. That day, Magic led everyone with 25 points, and he won the game's MVP. Magic also took and made the final shot of the game, a long three-pointer over his longtime friend and former NBA Finals foe, Isiah Thomas.

While there was still 14-some seconds left, we knew that was the moment to end the game. Everyone ran up to Magic to congratulate him for putting on a spectacle and beating the odds and showing you could live your life even with that diagnosis. Not only that, but the West won in a blowout, 153–113. It was the largest spread in NBA All-Star Game history. And while I didn't start, I was happy for my friend. The NBA, myself included, owes Magic a debt of gratitude. If it wasn't for him and Bird in the 1980s, the league wouldn't exist like it did in the 1990s and like it does today, generating billions.

* * *

After the All-Star Game, we went on an eight-game win streak and were the best team in the West. Even so, I refused to get complacent, improving every day. With each game, I was getting better at just controlling the tempo and understanding the ins and outs of my teammates. As a point guard, your job is to get your team in a position to win. It's about making plays—but even more than that, it's about being a floor leader. When it comes to basketball, leadership means talking to guys. Helping them out if they don't understand what the coach is trying to say or do. A leader makes people better any way they can. A leader is supposed to give you confidence that you can go out there and beat anybody on any day, on their court or yours. A leader has charisma, a twinkle in their eye that makes the team want to follow you. When they see you're all business, they will follow you into battle.

Completing my third season, I averaged 23.4 points, 10 assists, 3.8 rebounds, and two steals per game. Along with being an All-Star, I was named to the All-NBA second team the league's second-best point guard. That was a great honor. And while single-season stats are of course important, knowing that I had accomplished something not many had in the game's history was something almost impossible to comprehend. With my stats, I became only the seventh player in NBA history to average 20 points and 10 assists per game for a season.

In the end, we finished the year 55–27, which was good for third in the West, despite missing Mitch, who'd averaged 22.5 points per game in Sacramento. Mully averaged 25.6 per game for us, as we were the only two with averages above 20.

As the third seed, we faced off against the SuperSonics in the first round of the playoffs. Seattle boasted a great one-two punch with Gary Payton and Shawn Kemp, and were only getting better—they were a little too good, actually. I'm not sure if we thought it'd be an easy series based on how we'd played on the season, but we lost Game One, at home, 117–109. Kemp and Ricky Pierce each scored 28 for Seattle, while Billy Owens had 25 points and 11 boards. I added 22 with six assists. But it wasn't enough.

Two days later, we battled back from a six-point deficit at the half to win the game, 115–101, tying the series at one game apiece. Mully had 20 and I had 23, with Billy getting 16 with 12 boards.

But it was all downhill from there. Seattle won the next two at home—the first game by a single point (I had eight costly turnovers in that one) and the next by three.

And, just like that, our season was over.

Afterward, the trash-talking Payton told it like it was. He said they weren't afraid of us. If we'd had Run-TMC, he said, it would've been different. They wouldn't have been able to stop all three of us. But two? That was doable. All Mully and I could do was shake our heads. Kemp killed us on the glass. We didn't have the juice. Our mystique was gone. What made the experience worse was that Kemp turned the series into a photoshoot. He had two of his most memorable dunks against us, which is really saying something. In one of the games in Seattle, he came down the line, cradled the ball like a running back, and then uncorked a giant slam over our center Alton Lister. His head was at the rim like he was really flying. As Lister fell to the ground, he pointed at him like he was shooting lasers from his fingers. Another time, Kemp got the ball after our big man Chris Gatling blocked a shot. And in one powerful move, Kemp rose up and slammed it one-handed over Chris.

Incredibly, though, and this made me mad, Chris dapped him up after that! They slapped five like they were meeting up for dinner. I told Gatling after the game that if he ever did that again, if he ever gave a motherfucker five after someone dunked in his face on TV like that, I would kick his ass. You don't do that there. If anything, you wait until after the game when you meet the guy in the hallway. You say good game then. Not when millions are watching. That just made him and us look so weak. It showed Seattle they could do whatever they wanted, and we'd take it. "Yeah, you're right, Tim," Chris said to me. But man, that pissed me off.

* * *

Later that summer, Mully got some good news: he was named to the 1992 Olympic "Dream Team." It was to be the first time that a US Olympic men's basketball team would include active NBA players. And eleven of them had been All-Stars in the 1992 game in which Magic got the MVP. I was so happy for Chris. It was well deserved. He was a hard worker and exactly the type of shooter the team needed. He was someone who motivated me as a player. Mully was a real leader thanks to the example he set in practice. I knew he would be a big help to the team in Barcelona, Spain, that summer.

And while the fellas were ripping off win after win in Spain, going undefeated and winning gold, I was working to keep things going at home. My dad, who had quit basketball by now after tearing his meniscus, had begun drinking again. It had started up during my first few years in the pros. My brother and I could tell he was falling off the wagon. I approached him. "What's going on, man?" I asked. "Donald and I can't be around you if you're going to be like this again." He said, "Yeah, I know, I know." He felt low about it. So my brother and I said he had to take a step away. We had to show him we were serious about boundaries. It hurt, but it was necessary.

I told him, "Let us know when you get it under control." To his credit, after several months, he started to get sober again. It's hard for an addict. Sobriety isn't linear. But you have to make sure you take care of your own self as they're dealing with their issues. In his early forties, he got himself under control again. He didn't want to be without his sons. It took him six months, but he managed to finally beat it. For as much as I love my father, he can often set the example for me of what *not* to do as a man. But even with him sober, I had a lot on my plate during the summer between the Warriors falling apart and me and Yolanda becoming first-time parents.

7

CHANGE, FAMILY, AND MY ACL

THE chickens came home to roost for us during the 1992–93 season. It was strange. On the one hand, I was becoming one of the biggest stars in the NBA thanks to my style of play, charisma, and killer crossover. But on the other, my team was crumbling in front of my eyes. It seemed like the 1992–93 year took place in a hospital ward—so many of us were hurt. Mully, who'd just won gold in the Olympics, missed half the year with a thumb injury. Šarūnas broke his leg and dislocated his ankle, and later blew out his Achilles. Billy Owens had knee issues. Even I missed 16 games due to a bruised right knee.

The only bright spot for the franchise was that it drafted Latrell Sprewell from the University of Alabama with the 24th pick that summer. Things were going okay for us through the beginning of January, as we were treading water at 18–14. But then the spiral began, as we lost our next five games and 15 of 17. We entered the All-Star break at 23–30, and finished the season with a dismal 34–48 record. Just one season removed from our 55-win campaign, it was a hard fall.

A lot of things just weren't working in our favor. Nellie was frustrated, too. By now, he thought we should be title contenders, but we'd gone south. Losing Mitch killed us and the injuries buried us (back then, if you were on the injured reserve, you had to miss five games—you couldn't just miss one like today's players do when they sit out for "rest"). Coach also thought some of our young guys would be further along, but they weren't.

Billy wasn't moving the needle, and while Latrell was good, he was still too young to help lead the team. As a rookie, he was a reserved guy. He was very, very quiet at the beginning. To his credit, though, he came in wanting to learn. Latrell was already a good defender. He had long arms and good instincts. But his shot and his handle weren't quite where they needed to be. With each game, though, you could see him getting more confident. He was a fast learner and, for the year, he started in 69 of the 77 games. He shot 37 percent from three and got 15.4 points with 3.8 assists, 3.5 rebounds, and 1.6 steals per game. He was a rising star.

Another rising star in the franchise was our assistant coach, Greg Popovich. Pop had been an assistant with the San Antonio Spurs from 1988–92, and then came over to Oakland to work with Nellie for two years, beginning in 1992–93. Later, as many NBA fans know, he'd become a five-time championship coach with the Spurs. But when he was with us, you could tell he was an energetic, innovative guy. He was young and always thinking outside the box. He was excellent with defensive strategies and wasn't afraid to go against the grain. He and Nellie were a perfect fit, one a defensive genius and the other an offensive one.

When you hire an assistant coach, you have to trust them. You have to feel comfortable with them on the bench and believe that they won't backstab you. Pop was that for Nellie. He just wanted to soak up his ideas. Perhaps he knew he'd go back to San Antonio and take over there one day, and so working with Nellie was like his offensive PhD program. Either way, despite the fact we lost more games than we won, it was good to have Pop around. A former military man, he would deliver a message with a certain authority that made you perk up. He was the type of person you *wanted* to hear from. Later, with the Spurs, he ran a well-oiled machine.

* * *

Despite our losing ways, I made my third All-Star team in a row. The game was held in Salt Lake City, so of course John Stockton and Karl Malone were in the West's starting five. So was Clyde Drexler, David Robinson, and Charles Barkley. I came off the bench with Sean Elliott, Shawn Kemp, Dan Majerle, Hakeem Olajuwon, Mitch Richmond, Mully, and a few others. Run-TMC was reunited again (though Chris and Mitch didn't play due to injury). For the East it was Isiah Thomas, Michael Jordan, Scottie Pippen, Larry Johnson, and Shaquille O'Neal. The bench included Mark Price, Detlef Schrempf, Dominique Wilkins, and a couple more.

Our side won a close one in overtime, 135–132, and Stockton and Malone took home co-MVPs. It felt good to make the squad again. At the end of the year, I was named to the All-NBA team for the second time in a row, too. For the season, I averaged 21.5 points, 10.6 assists, and 1.8 steals per game. I was second in the NBA in assists (behind Stockton). Also on the year, Mully averaged 25.9 per game and Sprewell scored 15.4. While we

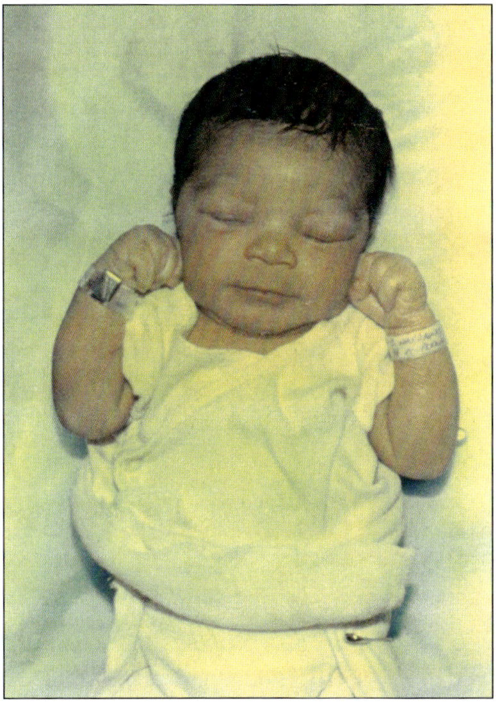

Baby Tim Bug, born September 1, 1966.

Three years old and already prioritizing cardio, with Yogi Bear coaching.

Around seven to nine years old, looking sharp for the camera.

Cheesing with my brother, Donald, then around six months old.

Me and Donald sitting with Santa at Christmas, around 1975.

Me and Yolanda with two-year-old Tim Jr. and nine-month-old Nia.

Beautiful shot of Yolanda with Tim Jr. and Nia in 1996.

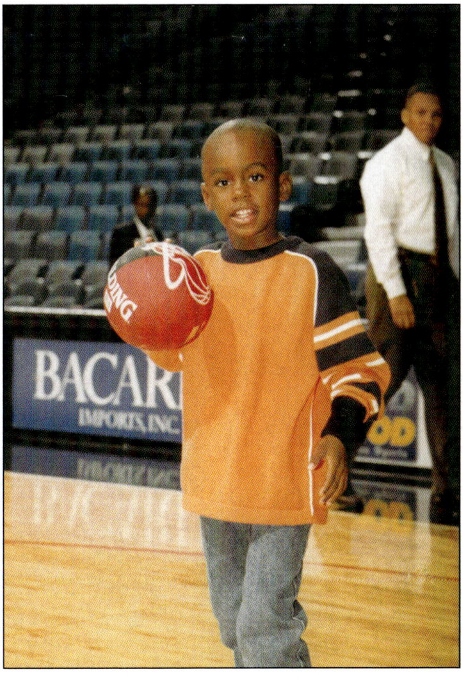

Tim Jr. showing off those skills on the court before a Heat game in 1996.

If you're not having fun, then why play the game? Scored 15 points that night against the Raptors in a game we won, 89–88, on December 14, 1996. *(Zoran Milich/Allsport/ Getty Images)*

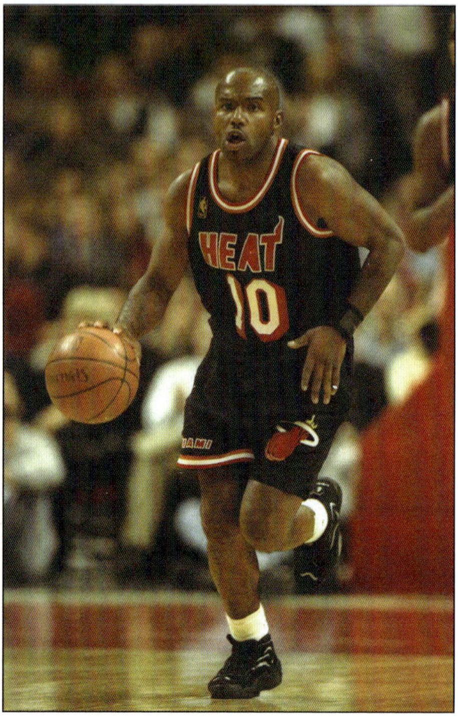

Going against the Bulls was always a welcomed challenge. Though we didn't always win (like on this night), I always made sure to give it my all. *(Jonathan Daniel /Allsport/Getty Images)*

I always enjoyed my "conversations" with the refs. On this night, in December 2000, I'm just chatting it up with ref Joe DeRosa in a game against the Jazz. *(Eliot J. Schechter/Allsport/ Getty Images)*

One of my proudest moments. When you get that jersey with "USA" on it, you just smile. Team USA took gold during those 2000 Olympics in Sydney, which was one of the highlights of my career. *(Harry How/Allsport/Getty Images)*

Our rivalry with the Knicks was one of the greatest in basketball during the 1990s. I scored 27 points with eight assists on this night, beating Allan Houston (#20) and his boys, 86–82. *(Andy Lyons/Allsport/Getty Images)*

There's no better feeling then hitting a game-clinching shot. My big three on this night came against the Spurs and put us ahead, 86–81, with just 20 seconds left. *(Eliot Schechter/Allsport/Getty Images)*

My brother for life: Alonzo Mourning. We shared a lot of blood, sweat, and tears during our time in Miami, and it was an honor to battle with Zo by my side. *(Logan Fazio/Getty Images)*

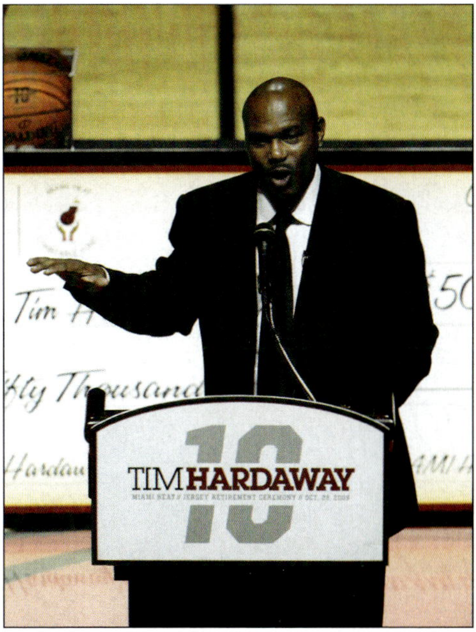

On October 28, 2009, I got the honor of a lifetime when the Heat retired my #10 (against the Knicks of all teams). *(Doug Benc/Getty Images)*

The ultimate acknowledgment of your hard work is seeing your number hanging in the rafters—especially with "Hall of Fame" right under it.

One of the toughest lessons I had to learn as a father was when to be a coach and when to be a parent. Watching my son play in the Final Four was that type of special moment, and I'm glad I was able to be there to support him.

Seeing your kid make the NBA is not something I can put into words. I've made sure to share all the knowledge I have, while remembering that we're two different people and, sometimes, I'm more help as a dad then as a coach. *(Ronald Martinez/Getty Images)*

The day I always hoped would come, but didn't know if it actually would. I had finally made it. I was a Hall of Famer.

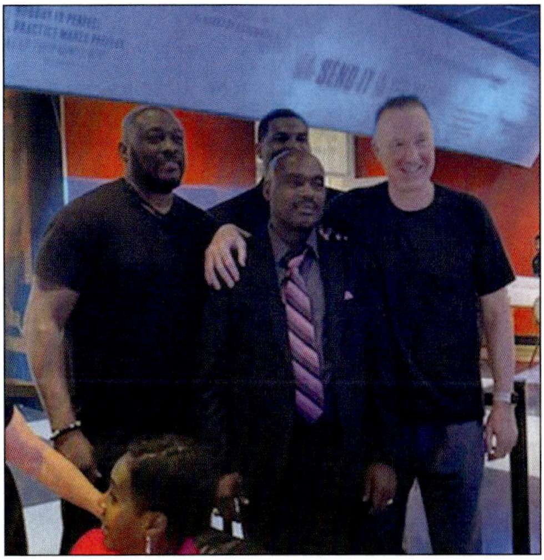

Nothing better than sharing my special day with those who helped me get there: My "Run-TMC" brothers, Mitch Richmond (left) and Chris Mullin (right).

Sharing this special moment with my parents, Donald and Gwendolyn Hardaway, and my brother Donald Jr.

I wouldn't have made it to the HOF if not for my parents, and no better people to put on that illustrious blazer than them.

The Hardawy fam (L to R): My daughter Nia, me, wife Yolanda, daughter Nina, and son Tim Jr.

Hard work pays off!

Showing off the inside of my HOF blazer with photos of the people who helped me get there: family, friends, and teammates.

Cheesing it up with my baby girl Nina while rockin' that "Naismith Orange" blazer.

My high-school sweetheart, wife, and amazing mother of my children. Words cannot express the love I have for you. *(Alexander Tamargo/WireImage for Plum Magazine)*

Enjoying the Olympics with basketball greats and *the* president! (L to R: Gary Payton, Reggie Miller, Shawn Marion, President Barack Obama, Steve Smith, myself)

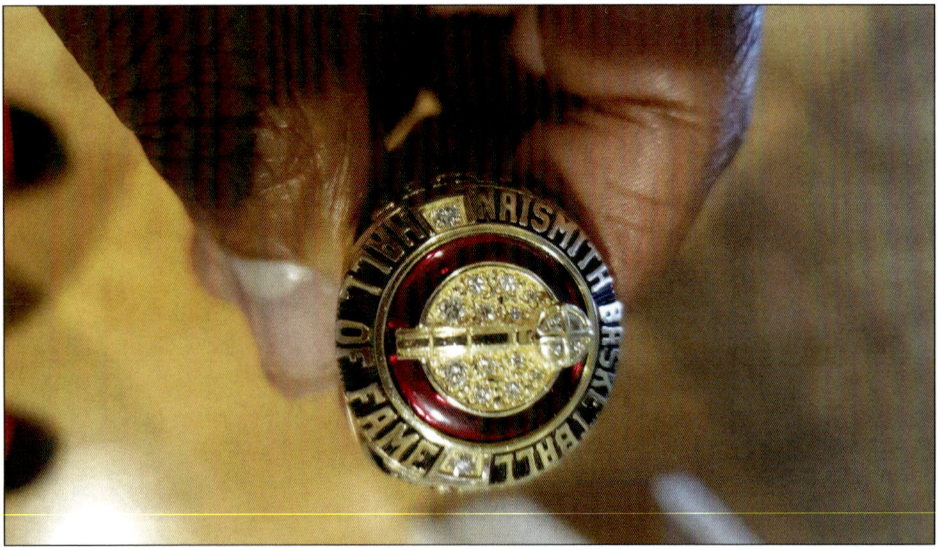

Hall of Fame, Class of 2022.

didn't make the playoffs, finishing 34–48, after the season, the Warriors finally got a bit of good luck. The NBA Draft Lottery ping-pong balls bounced so that we got the No. 3 pick. That gave us hope and made Nellie grin.

During the summer, he approached me and asked what I thought we should do with the pick. There were a lot of talented college players coming out, including University of Michigan star Chris Webber, along with big Memphis guard Anfernee "Penny" Hardaway and Kentucky scoring forward Jamal Mashburn. "Which one do you want?" Coach asked me. "Can you play alongside Penny?" I said, "Hell yeah! I can play alongside anybody!" In the end, Golden State made a big trade with Orlando. The Magic already had Shaq and he didn't want them to take another big in Webber, the projected top pick. Shaq had also filmed a movie with Penny and they got along well.

So the Magic and Warriors made a trade. They picked Webber and dealt him to us for Penny and more future draft capital. Now we had the star power forward to go along with me, Chris, Latrell, and Šarūnas, assuming all of us would be healthy for the upcoming 1993–94 year. With the "Year From Hell" behind us, I was able to take the summer to focus on family. Yolanda and I had welcomed our first child into the world, Tim Hardaway Jr., on March 16, 1992. Then, on May 15, 1993, Yolanda and I tied the knot. At the time, she was also pregnant with our second child, Nia, who was born that winter, on December 1, 1993. It was a special time for us.

I was experiencing success with the Warriors and our family was expanding. Baby Tim was a funny little guy. He was a skinny kid with a big head. And by the time he was six months old, I was taking him to Warriors practices in his stroller. He watched us play. Little Tim, who would grow up to play in the NBA as an adult, was crying when he got to our practice, but as soon as he started to hear the basketballs dribbling against the hardwood of the court, he would get quiet. He'd peek out of his crib, like, *What's going on?* I would prop him up and he'd watch, not making a sound. Then when we stopped, he'd start to cry again.

It was so fun having a baby. I loved it. It was also a trip watching Yolanda go through all the things she had to go through while pregnant and then giving birth. We don't give our women enough credit for what they have to do to bring life into this world. It's an amazing thing and takes great sacrifice. As a parent, your life changes dramatically. It's no longer about you. It's about the family and what you can do for the baby. I had to learn all of that quick, but I took to it—I appreciated every minute. I also couldn't help but compare myself to my own dad. You always want to be better than your father and provide an even better life for your kids.

* * *

Remember when I talked about all the promises the new season had, assuming we'd all be healthy? Well, what's that expression? *Man plans, God laughs?* He sure must have been yukking it up with us because we had a ton of bad luck in 1993–94. Ahead of the season, I inked a big new deal for three years and $10.5 million. That was a ton back then, and I was glad to sign. But I didn't have a whole lot of time to savor it because, during our first practice—which was the same day we signed Chris Webber—I went in for a routine layup and hurt myself. At the time, I was going hard but it was all routine stuff. The next thing I knew, I saw the bottom of my left knee move in the wrong direction.

It wasn't pretty. I'd come down the lane—something I'd done thousands of times in my life. I picked up my dribble and took two steps toward the basket . . . and then it just felt like the floor grabbed my foot and ankle and held onto it. Everything just stuck for a second. The bottom of my knee went in and out, and I knew at that moment that I'd torn my ACL. The trainer rushed over and asked what happened. "I just tore my ACL," I said, pained but confidently. He said, "Don't say that, don't say that! How can you know?" And I replied, "Man, I just know it." And sure enough, I was correct.

It was a huge blow for me and a huge blow for the team. I knew I'd miss the entire season rehabbing. Thankfully, it wasn't the same knee that I'd had that cyst operation. If it was . . . well . . . I probably would have needed a knee replacement, which would have ended my career. But thankfully it was my other knee. Small victories, I guess. I still recall the feeling of it giving out under me. I saw the whole thing happen in slow motion. It was devastating. It had taken all summer to sign Webber—back then, there weren't rookie contracts, so top picks negotiated with teams for what they could get. And now we couldn't play together.

Chris and his agent had fought from June into October. And it was in that first practice with him when I'd torn my knee up—day-freaking-one after we signed one of the most exciting young players in the NBA. When the 1992 Dream Team was scrimmaging with college players to get them ready for Barcelona, Webber was on the select team. Larry Bird said of Chris then that, if he was going to be in the pros, he'd have to get out of the league soon. That's how good Webber was. But now all I could do was lean on my sense of patience and try to heal. (Sadly, Šarūnas also missed that entire season with knee issues.)

In my absence, the Warriors signed free agent Avery Johnson to be the starting point guard and gave Latrell a bigger role. Spree really clicked with Mully. They were excellent in pick and rolls, and Sprewell was playing great defense. His shot had improved, and he was making plays up and down the court. We relied on his athleticism, and his strength and his confidence increased almost daily. It was very hard to watch the team play without me. I wanted everyone to do well, of course. But to not be out there . . . it killed me. We had so many great players and I could have been the one to tie everyone together.

Beyond how difficult being out was—have you ever tried to rehab a torn ACL? It's brutal. While I was able to come back stronger after it all, that's not a guaranteed thing. I knew I needed help. I prayed a lot. I leaned on my friends and family, who encouraged me. There were a handful of low points throughout my recovery that season where I almost gave up. The only person who saw it was my wife. Getting my leg to work again properly was no easy task. Believing you can run on it, bend it, be flexible—it's all a leap of faith. The one thing I tell people is to listen to the doctors. Don't push beyond what they tell you.

In my absence, the team had a good regular season, going 50–32. Billy Owens had a solid year, averaging 15 points and 8.1 rebounds. Avery averaged 10.9 points and 5.3 assists. Mully, though, missed the beginning of the year with injury and only averaged 16.8 points to go along with 5.1 assists and 5.6 rebounds. But the stars of the show were Sprewell, who scored 21 points with 4.7 assists, 4.9 rebounds, and 2.2 steals, and Webber, who scored 17.5 points with 9.1 rebounds and 2.2 blocks, along with taking home Rookie of the Year honors. While things seemed rosy on the surface, there were a lot of internal problems. Entering the playoffs as the sixth seed, we faced off in the opening round against the third-seeded Suns . . . and got swept. Losing that quickly after a 50-win season is indicative of a team that had internal issues.

For much of the year, Nellie and Webber were at odds. The power forward had spent two years at Michigan as part of the famous Fab Five, along with Jalen Rose and Juwan Howard. After back-to-back losses in the NCAA championship game, he left school and was taken No. 1. He was super talented, but was still raw as a player in certain areas. On offense, Chris liked operating down low, going one-on-one and using his athleticism to dunk and score. But Nellie wanted to expand his game all over the floor. He wanted to make him more of a passer, put him at the free-throw line, and let him be the focal point of the offense.

Later in his career, when Webber was in Sacramento, he would do all these things to great success, challenging the Lakers in the West for NBA titles. But as a youngin, he was less confident in those skills and Nellie just couldn't reach him. The hard part for me was knowing that if I'd been with the team and able to play, I could have been the liaison between the two and helped the rookie. I could have pushed him to become the NBA's next great point forward. And who knows what would have happened with him, Latrell, Mullin, me, and the crew? But I wasn't playing. I wasn't even with the team most of the time. I was home, rehabbing and working out.

One of the things I did most while injured was shoot. I wouldn't take jump shots, as my knee wouldn't let me get off the ground while I was still healing. But I could stand there and get up on my toes and take set shots. So, I shot and shot. A thousand a day. Outside with a friend of mine at a sports complex in Los Angeles. Set shot after set shot. That's how I got to be a better shooter. I'd shot 33 percent from behind the arc in 1992–93, and I knew that wasn't good enough. And, as I had always seen, hard work meant results. The next season I not only doubled the amount of threes I took per game, but raised my average to nearly 38 percent. It was like night and day, and I gave myself more confidence with each set shot I took. If you shoot a thousand shots a day for five months, it better pay off!

I was able to observe the game while I was injured. Doing that, I actually picked up a few things that I used later on the court. I saw how to better control the tempo of a game in certain situations. When to slow it down versus speed it up. Once I got my leg stronger, I started to run on an outdoor track. I'd bring Tim Jr. with me—he was maybe two or three years old. I'd park him at one spot and run around the oval track. When I was running away, he'd cry. "Why are you leaving me, Dad?" But as I came back around, he'd smile again. It was very cute. And it helped those long days as I tried to get my wind back and my legs under me.

It was only late in the year with maybe a month or two left in the season—well, after the All-Star break—that I returned to the Warriors. After spending much of the first four months of the season away from the team, Nellie and Mully had asked me to start to come around. "I need you to help the young fella," Nellie said. But by then everything had already gone sour. The two just weren't on the same page. Webber was out there doing his own thing. The season hadn't quite turned to chaos, but it was not what it could—or should—have been. Despite winning 50 games, no one was seeing eye to eye. Guys were playing more as individuals and not as a team. And while that might work in the short term, when you get to the playoffs it's the opposite of what you need to have success. Webber had all the talent in the world, but he just didn't believe in what Nellie was telling him. It was Billy Owens all over again, but even worse.

On defense, Coach wanted Chris to play center, too, knowing that if he could play that position, the team would be even more dangerous because he had a nice jump shot. But Chris didn't want to bang down low on defense with guys like Olajuwon and Shaq.

Then, adding insult to injury, Webber decided that he'd had enough, and so used a clause in his contract that stated he wouldn't be coming back to the Warriors for the upcoming season. The team really didn't have any options, and so a few games into the following season, we traded him to the Washington Bullets for Tom Gugliotta and three first-round picks. If you ask me, that trade should *never* have happened. If I'd been there to help Nellie and Webber coexist, it could have all been different. I would have kept the tension down. Webber and Don Nelson could have stayed with the team, and we'd be able to make a deep run into the playoffs. But hindsight is always 20/20.

8

FROM THE BAY TO SOUTH BEACH

I DIDN'T know it at the time, but the 1994–95 season was my last full year with Golden State. Before the season began, the Warriors traded Billy Owens for Miami center Rony Seikaly, ending that experiment. To kick it off, the Warriors sent Webber to the Washington Bullets for Tom Gugliotta, who only ended up playing 40 games with us before being dealt to Minnesota.

Things just got worse from there. We started off slow, and went into the All-Star break with a dismal 14–31 record. Then, a day before we came back from the break, on February 13, 1995, Nellie resigned as our head coach. Then, three days later, our GM Ed Gregory traded Gugliotta to the Timberwolves for Donyell Marshall, turning a bad situation worse. But that's NBA life. Things can turn on a dime. It happened to us with Mitch, and it happened again with Chris. Bad move after bad move. It was terrible. The only bright spot for the season again was Latrell, who made the All-NBA First Team, which was a huge honor. Some NBA seasons for teams can be fool's gold and, sadly for us, the 50-win 1993–94 campaign was just that. What made it harder was that it was difficult to imagine improving next year. Over the summer, we lost Šarūnas, Avery, and Pop. Everything just seemed to be wrong.

Even though the news off the court was louder than it had ever been, we did our best to start the season off on the right foot. When I came back to the team, I felt confident I could return to my old self. But I would've had to become Superman to get us off the mat . . . and open the year, we won seven of our first eight games! I began the season averaging more than 20 points, to go along with almost nine assists per game.

But then, the wheels fell off. We followed our hot start by dropping 14 of our next 15. Then, after winning two straight against the Bullets and Lakers. We dropped 13 of 15, finishing the calendar year at 12–28. It was miserable. Along with that, I was still shaking off some rust from my injury and it was hard to get excited to play. (I'd developed bone spurs during my rehab and had to get arthroscopic surgery in June before the season.)

NBA legend Bob Lanier, who'd been an assistant, was named interim head coach. A former eight-time All-Star and the 1973–74 MVP, Lanier had a history of success in the league as a player with the Pistons and Bucks. As a coach for the remainder of the year, he was solid. But with Mully missing most of the year again, there was little hope to turn the year around.

Though Lanier brought enthusiasm to our locker room, we went just 12–25 with him at the helm. But at first, he was telling the press he didn't want the job. I told him to go for it. "Stop saying you don't want it! If you want the job, go for it!" I said. "Never tell these reporters and owners that you don't want to be a head coach, that's crazy! This is your opportunity." I was trying to talk him up. And when he did get the job, I worked with Bob to get him straight with the offensive and defensive schemes. He'd only been an assistant with us for a short time, so I also helped him with running practices.

But in mid-March, I tore ligaments in my left wrist and had to get more surgery, which kept me out the rest of the season. Doctors told me it wasn't going to heal unless I got the operation. So with our team far from making the playoffs and their guarantee that I'd be ready for next year, I agreed and went under the knife. For the year, I played in 62 games and averaged 20.1 points, 9.3 assists, 3.1 boards, and 1.4 steals. Latrell Sprewell, who was an All-Star again, averaged 20.6 points with four assists and 3.7 boards. It had been a lost year for the franchise, which was still suffering from trading Mitch, now a three-time All-Star and two-time All-NBA player. Our 26–56 record was the franchise's worst in almost a decade.

* * *

Off the court, life was a bit better. Ever since the mid-1980s, the NBA has been a globally popular league, and I was the beneficiary of that a decade later. In 1995, *Sports Illustrated* put out its *Below the Rim* VHS, which highlighted the league's top point guards, from Mark Price to Kevin Johnson to me. It was the era of NBA video tapes, which included Michael Jordan's *Come Fly With Me*. Around that same time, I was picked by the league to host its *NBA Rising Stars* VHS, which showcased the NBA's up-and-coming talent, from Alonzo Mourning and Larry Johnston to Shawn Kemp and Gary Payton.

The '90s were truly an incredible time for the NBA and its marketability thanks to David Stern taking the game global.

Video games were popular, too. EA Sports came out with their *NBA Live 95*, and one of the commercials showed me and Mully playing video games in the locker room, dunking on each other. Then Nellie came in to stop us like an angry dad and put an end to our fun. A few years later, EA Sports put me on the cover of their *NBA Live 98* game (Mitch had been on the cover the year before). And five years before that, one of the bigger video games of the 1990s, *NBA Jam*—a two-on-two full-court basketball game—included me and Mully as the main duo for Golden State.

As it turned out, we were one of the more popular pairs used in that one over the years. To this day, people still come up to me on the street saying how much they loved having me in the game, running up and down and passing the ball to Chris for three. I was in my fair share of commercials around this time, too. From Cheetos to sneakers. There was the Nike ad where I was "Professor Hardaway," and took everyone to school with my dribble. There was another Nike ad where me and Kevin Garnett played "The Fun Police." I was even in a barber shop–themed commercial for Nike with Dennis Rodman and David Robinson talking smack.

There were commercials with the famous movie director, Spike Lee—one about talking trash and another where I was on a big bright outdoor court called "Spike's Urban Jungle Gym" for the Nike Air Raid. That shoe was meant for outdoor use only, which was perfect for me as I grew up playing the game on the hardtop of Chicago. The sneakers would be good for families who couldn't afford multiple pairs every year, since they were tough and didn't wear out quickly. The commercial for the Air Raid shoe was probably my most famous, and ended with me saying, "I got *skeeeellllls!*" (One time a guy came up to me in the airport and said, "I just need to hear you say it!" and I repeated the line. "Thank you!" he said.) Later in 1996, I also had the red and black Air Bakin', which were so beautiful.

The problem with all these shoe commercials, though, was that Nike didn't pay much for them. The money was in the royalties if you had a signature shoe, and a lot of guys—myself included—didn't have their own dedicated pair. We may have endorsed sneakers, but only names like Jordan and Shaq got those great deals. My agent Henry Thomas didn't have his own marketing firm like some athlete agencies had, so I never really got the payday I wished I could have. And it could be difficult to find one that could handle you right or that you could trust. Still, I put in the work where I could. But Gatorade and Fruit of the Loom never called!

I remember one ad I did for Hibbett Sports about patenting my killer crossover. The tag line for that one was, "You don't need a patent on something nobody can copy." Those were fun. I grew up talking a lot on the court, and to take advantage of that for Nike and video game ads was a bonus—not something I could have ever predicted when I was just a kid playing ball for fun. But they were something I took to like a duck in water, which is why I always wanted more. I like to think I'm a pretty personable guy. Even during NBA games, if fans called out to me I'd engage with them. One time I remember a guy in the stands said, "Man, Tim you look tired." And instead of mean mugging him, I replied, "Shit, I am! You know how hard it is to win a game?" I'm not the type of person to say, "Man, shut up, you don't know shit!" What good is that going to do? That doesn't help anyone—not the fan, not me, not the game of basketball or the NBA. If you have a good relationship with the fans, it will pay off. It's like that movie *Gladiator*—win the fans and you'll be loved.

One of the most fun moments in my career was playing in the MTV Rock N' Jock game in the summer of 1995. MTV put those on at the UCLA campus and they included NBA players and celebrities. The games were famous for the 25- and 50-point shots, and hot spots around the court. People like Kemp, Queen Latifah, and Mark Curry from *Hangin' with Mr. Cooper* (a show I was a guest on in '92 when Mark tried out and played for the Golden State Warriors) would lace 'em up in the exhibition. They were a blast and quite popular when broadcast on television. As I've said, music and basketball have long been related. I was even mentioned in several rap songs, from Common Sense to Kanye West. That was a badge of honor for me coming from those Chicago-born hitmakers.

* * *

Getting back to basketball, with the trainwreck that was the 1994–95 season—from our terrible play and losing Nellie to my injury—I knew that the 1995–96 was going to be one of the most important seasons of my career. The previous season was one to forget, so in the offseason the team had made some big moves. Heading into the summer, the Warriors again saw good fortune in the draft. We got the No. 1 pick, and this time the team took sophomore Joe Smith, a slinky forward from the University of Maryland. The team also brought in point guard B. J. Armstrong. A six-year veteran, he had been selected by the Toronto Raptors in the 1996 expansion draft, but refused to report and so was traded to us.

It was clear that the team was headed in a new direction when the franchise and GM Dave Twardzik brought in Rick Adelman to coach, replacing Lanier. Adelman, who'd had success earlier in his career with the Portland Trail Blazers, taking a squad led by Clyde Drexler to two NBA Finals, decided to put me and Mully on the bench in favor of Armstrong and Jerome Kersey. It was the mark of a new era. Everything just felt different. Going into training camp, though, I tried to be optimistic. I've only ever wanted to win, and while I thought I was still the best option at point guard, I did what Coach thought was best for the team.

Even though Adelman wanted to start B. J., he came out and said he would be fine coming off the bench, which is something he'd done earlier in his career. A former All-Star, Armstrong had won three rings with Michael Jordan and the Bulls. Adelman saw what he had done in the 1992 Finals, and I guess he Armstrong was now the man for the job in Golden State. It was hard for me and Mully, who was also on the outs, to see what was happening with the team. Not long ago, we were Run-TMC. Now we were yesterday's news. We both knew we were still starters and key contributors. But we also saw the writing on the wall, saw how the year would play out, and I knew I had more to give a team. Knowing that I wouldn't be given a chance to really help the Warriors, I felt Rick was doing me a disservice. Plus, being in the last year of my contract, I decided it was time for me to go.

There was one game when it all crystalized, which was on February 7, 1996, in Oakland. The Chicago Bulls were in town, which meant going against Michael Jordan and Scottie Pippen. Two guys I'd played against in All-Star games. Now I was diminished, coming off the bench. What made it worse was that they were relentless with me. At one point, I was running down court and Scottie and Mike just started laughing at me. *Why are they laughing?* I wondered. Then one of them said, "Yo, fat ass, you put on a lot of weight! You not working on your craft?" They were joking about me and, well, it pissed me off.

But they were right. After my ACL tear and the pitiful prior season, I'd come back overweight and wasn't the same explosive person I'd been in previous seasons. On top of that, Adelman was hardly playing me. I'd gotten used to playing 35 to 40 minutes a game, but now I was lucky to get 30. In that game against the Bulls, I only played 14 minutes and didn't score a single point. I was having trouble getting my weight back down and myself right. And being the sharks that they were, Scottie and MJ were laughing at me. In one way, though, it was a compliment. They wouldn't take the time to point that out about a benchwarmer. They knew what I was capable of.

In hurt my pride, but most of all it just pissed me off because I knew they were right. Today, lots of young players can't take criticism. They say you're just "hating" on them. But I knew I had to listen to Scottie and Mike and make a change. I've always been the type to take constructive criticism and use it as fuel—whether that meant I had to be a better leader, a better player, or get in better shape. So while I was madder than a motherfucker at what Scottie and MJ were saying, I had to take it the right way and use it to better myself. I wasn't no scrub, and so I had to show the world what I could do. That meant, sadly, I had to move on from Golden State, where there was no room for me at the Inn.

First, I went to my agent to tell him what I needed. Then in late January or early February, before the NBA's trade deadline, I talked with Golden State's Dave Twardzik and Al Attles and told them it wasn't working with me and the team anymore. "I see y'all going in a different direction and that I'm not in your plans anymore," I said. "So, I need a change of scenery."

To their credit, management said, "Okay, what are you thinking? What can we help your agent do?" By that time, I had my eye on the Miami Heat. Pat Riley, the former head man with the Showtime Lakers and the Patrick Ewing–led New York Knicks, had come in and begun a quick and effective rebuild. I knew they needed an All-Star guard like me. Now, that wasn't a slight to their starter, Bimbo Coles, who was averaging 12.8 points and 5.7 assists per game, but I knew I could help to take them to the next level.

Now at the helm of the Heat, a team that had just one winning season since its inception in 1988–89, Riley immediately began to shake things up. His first big act was to bring in Alonzo Mourning from Charlotte after a contract dispute, trading away sharpshooter Glen Rice. With Zo as the foundation, there was a lot of room to grow.

When things had begun to go south in Golden State, I'd talked to Mourning and asked him to put in a word for me with Riley. When we played the Heat on November 22 in Miami, I'd put the bug in his ear after scoring 15 points. Then I did the same thing on December 12 in Oakland. They were the only team I had my eye on. They needed what I could bring to the table as a point guard.

As the NBA season neared the trade deadline, I told Zo, "Man, y'all need to trade for me. I can take y'all into the playoffs! You got a good team, but I can make y'all better." He said, "Yeah, yeah, okay." But I pressed, "No, for real, man!" At the time, we didn't have any kind of relationship. We were cool with each other, but it wasn't like we went to dinner together or kicked it in the summers. We just knew the other could ball. In December, though, I doubled down and said, "Man, y'all ain't going to make the playoffs. But I can help. Pat doesn't want to mess up his streak, does he? Let's try it!" And two months later, I was in South Beach.

What I didn't know at the time, though, was that Randy Pfund, who worked for Riley, had been buying tickets in the stands in Oakland to watch me play. He was telling Pat that I still had gas in the tank, but that Adelman just wasn't giving me minutes. I needed to lose a few pounds—that's what happens when you don't play often and the team doesn't practice enough—but outside of that, I knew I could contribute with the Heat.

After 52 games that year with Golden State, on February 22, 1996, I got the team to deal me and Chris Gatling to Miami for Coles and Kevin Willis. That same day, the Heat also traded for Walt "The Wizard" Williams and Tyrone Corbin, sending out Kevin Gamble and Billy Owens to the Kings. Miami also got Tony Smith from Phoenix for Terrence Rencher. And just like that, Riley had remade his roster, bringing in more talent and also a number of expiring contracts to give him options for the future.

I'd never wanted to leave Golden State, but the circumstances had changed. Mully and I had talked about the possibility of either of us going, but we also knew that we had to do our best while with the team. Being professional means fulfilling your contract. Even when you don't agree with your situation. And while I didn't want to leave the fans in the Bay Area, I was happy my landing spot featured Pat Riley. It's what needed to happen for my career and for my family. (Note that Mully would play another year with the Warriors before they traded him to the Pacers in August of 1997.)

Landing all those deals was masterful work by the five-time NBA champion. With me, he brought in a floor general and someone who could score. Gatling was another potent scorer who had one of the best pump-fakes in the NBA. He'd get on his tip-toes and guys would fly by him. Walt Williams was one of the best three-point shooters in the league. There were also rookies Kurt Thomas, who would become a strong player, and Voshon Lenard, a skilled shooter. Together with Zo, we knew we had a chance. When I joined the team they were 24–29, and I knew we would have to go on a big run over the final 28 games of the year to make our way into the playoffs. But with our goal in our sights, we began to go for it.

Along with the youngins that could ball, the team also had talented veteran guard Rex Champan. Rex helped acclimate me in Miami, showing me the ropes of what Riley liked. In my years with the Warriors, I was used to running up and down the court and scoring. But in Miami, we played slower. That suited me fine, as I was no one-trick pony. Riley was also known for holding tough, long practices. I remember one during the season when Chris Gatling kept messing up. Riley told us to do a drill where three people came down the court, passing to one another. The idea was to start at one end of the basket and make it down to the other end in just three passes for a layup. Chris kept passing it a fourth time. Riles would blow his whistle and make us start again. "Nope!" he'd yell. "Come back!"

Chris kept fucking around. After enough whistles, he took the ball and threw it at Riley, but Pat wasn't fazed. "You're mad at me," Riley said, "but you're the one fucking up! You're the one that's not following instructions! If you paid attention to detail, you'd be done by now! Do it again!" I was over in the corner dying of laughter. "You're frustrated with me, but you're the one who isn't doing it right," Pat howled. It was 10 minutes of them going back and forth. Finally, Chris got it right. But I knew what Chris was doing. He was tired or hungover, so was trying to get his ass kicked out of practice.

Pat, though, wasn't going for it. He'd been around too long and was too caught up in trying to build something in Miami. Now, with all those trades, he knew it was time. It was his first year in South Beach and he'd made a ton of big moves. He wasn't going to let a role player like Gatling show him up or throw him off his perch. And Chris benefited from it, too. He had his best stretch of games in his career in Miami, and that set him up to make more money in Dallas in New Jersey and have the best years of his life. He even later made an All-Star team. That's what happens when you learn to pay attention to detail.

* * *

On February 25, 1996, after 422 games with the Warriors, I suited up for the first time as a member of the Miami Heat—the same day I arrived in the city. It truly felt like a breath of fresh air. Knowing I had a chance to get back out on the floor and lead a team was a dream come true after the way my time in Golden State ended. I'd second guessed myself a lot sitting on the bench with the Warriors. I'd been frustrated and at times lost confidence. Now here I was, back in the fold.

At the time, Riley's assistant coach was the thirty-six-year-old Stan Van Gundy (one of the team's great assistants, along with the likes of Bob McAdoo, who could still embarrass guys in practice with his two-handed jumper). Ahead of the matchup against the 76ers, we were all going over the game plan. Miami usually went into each night with five different plays. Over time, I'd learn that they would switch the five they used from game to game, but it was always five on a given night. Pat asked Stan which plays he could use that night and which of the five he had to drop, since the Heat had so many new players. But Stan said, "Tim can run all of them. He knows all five plays. You call them out and he'll run it." Pat's eyebrows jumped when he heard that.

He thought I'd take a longer time to pick up on the schemes, but Stan was confident in what I could do. Pat was like, "Okay, cool, let's play then." And we were off. We won that night and I killed it, of course, scoring 20 points, dishing nine assists, and adding two steals in 32 minutes. We won the game, 108–101, and I was excited for what this team could do.

It only took me about two games to get used to playing with Zo. The big thing with him was that I had to wait until he got set in the post. That was the key. If I rushed him the ball, it would lead to a turnover. So I learned to be patient with him. I paid attention to detail. Zo had to get in the lane, establish position, get his feet set, lock in his defender, and then throw up his hand. If he did that, he'd catch it and almost always get us a bucket. In fact, in a game on March 29 against the Bullets, Zo had a career game with 50 points and 12 rebounds (and I know some of my 12 assists helped him get those points) in a 112–93 win.

With Mully and Mitch, we could do a lot on the fly. They'd come off screens ready and know how to get set as they caught my pass. But Zo, a big 6-foot-10 center, took a little more time—but that was fine with me. You have to learn your personnel—especially if you're a point guard. With Zo, sometimes it took three seconds for him to get ready. But I knew that if I waited, I'd almost always have an assist on the other end. Either that or it would lead to a good bucket, including a kick out for me for a potential three-pointer. He'd communicate with his eyes that he was ready, and I'd hit him in the hand. Then he'd make a move and dunk on somebody.

When I joined the team, we were in ninth place and three games under .500, but that didn't last long. In fact, for the month of March we won 10 of our 14 games and headed into April as the eighth seed with a 37–34 record. We finished the season at 42–40, and were able to sneak into the playoffs. It was just the turnaround the team needed, just the turnaround Pat wanted and just the turnaround I'd predicted. I had some of the most fun of my entire career trying to win games that half-season in Miami. We got in sync really quick as we aimed to make the playoffs.

For the season, I averaged 14.1 points and 6.9 assists per game in Oakland but in Miami those numbers jumped to 17.2 points and 10 assists. I proved to everyone, including myself, that I had a lot of game left, and that Golden State should have been playing me more. My magic had come back, and patience had paid off once again.

Coming down the final stretch of the year, the biggest win we had to solidify our playoff berth came against the Charlotte Hornets. The matchup came with seven games left in the season, and both our teams essentially tied for the final spot.

From the moment Zo had just been traded from Charlotte to Miami the summer before, there had been bad blood between the two teams. Charlotte didn't want to pay Zo, and he and

Larry Johnson had feuded over who was the "man" in Charlotte. Now Glen Rice was a star with the team after Riley had dealt him out of Miami.

We knew that if we beat Charlotte on April 10, we'd be in the driver's seat in the playoff race. The game was in Charlotte, and we both had near-identical records (we were 37–38 and they were 39–37).

The Charlotte Coliseum, also known as "The Hive," was *always* packed. Ahead of the game, Riley hyped us up. *Winning was the only option*, he made clear. We jumped out to a 10-point lead after the first and headed into halftime up 11. Even with a good lead, we knew we couldn't take our foot off the gas. Keeping that momentum, we came out strong again with 41 points in the third, and at the final buzzer beat them by 21, 116–95. I scored 29 points and dropped 11 assists while Zo scored 26 with nine rebounds. Rex Chapman, who was another former Hornet, added 19 and Walt scored 15. Rice had 21 points and sharpshooter Dell Curry added 22 off the bench, but it wasn't enough to stop us that night.

For us, it was an all-around team effort butt whooping, and put us in position to make the postseason. After the game, we felt we were good enough to beat anyone. We won four of our final six games, making the playoffs as the eighth seed. And with that, we were able to keep Riley's personal postseason streak alive. But in the opening round, we faced the dreaded 72–10 Chicago Bulls and my old Chicago foe Jordan, now a full season back from baseball. And while we knew we'd improved in the few months since the "new Heat" had come together, we were still facing off against giants.

The Bulls were no nonsense, and they blew us out in Chicago in the first two games, 102–85 and 106–75. I scored 30 points in the first matchup along with seven assists, but I only scored nine with four assists in the second. Now in Miami in a potential elimination game, we were hoping that a change of scenery would aid us in our battle. Unfortunately, we were again going against giants. Though I had 14 points and six assists, and Zo scored 30 points and eight rebounds, Chicago's Scottie Pippen had a triple double with 22 points, 18 rebounds, and 10 assists (to go along with 26 from Jordan). The game was never close, and we fell to the future champs, 112–91. Still, advancing in the playoffs at that point wasn't our main focus. We'd just wanted to get in after all those trades, to get a taste of the postseason together and then regroup for next season. We'd achieved what we set our minds to and had momentum for the future. All in all, it was a success.

* * *

These days, a lot of people talk about "Heat Culture." This hard-nosed, attention-to-detail style the team is known for. It started with Riley, but it also started with me and Zo in the mid-1990s. It may have been perfected by Dwayne Wade, Shaquille O'Neal, LeBron James, Chris Bosh, and Jimmy Butler later on, but it started with us. We knew the way the Heat would win games was by playing rugged. Riley dug into the philosophy while with the Knicks (though his "Showtime" Lakers with Magic Johnson were more run-and-gun), and he brought that workman-like sense to Miami. Me and Zo took it upon ourselves to bring it to the floor. We poured the concrete.

Pat learned a lot from us. The city of Miami is known for its beautiful people, sunny beaches, and vibrant nightlife. But on the court, we were anything but glamorous. We wanted to win. To do that in the NBA takes defense, rebounding, and confidence. We knew our opponents would have to bring their lunch pails to play every game. Sometimes, they'd come in tired and hungover, too, having enjoyed our nightlife the night before. We used that to our advantage. If they outdid themselves among the bikinis and six-pack abs, we'd smother them on the floor. We knew discipline was the key to our future and to take advantage of any weakness.

Thanks to my previous coaches, I was sure I could play any way my team needed me to. My time with Nellie, it might surprise some, helped me prepare to work with Pat. Nellie, for all his innovation and offensive gimmicking, was all about attention to detail. He knew the rules of the game in and out, and was even often trying to get them changed in the 1990s. He wanted zone defense to be legal, he wanted to be able to double team a player before they got the ball. Many of the rules used in today's game are ideas he had back then. But it wasn't until there was an influx of European players that the NBA decided to change.

Many of the rule changes came about in the early 2000s when Nellie was with Dallas coaching Dirk Nowitzki. European players came over here with an entirely different sense of the game, and it was difficult for some to adjust, so Nellie (and Jerry Colangelo) helped get the league's rules committee to alter things. The new rules opened up the game and made it more free flowing, which is one reason why the Steve Nash Suns were able to run and score. It has only increased over the years with guys like James Harden, Luka, and Stephen Curry's Warriors. But when I played with the Heat, while we could match up with anyone, games often turned into low-scoring wars.

Growing up in Chicago, I learned how to play fast on the playgrounds and run an offense like a floor general in organized games. My grammar school coach gave me the fundamentals, and my high school coach taught me how to lead. Don Haskins at UTEP taught me to be patient and understand my teammates. It's important to know where a guy likes to get a pass, when and where he's most able to score, who can handle the ball, who is a shooter, who can defend and rebound. I brought all these tools with me to Miami, and it made me a perfect fit for Riley and the burgeoning Heat Culture.

But after that first half-season, my contract was up. The Heat had a lot of salary cap room when a number of our players became free agents. Up north, the New York Knicks signed New Jersey Nets point guard Chris Childs to a five-year, $20 million deal. And though I was playing for the Knicks' blood rival (thanks to Pat), I wondered if they might show interest in me. But I guess they just assumed I would stay in Miami because the Knicks never reached out. I was surprised they didn't pick up the phone . . . and so were their fans. I thought I could have thrived in New York and Madison Square Garden with those rabid fans. If the money had been right, I could have been playing in blue and orange, which might surprise some people today. That could have been wild!

The Knicks, though, chose Childs instead, but everything worked out for the best. Things happened for the right reason. So I stayed in Miami on a four-year, $18 million deal with lots of incentives. Part of me was mad that I signed for such a conservative deal, though. I thought Pat lowballed me and that I could've gotten more (especially when Childs had only started 65 games in his two years while I was already a three-time All-Star). I signed a similar contract to the one Scottie Pippen got with the Bulls, which he ended up also not being happy about. We each chose long-term stability over the possibility of bigger paydays down the line. Maybe I should have signed a one-year deal and bet on myself. Thing was that I'd been hurt, coming off my ACL injury, and I wanted the security of a multi-year deal.

If you bank on yourself and something goes wrong, that could be it. For example, during the course of that first half-season in Miami, my back went out on me. That was a first. And coming off some weight issues, Pat wanted to put incentives in my contract that I would stay trim and would average better than a three-to-one assist-to-turnover ratio. If I achieved both, I'd get one million dollars. And if I played well during the deal, I knew I could be rewarded with another big contract later. Besides, I was excited about our prospects in Miami. With the team's extra cap space, Pat signed bruiser P. J. Brown from the Nets and shooter Dan Majerle from the Suns.

He even considered signing Gary Payton from the SuperSonics, but Gary was not a fan of long practices. He famously used to sit most of them out in Seattle, so I knew he wouldn't feel at home under Riley's rule. That's the NBA. There are always a lot of moving pieces. It was the same for me after the initial trade. The news had come in while the Warriors were in Seattle preparing for a game. So after I found out the Heat got me, I got on a plane and flew back to Oakland. The Heat had said I could report in a day or two. I didn't want Yolanda and the kids to uproot their lives until I knew where I'd be for the following season, so I lived by myself for the first few months in a decently sized hotel room. After the season, I decided to go out driving to look around a few neighborhoods in Pine Crest. I walked around and checked out some of the houses for sale when I stumbled upon this one home on a 2.5-acre plot. When I talked to Yolanda that night and told her about it, she was excited to see it. Later, when she and the kids moved out from Oakland, we bought it and lived there happily for many years. One of the nice aspects of the area was that there were a lot of families with kids, and ours got to grow up with lots of friends.

In the end, it had been a long year that had started in Northern California and ended in Southern Florida, some 3,000 miles away. I loved my time in Oakland. I'd tallied 5,000 points and 2,500 assists there faster than any player in NBA history (except for the great Oscar Robertson). And while I was sad to leave the Bay, I was hyped about my new home in South Beach. Sadly, after trading me, over the next fifteen years, the Warriors would become one of pro sports' biggest laughing stocks, losing big every season. They'd just lost too much talent. Oh well—nothing I could do about that now.

9

PAT RILEY

I WAS small growing up, so my cousins nicknamed me "Tim Bug" because they said I scooted around the house like a little bug. I'd run through people's legs and was almost too small to tackle when we played football. On the basketball court, I could dribble everywhere because I was so low to the ground. In the NBA, though, my Miami Heat teammates started calling me "Bigs" as a nickname. At first it was because I was a bit overweight. Like I said, that's what happens when you don't play a lot for a while, which was the case due to my last year on the Warriors. In Miami, Voshon Lenard called me Bigs first, because I was a little bit chunky.

But as my career went on there, I started to hit big shot after big shot. When that happened, I flipped the name Bigs and it came to mean all the big buckets I got. Reporters would ask, "Oh, they call you Bigs for all those buzzer-beaters?" I'd smile and nod, "Yup!" But even as I slimmed down, I was still burly. I was strong and played that way. It's how I was raised in Chicago. No crying, no backing down. Like my dad said, there are no positions on the court. If you want to play down low, play down low—but you have to be ready for it. In grammar school, I learned how to post up. Drop-step. I did the George Mikan layup drill repeatedly. The game can be dirty, so I made sure to always be ready for anything. Some guys might be 6-foot-2, but they make a seven-footer look tiny. That's what confidence—or lack thereof—can do for you.

With a new contract and the starting job, I knew this was my redemption year. My first full year with the Miami Heat was my best in the NBA. Pat brought in a slew of great talent, too, including Dan Majerle, P. J. Brown, and center Isaac Austin (who won the Most Improved Player that season). Pat also tried to sign Juwan Howard but the league vetoed that move for esoteric salary cap reasons and he later signed with Washington to be with his friend Chris Webber.

Majerle was the consummate pro, a great teammate, and an excellent shooter and defender. He made big shots, but was also dealing with back issues at the time. P. J. was our best low-post defender. We had a formidable roster for the 1996–97 season, and it was bolstered midway through when Pat traded Kurt Thomas for the 20-point scorer Jamal Mashburn from the Mavericks via the University of Kentucky. We had a good crew, but we just couldn't stay healthy the whole way through. Dan, Zo, and Mash dealt with injuries, but thankfully we were all healthy around playoff time. The NBA season is long, and durability is an important part.

We were winning and having fun doing so. But I wasn't looking at the season through the lens of number of wins. We wanted to win the whole thing. Yes, victories are important for seeding, but I had the long view in mind.

Some might ask how I developed chemistry with my team. I'm one of those guys who prepares ahead of the season. As a point guard, I study my roster. I know where each guy likes to rock, when they like to catch it. Point guards have to know their personnel. The thing I focused on ahead of the season was conditioning. Pat's famous five 17s. That's when you run from sideline to sideline on the court 17 times faster than basically humanly possible. I'd heard how gruesome they were. With only a two-minute break in between. They were tough, but I got through them. I proved I was ready for the new year.

That season, I was able to play in 81 games and had my best overall year as a pro. I led the team in scoring, assists, and steals, I made First Team All-NBA, finishing fourth in NBA MVP voting. For Riley, the season was all about having something to prove. He assembled a group of guys he thought all had chips on their shoulders; players who he thought the league had all but written off. But that wasn't my personal take on it. I just thought he put a good team together, and I was ready to come out and play. Do what we needed to do, what we'd done our entire careers. I knew we could win at a high level.

Riley, who often seemed like a General, never gave the team a speech about me getting the car keys like Don Nelson had when I was a second-year player in Golden State. It was just assumed that I was the lead dog. For a while, Pat never thought anyone could match his Basketball IQ, other than Magic. Thought that no one could have control of a team like him. But when he saw what I could do, that took him back to his old Showtime days. He knew he had a six-foot guard that could do what the 6-foot-9 Johnson could. I think it surprised him a little that I could go out there and command the team. But it created quick trust.

For Pat, who took over the Heat at fifty years old and became "The Godfather" of the team, Miami was his new home after years in Los Angeles and New York. (People ask me if he has mafia ties and I'll just say he knows a few people.)

Pat liked to dabble in mind games. Sometimes that meant him talking about the contract I'd signed. "I know it's not where you want it to be," he said to me, "but I don't want to hear you talking about it in public." I told him I understood, but there were times during the year when the press came up to me saying Pat was talking about it to them. I had to approach Pat and say, "If you tell me not to talk about it, what makes you think I want to hear you talking about it?" I wasn't upset, but I wanted to clear the air. I knew I'd signed a below-market deal, which I did for security. And that was that. I just wanted to keep moving forward. But that was Pat. He would poke and push—everything to try and get the most out of his players. During the course of a season, he liked to sit us down and preach. On one occasion, after one of our practices—which were always closed to the outside world—he sat the whole team down.

He was hooting and hollering about something and during his talk, he looked at me and said, "What do you think, Tim?" I looked up and replied, "Pat, you know what, man? I hear your message. I hear what you're saying. But I'm just not with *how* you're saying it. Your demeanor. Your face. You're upset, you're yelling. But I'm just not that type of person." Know that I'm the type of guy where I'll do what the coach says, but I'm not going to get all revved up about it. I play. I know what a coach wants, and I'll go out and do just that. I'll give my team confidence and put us in a good position to win. But I'm not going to tear my teammates' heads off doing it.

Ever since the eighth grade, I've been through coaches who would yell and scream. That doesn't faze me. I listen to the message, not the shouting. Pat, though, didn't like that response because he thought I was calling him out in front of everybody. He wanted me to say, "Yeah, yeah, sounds good, Pat!" So after practice, he brought me up to his office. "Tim, I didn't like that," he said. "You didn't like what?" I asked. He replied, "I didn't like you saying that back to me because we've got young players and I need them to buy into the program." After our meeting, I decided to use that conversation as a learning moment for us both.

Pat was a good coach and a good man, and there was no sense creating barriers or getting us off on the wrong foot as head coach and point guard. I said, "Pat, you know what Nellie used to do? When you're going to ask me something, why don't you tell me beforehand? Tell me you're going to come to me during practice with such-and-such and that you need me to agree on it. And that will be that. When I don't know what you're going to say and you ask me for my opinion, I'm going to speak honestly about it. But I didn't know you were going to point to me, so I'm sorry for how I responded."

I added, "Next time you're going to do that, just let me know first. Then I'll go with it." (Fun fact: Nellie actually replaced Pat in New York for 59 games when Riley had left.) Personally, I didn't mind getting yelled at. If it has to be my day to take it, so be it. But if anyone asks me for my opinion, I'm going to give it honestly unless I know we need to be on the same page ahead of time. That day, we both learned something about each other, which benefited us moving forward.

When I was first traded to Miami, Rex Chapman was quick to tell me that New York hated Pat. "You're going to hear boos,

boos, boos, boos, boos," Rex said. "They're going to let him have it. They're going to let us have it. They're going to let everyone have it when we come to town."

* * *

Now a full team, one that would start the season as a single unit, we began from the jump and kept our feet on the gas. We were . . . well, on fire. Starting the season, we took five of our first six games, and though had a three-game losing streak after that, won seven in a row heading into our first matchup against the Knicks . . . which was at Madison Square Garden. I remember Knicks fans booed Pat relentlessly, and he slyly waved them on.

Even if Coach didn't say it, we knew this was a big game for him. We were 12–4 (with two of those losses coming against the Bulls), but that didn't matter as long as we beat the Knicks. Pat had crafted the Knicks into a well-oiled machine, and now took that mindset to Miami. Before the game, he even said to the press:

"We're gonna play a team that's a facsimile of us. This isn't going to be as much about strategy as it is going to be about energy and what I call 'big muscle movement.'" It would be Pat against his former assistant, Jeff Van Gundy. It would be Zo against Ewing. It would be me against Chris Childs and former Heisman Trophy winner from Florida State Charlie Ward. Plus Zo's former adversary in Charlotte, Larry Johnson, was now a member of the Knicks. Add P. J. Brown and Charles Oakley and you have fireworks ready to go off. Just before the game, Pat came up to me. I was the last one to leave the locker room and I was tying my shoes. He said, "Can you win this one for me?" Already, we'd beaten Golden State for me, Phoenix for Dan Majerle, Dallas for Jamal, and Charlotte for Zo. Now Pat wanted his revenge game. I looked him in the eye and knew he was serious. Out there on the court, I told the guys we had to do it for Pat.

MSG is crazy. "They think this is Gotham City," Pat told us. "They think they're bad! But the rim is still 10 feet tall and the court is still 94 feet. Just play your game!" While we were sloppy with the ball to start, we took a 47–38 lead into the half. In the third we kept pushing and were up by almost 20 when things began to get a bit chippy. I'm sure the Knicks didn't like getting pushed around at home, so of course Oakley and Zo got into it a bit. At the end we took them down, 99–75, which was a big chip on our shoulders.

Three days later, however, we were home against those very same Knicks—though this game would be a different story. New York wanted to beat us at our home like we'd done at theirs, and put a lot of pressure on. While back and forth heading into the third, they outscored us by 12—including a three by Allan Houston as time ran out to put them up 74–66 heading into the fourth. They kept their momentum from there, and even John Starks was trash talking our fans at one point. And while they were up, we kept up our physicality, which Larry Johnson didn't like as he swatted at our forward Keith Askins. It was his second tech of the game which meant he was thrown out, and as tempers were flaring I tried to calm him down, but he just pushed me away. Then as he was leaving the court some fans threw stuff at him, further igniting the bad blood between the two teams. Both Zo and P. J. fouled out of the game, and our winning streak ended at nine at the hands of the Knicks by a score of 103–85. We knew this would be a team we'd have to battle the entire season.

By the time the All-Star game came around in February, we were 36–12. I was named to the All-Star team again for the first time in four years. That meant a lot to me after my battle with the ACL injury and the issues in Golden State. For a while, I was the only guy to come back from an ACL tear and make the All-Star team. Most guys couldn't get back to that status, but I did so and, again, became one of the league's best players. I attribute that success to maintaining my confidence and hard work. Really, I'd just wanted so badly to come back and prove my career wasn't done after just a few years. I wanted to show everyone I was still that badass, that killer crossover king. That's what motivated me from the first day of practice. To Pat's credit, he kept me and the whole team in tip-top shape. But I pushed myself to be the best simply because I knew I could be the best again.

Fully clicking as a unit, we mostly coasted through the season, finishing 61–21 for second place in the East (behind the 69–13 Chicago Bulls). And I was fourth in MVP voting behind Karl Malone, Michael Jordan, and Grant Hill. Tell you the truth, though, I was mad.

This is the first time I've ever spoken on it, but I was fucking mad that I didn't win MVP. It was my best chance to do so. I'd played well, averaging 20.3 points, 8.6 assists, 1.9 steals, and 3.4 rebounds. I really thought the award was mine, but the Heat ended up losing three out of our last five games—we were exhausted—and I think that took me out of contention. I think I was at the top of the list before we slid. Malone ended up winning it. His Jazz team was first in the West at 64–18, and NBA writer Jackie MacMullan had written about Karl saying that it was his time. Fuck, I was pissed. I let it slip through my damn fingers. Right out of my hands.

* * *

One of the best parts of the season, though, was getting to know my new Miami teammates better, including Zo. There are cliques on every team. Sometimes personalities clash or sometimes certain guys just get along better with others. But for me and Zo, we got along real well. We were like the East's Stockton and Malone. In fact, our whole team was close, including Isaac Austin, Mashburn, P. J., Voshon, Askins, and Majerle. We played hard for one another, and despite the occasional spat during practice after an errant elbow—which is always bound to happen—we had each other's backs. We genuinely liked each other.

With the Heat, it wasn't all regimen and seriousness. In the locker room we could fool around, joke and bust each other's chops. Pat knew people had to cut loose once in a while. He also knew that, when we walked out onto the floor—whether it was practice or a game—once you went through those doors, all the bullshit had to stop. Your shoes had to be laced up, your uniform on straight. It was time for structure—and that's the way I liked it. That's what made for wins. It was time to work. And that was how Heat Culture was born. When it was time, you had to wipe the smiles off your lips and put on the serious face. You had to be ready to battle each and every night.

Still, though, we could have fun off the court. I remember times when we were all hanging out at Zo's house on the water in Miami, kicking it on his jet skis. On the court, he was intense. Zo was crazy about winning. Nothing mattered to him besides us going out to get the victory. In fact, a lot of people, from media to players, bristled at his personality. But I knew he was like that because he was mostly fed up with everyone. When you're a star like Zo, you're always asked for something. From the day you enter high school, people want something from you, and he was sick of it. That's why it was fun to kick it at his place on the water with the jet skis and no media in sight.

But people knew I had skills when it came to communication. So much so that Alonzo's parents even came up to me to ask me to help their son. Pat Riley and Heat owner Micky Arison did, too. They knew the world saw Zo as closed off. Gruff. But I knew he just hated to be around people because all they wanted was autographs or pictures or a quote for their newspaper article. So I began to work with Zo here and there, giving him little tips on how to work with the media and fans. To talk, to smile a bit—even if you didn't want to. Over time, he responded well to it and he's more personable now, thank goodness.

But here's a story that illustrates just how intense Zo could be. One night in Cleveland during my second year with the Heat, Zo, Isaac Austin, and I were set to go out on the town. We got on the elevator to go down to the lobby when we saw Pat Riley. He was just getting off the elevator to go to his room for the night. Once the elevator doors closed, Zo said, "Man, I'm not going out tonight, I changed my mind." Then I responded, "What? Why not?" Zo said, "Man, Pat saw us and now he's going to practice us extra hard in the morning." I shot back, "When does Pat *not* practice us extra hard?" (Truly, we were hardly ever tired in a game because of his two-and-a-half-hour workouts.)

Zo nodded, "You're right. But, Tim, he saw us. So, I'm not going to go." Well, me and Isaac called him every name in the book, from chump to worse. Still, Zo stayed in. So Isaac and I had a great time hanging out. The next morning, Pat ran us hard in practice and there were even extra shooting drills. It was just his voice and the whistle. At one point we were running the three-man weave when Ed Pinckney went down. He'd torn his meniscus, but no one knew that yet. Zo, still angry that Pat caught him the night before, said to Ed, "Man, get your ass up!" He wouldn't stop cussing Ed out, even though Ed was writhing in pain.

I shouted, "He's hurt!" But Zo said, "No, he's not!" When Pat blew the whistle, we went to another drill and this time Pat was putting money on it. We broke off into teams of two and had to shoot jump shots from the corner and then the elbow, back to the corner and back to the elbow, over and over. First for 30 seconds, then a minute, increasing all the way up to three and a half minutes. Well, Isaac and I made the most shots out of any duo and won the drill, and Pat gave us $2,000 a piece for our success. After practice, Zo looked at me and Isaac and said, "Man, aren't you guys tired?"

We just told him that we were tired *now*, after it was all done. But we got through it and were still able to enjoy the night out. And now we could go back and sleep. I told Zo, "Man, you were scared for nothing! And now you have to apologize to Ed! And I want to see you say you're sorry to him!" I was dying laughing, and Zo could only shake his head. But some guys are like that—almost *too* intense. Guys like Zo, Kevin Garnett, and others just can't get out of their own heads. It's what makes them great players. But sometimes you need a guy like me to cut the tension a bit with a hearty joke.

* * *

Playing for Pat Riley was a gift. We butted heads here and there like any great point guard and coach might. But like most people to come through the Heat organization, I would have run through a wall for Pat. He had the best motivational speeches. They were on point every single time. One time, Pat came into the locker room with a big bucket of ice water and put it on a table. Then he put his entire head into the bucket of freezing water and held it in there for 30 or 40 seconds. When he finally took his head out, he said, "You have to WANT to win! There are two things in life: there's winning and there's misery!"

Magic Johnson told me he did the same thing with the Lakers back in the day, and I heard from other Heat players that he did that to them in future years. But that was Pat. Dedicated. He'd do anything to win and anything for his team. But he also knew how to have fun. Sometimes on our plane rides, Ike Austin would bring out his boombox and we'd do soul train dances. Pat only had but one dance, but he'd bust it out and come down the line after a big win with his fists in front of his chest like he was riding a horse. Another time, he was giving a big speech in the locker room and Zo let out a giant fart that lasted about 10 seconds. You could hear Zo's stomach gurgling and then he lifted up his leg and just let it rip. Pat stopped talking and turned around and you could see his face that he was smiling, but he never said anything. Now if one of the bench players had done that, they might still be running sprints, but because it was Zo, Riley let it slide. But the biggest lesson Pat taught us was that winning was most important. "If you want the fans to come out, you got to win," he said. "There's nothing I can do, nothing Micky Arison can do. It's on you. If you want to fans to come, then you got to win."

* * *

Heading into the playoffs as the second seed, we knew we could make a big statement. During the regular season, teams approach games by running their stuff. Stick to the program, no matter who you're playing. Do what you do, mind your principles. Don't deviate. But when it comes to the playoffs, it's about adjustments. Each team knows all the plays of their opponent. You know the other players' tendencies and you try to cut them off. You try to stop their plan-A and plan-B and make them do things they don't necessarily want to do. You put schemes on top of schemes in order to outdo and outthink who you're matched up against. You get specific.

In the first round of the 1997 playoffs, we faced off against the Orlando Magic, our Florida rivals. For them, the series marked the first in several years without their all-world center, Shaquille O'Neal, who had departed the previous summer for the Los Angeles Lakers. And while that hurt Orlando, they still had a great team with Horace Grant, my old Chicago foe Nick Anderson, sharpshooter Dennis Scott, Brian Shaw, Kenny Smith, and, of course, Penny Hardaway. Still, they were the No. 7 seed. We thought we would take them out quickly . . . but we were mistaken.

We took care of business at home, beating Orlando big in the first game, 99–64. That gave us huge confidence and, if it was the Little Leagues, there might have been some sort of mercy rule. I scored 13 and dished out 11 assists, though Voshon Lenard was the standout, dropping 24 points on 6–9 from three. Both Zo and P. J. had double-digit rebounds. We beat them down again in Game Two, 104–87. Penny had 26 points, but I got 20 with 11 more assists. Zo and P. J. each scored 17, and we were quickly up 2–0 in a best-of-five series, having outscored them by a total of 52 points. But when we went up to Orlando for the next two games, we got a rude awakening.

In truth, we should have swept the Magic. But we were complacent. Two blowouts can do that to you. We made it hard on ourselves. In the games on his home floor, Penny went completely off. He hit shots from all over the court. We were looking at each other on the bench like, "How the hell did he do *that*?" He was doing his best Tim Hardaway impression, taking over the game, putting his head down, and not letting his squad lose. It was his time to prove he was the man—especially without Shaq. Though we were up 20 with just six minutes to go, the Magic won, 88–75, and Penny had damn near half his team's points, scoring 42.

Game Four was the same thing. They won a closer one, 99–91, but Penny got 41. Though I had 16 and eight assists, Zo had 23 with 13 rebounds, and P. J. had 20 with 13 rebounds, we still lost. Even Mashburn pitched in with 19 points. We couldn't get past the 6-foot-7 Penny, one of the best tall point guards since Magic. But that's why you play hard during the regular season to get home-court advantage. With the series now tied, we went back to Miami for the deciding Game Five . . . and took care of business. We were up by 16 going into the fourth quarter, but instead of putting them away, we let them come back. Orlando made a big run in the fourth, putting up 30 points in the quarter. But I was just a little too good.

With 45 seconds left, I hit a step-back jumper at the right elbow to put us up six. Then Penny answered with a three to cut our lead in half. Coming back down court, I got the ball at the top of the key, a few feet behind the three-point line. You have to know when to take shots at the right time, and this was mine. In a flash, I cocked it back and drained a three, which put us back up six. Orlando called a time out, and Dan Majerle came over and gave me a big hug. I pointed to the fans in the stands going crazy. That was the game winner for us, and we'd done it. We'd won our first playoff series as a team in Miami, taking out the Magic with a final score of 91–83.

Our next series would be one for the ages, setting off a rivalry that NBA fans still talk about to this day. In the Eastern Semifinals, we matched up against the New York Knicks. While it was Pat's former team and one he left essentially in the dead of the night after the 1994–95 season for Miami, the idea that he *hated* the Knicks, which was something many commentators said at the time, was not true. He didn't hate the Knicks. He'd just done what he had to do. He'd wanted to run a team, and New York told him he wasn't going to run their franchise. They'd said no, so he left. Miami's owner Micky Arison gave Pat a *Godfather* offer he couldn't refuse.

Pat had wanted to run the Lakers back in the 1980s, but that didn't work out. He wanted to run the Knicks in the 1990s, and that didn't work out. But Arison said he could run Miami, so he jumped at the chance and has been there ever since. Pat knew he could do it and has been doing a *great* job. He's won three more rings in Miami and been to the Eastern Conference Finals and NBA Finals many more times. He had confidence he could get the job done and bet on himself correctly. We knew we had a great team that could advance. But when our series with New York began in the 1997 playoffs, he warned us that Knicks fans were going to hate us and that it was going to be a *crazy* battle.

The rivalry began because of Pat, because he left New York. And throughout the season we'd gone to Phoenix where Majerle was from and won, went to Charlotte where Zo was from and won, went to Dallas where Jamal was from and one, went to Golden State and won, went to New Jersey where P. J. was from and won.

For me, now that we were in the playoffs against New York, it wasn't anything crazier than I was used to. I grew up in mad basketball moments. Chicago is the city of challengers, a region of trash talkers. So nothing bothered me in the NBA. The No. 3 seeded Knicks wanted to beat their former coach and prove they didn't need him. Even though they'd gone to the NBA Finals with him in 1994 and lost to the Houston Rockets, they wanted to prove the players were the reason, not him. We knew we'd have our hands full. There was so much buzz around Pat's return to New York, but I knew it didn't have anything to do with me. It wasn't on us players. It had to do with Pat and how he left. Still, though, we wanted to win.

The first game was on May 7, and we had home-court advantage. But we quickly squandered it. New York came out strong after beating Charlotte in the series before us, 3–0. They were rested and we'd just gone through a five-game series. We knew one of the keys to the series would be turnovers—as the Knicks had led the league—so by playing smart basketball we would have the advantage.

While we were pretty much even with them for the first half, things would change quickly. At one point we were up by eight in the third, but that's when Houston turned it on. Zo was forced to the bench with four fouls, and the Knicks went on a 13–0 run. Despite my 21 points and six assists, we missed 13 free throws as a team, which really hurt. Allan Houston was the high scorer with 27 and Ewing had a big dunk on Zo to put the Knicks up for good.

Not ones to be pushed around, we shook off that loss for Game Two, edging the Knicks by four, 88–84. I knew I had to step up my offensive game, and so got 34 points.

With the series tied, we boarded a flight to New York for Game Three. When you lose a game and have to get on the plane, most of the time you end up talking the whole way back about what you could have done differently. Or you're watching film to prepare for the next game. Sometimes you see if a different play needs to be run in a certain situation, or if you and your teammate should play off your defenders differently. Or maybe you need to defend them differently—pushing Patrick Ewing right instead of left. If you won the game, you aren't partying on the plane, but you're happy. You're calling out what worked and building confidence for the next game. It's intense either way.

We started Game Three strong and were up by eight at halftime, but again faltered in the second half. Madison Square Garden is crazy in the playoffs. You can hear fans shouting at you, calling you names, trying to get you out of your game. Sometimes I'd shoot a glance back at them, but I never talked trash. At the same time, fans in every arena, including MSG, knew not to lean into me too hard because if you get me started, I might get hot and score 18 on you real quick.

That game, though I had 17 points, eight assists, and four steals, I also had six turnovers—something that can't happen in the playoffs. Even though they battled back, the game was still tied with three minutes to go in regulation. Then, after forcing a *huge* turnover, we had the ball at midcourt with just 13.4 seconds on the clock. With Jamal inbounding to me, I had Chris Childs in my face, trying to prevent me from hitting a game-tying trey. I lined up with a minute left, we were down by three and I had the ball in my hands. I passed it off to a teammate and was able to use a screen to get the ball back with six seconds left. I'd shook Childs, but now had the 7-foot Ewing in my face with the clock ticking away. I hoped that I'd be able to juke him to get the shot off, but his big arms swatted the ball away and he grabbed the rebound. The MSG crowd went nuts as Ewing egged them on, and I knew we'd let another opportunity slip through our fingers. Along with that block, Ewing had 25 points with 11 rebounds. We lost, 77–73, and were now down in the series with still another to go at the Garden.

To say it was a tough loss for us is an understatement, but since the series had gone back and forth, we had hope that we could win Game Four in New York to tie the series. You never knew how Pat was going to address the team after a loss. Sometimes he could be loud, other times he was calm, cool, and collected. But he always had these little notes on blue pieces of paper. Whenever we practiced, he took out his notes and read us his detailed thoughts on what he saw.

Yet, there was nothing he could say to help us now, because they took it to us again.

It wasn't even really close. The Knicks outscored us by 14 in the second quarter and we couldn't get much closer, losing 89–76. Now, all of a sudden, we were down 3–1 heading back to Miami. Pat wasn't happy at all. He tried to rally us and build up our edge. He asked if we wanted our season to be over, if we were ready to lose. If Alonzo was going to let his fellow Georgetown alum Patrick Ewing walk all over us. We knew we were in for a war, but none of us could have known what would happen next.

"You guys are going to have to scrap!" Riley warned us ahead of Game Five. "You're going to have to fight!" P. J. Brown, a guy who in the offseason read to children at libraries and provided meals for the homeless, was taking everything in. Smoldering. He even said after Pat walked out of the locker room, "Man, if somebody does something to me, I'm going to go off." This was a bit new for someone who'd received the NBA's Citizenship Award that season. Ahead of Game Five, P. J. had even been praying in the team chapel with Knicks guard Charlie Ward, the two of them devout Catholics. That would prove ironic as the game unfolded.

The Knicks were a physical team with a lineup that included Houston, Ewing, Charles Oakley, Larry Johnson, Chris Childs, John Starks, Buck Williams, and Ward. If they beat us in Game Five, they would go on to play their rivals, the Chicago Bulls, in the Conference Finals. But we had something to say about it. We weren't going down that easy. We knew our defense would save us. Back on home court, we knew we had to step up. The game was back and forth for the majority of the first half, with us edging them at halftime, 35–34. We knew we couldn't allow another third-quarter flop, so we found the hot hand—Voshon Lenard—and let him ball out, getting 12 points in the third. We went up seven heading into the fourth, and the Knicks just couldn't score.

With five minutes left in the game and us up by four, we started a fast break after Oakley missed a jumper, but Jamal's pass to me was tipped by Starks and I dove on the ground for the ball. Still on the floor, I was able to grab the ball and get it to Lenard for a wide-open three, which he hit and we were up 79–72. New York called a time out and we knew we were in the driver's seat ready to lock this one down.

We were playing smart and our lead kept growing, where we were up by 10 with two minutes left. However, the Knicks seemed more interested in knocking us around then actually trying to win. Their fouls got harder and more intentional. So after a great offensive rebound and score by P. J. to put us up by 12, I was guarding Charlie Ward when Oak dropped me *hard* with a screen the refs called as an offensive foul. Being the good teammate he is, Zo came over to help me up while Oak was idling by me, and started pushing and talking shit to Zo. He knew what they were trying to do and just smiled it off, not playing their games. That's when P. J. and Childs started chirping back and forth. Meanwhile, Oak and Zo were still going at it, and even after he laid me out, I tried to get between them to calm things down, though it didn't help and Oak got tossed. I remember talking to him as he was walking off the court, and he said, "Man, what is your boy P. J. doing?" And I remember saying right back to him, "Man, what's Childs doing?"

Despite all the craziness on the court, Oak is a friend of mine. We'd actually been talking all game. He told me when it started that Van Gundy had been on their asses about being more physical. "Done come down the lane here today," he'd warned me with a smile before the game. "Not a good day for that." But I was a veteran and I knew you just had to give it to them before they gave it to you. Still, I guess toughness was on their minds. And sometimes the chaos of a game can outweigh any previous friendly relationship. And that's what happened next . . .

On the next possession, they fouled me immediately and I headed for the free-throw line. After hitting the first, I sunk the second and began backing up to get on defense. That's when all hell broke loose.

With the ball in the air, Ward, the former football player, boxed out the 6-foot-11 Brown in a way that could have seriously injured him. Brown didn't like it and, well, he picked up the 6-foot-2 Ward, flipped him in the air, and dropped his ass on a few photographers under the basket like a sack of potatoes.

Ward, now on the floor, started grabbing after P. J., and Scott Brooks grabbed him from behind. And just like that the benches cleared—something the league had been trying to curtail. Riley and Jeff Van Gundy came into the fray and tried to stop it. I didn't know what to think at the time, it happened so fast. I just wanted the fight to break up. I could hear some guys on the court blaming Charlie and some blaming P. J. It was only later watching the replay that I could see what Ward had down to Brown. Ward, Brown, and Starks were tossed. The fans were chanting "New York Sucks" and some even threw cups at John as he left. After the game, I asked P. J. what happened. "That fucker," he told me. "Ward tried to clip me like he was playing football." I went back and looked at the tape and he was right. Ward went for his knees. It was a stupid move. The Knicks had us on the ropes and were going home to New York for Game Six. Maybe he thought P. J. wouldn't retaliate. But some people do shit just to do it.

I was glad P. J. handled his business. Jeff Van Gundy said they gave us life after that, and they had. The league came down hard on the players after the game. P. J. was suspended for the rest of the series, but New York got it worse. Ewing,

Houston, Ward, L. J., and Starks were *all* suspended for one game for leaving the bench and participating in the fight. But since there were so many guys, the NBA split the games up. Ewing, Houston, and Ward would miss Game Six while Starks and Johnson would miss Game Seven. That gave us a huge advantage. I was telling on people, too! Listing in the post-game press conference everyone who came onto the court. The Knicks got mad at me, but I was pointing people out to the league who came off the bench. The Knicks called me a snitch, but I just said, "Hey, man, rules are rules and I'm trying to win! You don't like it, you shouldn't have got your ass off the bench!" I used their idiocy to our advantage.

Back in New York for Game Six, we knew we had a chance thanks to our renewed toughness and their suspensions. Majerle started in place of P. J. and had a great game, rising to the challenge and scoring 18 points with seven rebounds and six assists (along with making four of eight threes). I scored 20 to go along with eight assists and six boards and Zo had 28 points with nine rebounds. The Knicks played well without Ewing, but we got the win, 95–90.

Just like with the Orlando series, we had the deciding game at home. And just like in the Orlando series, I took over. One of the more special moments of my career came before Game Seven got going. My son, who was just five years old, came to watch the game. Most of the time, since he was so young, he didn't watch the games too closely when he was there. He'd be playing around with toys or something. But ahead of Game Seven, he asked me in the car to the game, "Dad? What's the 'killer cross-over' thing everybody keeps talking about? They always ask me about it, but I've never seen it."

I said, "You never seen it?" And he shook his head. "Son, you just make sure to stay in your seat tonight, you can't go nowhere unless it's halftime. And I'm going to show you what they're talking about. I don't know when it's going to happen, but I'll make sure it happens for you." He nodded and said, "Alright, Daddy." But Tim Jr. didn't have to wait long. Five minutes into the first, I stole the ball from Houston at center court and as I came down dribbling, I remember clearly thinking *I hope he's in his chair*. I knew what was about to happen. Chris Childs stepped up to guard me in the paint and I froze him—*boom-BOOM*—and went up for the basket.

I got the layup and my son got to see it. I pointed at him in the stands after it to let him know I remembered our talk and he was jumping up and down. That was special. And it was the start of maybe my best game as a pro. If you've played basketball, chances are you've heard the phrase "in the zone." It's a feeling when you're on the court and everything you shoot goes in. Players can have cold games where the opposite happens. And in the series against the Knicks, I had bad games when I shot 6–22 and 3–17. But in Game Seven, I was in the *zone*. I made three after three. I drove to the hoop, scoring among the Oakley and Ewing trees.

And I played it up to the home crowd, waving my arms. Being in the zone, you feel like you can't miss, you're unstoppable. You're in a groove and no one can take you out of it. It's a lot like a baseball pitcher throwing a no-hitter. Your teammates are talking to you, but you aren't really engaging with them. You're doing your job at a high level and tuning everything else out. I'd had this same feeling once earlier in the season in a game against Washington in March. The Bullets had a good team then with

Juwan Howard and Rod Strickland, who each had 28 points that night. But it wasn't enough.

Just a quick flashback: We'd played Washington the night before. We'd been up in that game by 16 points after three quarters, but we got too comfortable and let them come back in the fourth and beat us. Pat was livid. He hated when an inferior team stole a win from us. So the very next night we had another game against them. We got up big and led at the half, 59–38. But in the fourth quarter we let them come back *again*, this time sending the game into overtime. But I knew I had to make sure we won it and didn't have Pat screaming at us. So I finished the game with my career-high 45 points. I knew for us to win, I had to take over.

We won by three after I hit the game winner against Washington with four seconds left to notch my 45th point. I also had seven assists, seven rebounds, and four steals. We won, 108–105, to earn our 45th win against only 16 losses. Pat might have held a 24-hour practice if we'd lost that one. But that wasn't the only time I was ITZ that season. The second time came in Game Seven of the Eastern Conference Semifinals against the New York Knicks.

In that third quarter, Zo, who'd been playing really well with 16 points, got his fourth foul and had to be taken out for a while. When that happened, barely three minutes into the quarter, Pat was worried. At a loss; I'd never seen him like that. The look in his eyes said: *What am I going to do?* Pat was in the huddle during a time out, and he didn't say a single word. He was trying to figure out a gameplan in his head, trying to figure out what the hell we could do against the Knicks at home in a deciding Game Seven. The team was sitting there on the bench waiting for anything from the coach. So I said, "Shit, I'm going to take this over. Just like in a summer league game. Let me take this over. Let me revert to old school Tim." So I started to hit shots. I got myself in a groove like never before. This wasn't no March regular-season game against the Bullets. This was Game Seven against the Knicks.

After the game, people asked me, "Damn, Tim, where did that come from?" And I said, "It came from Pat not saying nothing. He needed someone to step up." I knew that if I didn't take over and we had lost, I would have always wondered what I could have done. As a point guard, you want to get other people involved. But sometimes it has to be *your* game. That was that night for me. No one could touch me. It was just *swish, swish, swish.* The announcer said over the loudspeaker after every basket, "TIM . . . HARDAWAY!" I was busting Ward with my killer crossover, hitting three after three.

The legendary play-by-play man Marv Albert kept saying on TV, "Oh my!" And later, "It has been a Jordan-esque performance!" That night I scored my playoff career high of 38 points, and we won the game, 101–90. For me, there was nothing like it before or since. I'd had 13 at halftime but scored 25 in the second half. I also added seven assists and five steals. The win made us only the sixth team in NBA history to come back from a 3–1 series deficit. Now, we were in the Eastern Conference Finals against the Chicago Bulls. We'd made the NBA's Final Four, which was a first for me.

But the Bulls were rested.

They'd beaten Washington 3–0 and Atlanta 4–1 in the two series prior, whereas we'd gone the distance in both of ours. Chicago, which had won the NBA Finals the year prior against

Seattle, had home-court advantage. It was a rematch against the team that had beaten us in the playoffs the year prior. But instead of meeting in the first round, we were now in the Conference Finals. Unfortunately, though, the series still wasn't all that close. You could feel the rivalry between Pat and Chicago's coach, Phil Jackson. They didn't talk about it, but you could sense it.

Phil had beaten Pat's Lakers in the 1991 NBA Finals, and the two had squared off three times in the early 1990s when Pat was with the Knicks. Phil won a lot of games and a lot of series, which is what happens when you have Michael Jordan on your team. But for me facing the Bulls, I was happy. I was headed home to Chicago to play in front of my friends and family and a city that loved me. Sadly, though, the Bulls were just too good. They knew how to win, and they'd been there before. They had the confidence of champions. The only way we could make any dent on them was in the pick and roll.

If you posted up against the Bulls, they had you dead. Dennis Rodman was great on the block, and they were so long with MJ, Scottie Pippen, Ron Harper, and Toni Kukoč that they could cover a lot of ground. But they were also an older team, so if you got the Bulls moving around the perimeter, you could try to exploit what little weaknesses they had. They were great on defense, but they didn't want to play it much since most of them were in their late thirties. If you got the ball to spots around the three-point line, you could find openings. But it didn't do us much. We fell down 3–0 before winning our first game at home, 87–80 (which was also the first game in which we'd scored 80 points).

Two days later, back in Chicago for Game Five, they finished us off. Despite the loss, we'd turned around the Miami Heat franchise and became contenders in the league. For the season, I'd become the best point guard in the NBA after being benched and traded by Golden State. That meant a lot. We'd set a franchise record with 61 wins and earned the league's best road record at 32–9. Pat won Coach of the Year for the third time in his career. He'd set us up for years of success. We had championship aspirations. We were all about hard work and improvement. But little did we know how hard the road ahead would be, and how many times we'd face our blood rivals, the Knicks.

10

F*** THE KNICKS!

MIAMI and The Big Apple are separated by nearly 1,300 miles of Atlantic coastline. While many New Yorkers fly down to Florida for the winter, it was in May and June that the Heat and the Knicks saw one another most often over a four-year span. And each season, we ramped up knowing we'd have to go through each other in order to move on into the playoffs. It was the case the season before, and would be the case, incredibly, for the next three. But while the Knicks-Heat rivalry was always seemingly at the end of the road, the path to get there was long and fraught. To begin the 1997–98 season, for example, we suffered through injury after injury.

Ahead of the year, Pat Riley picked up three-point shooter Terry Mills and slasher Todd Day. Day, though, only lasted two months before getting into a spat with Pat and then was gone. The big blow to open the year, though, was Zo, who missed the first 22 games due to a knee injury he suffered over the summer. Thankfully, we had center Isaac Austin to step in and carry the load. That's the benefit in having a good bench: when the starters are out, they can fill in for a spell. They might not be All-Stars, but they can play that way for stretches. It also helped that Austin, who'd won the Sixth Man of the Year Award a year prior, was one of the best bench players in the league.

I was having another strong year. But a great year for an All-Star is no easy task. Point guards don't get a lot of open looks. We're usually the ones setting up our teammates for open jump shots, so have to take the contested offerings. Sometimes Pat got on me and told me to shoot fewer threes, but I liked to use the shots as weapons. "Hey," he'd say, "you're jacking up too many, Timmy." I understood what he was saying—threes are, after all, tough to make by definition. As Pat was the general, I understood his request and scaled back.

But I knew they were also daggers—especially at the end of games. Pat had us practice long-distance shots all the time. During the course of a day, he might have us take 300 threes. He'd designed our Heat team to be a collection of marksmen, from Dan Majerle and Voshon Lenard to Jamal Mashburn and me. It was a way to space the floor for Zo and our other bigs. That's why he'd have us stay late to shoot them, to hone our rhythm. He encouraged it if you were open, but he also made sure that we weren't abusing the privilege. There's always a balance. But, in the end, the best part about my game was that I was a versatile scorer.

I could shoot but I could also post up, thanks to the early lessons my grammar school coach Donald Pittman told me, and from my dad who told me there were no positions in basketball, just great players. I remember one game when I had Reggie Miller guarding me and I took him to the post. I shot a jump hook right in his face. Then, as we were running back the other way, I told him, "I'm coming back at you again!" But Reggie said, "No way, that's fake! You got lucky!" So I had to take him down low again and give him another hook from the block to prove I wasn't just a short guy with no inside game to my name.

In every contest, no matter the opponent, I wanted to tear your heart out and make the opposing crowd sit down. So I'd come down the court and size my opponent up, and sometimes just rise up on him or take a step-back three. That's what I used to do on the courts in Chicago, and it transferred over to the pros. Maybe I took a few too many in the early parts of the game but, by the end, I wanted to be ready to sink a game winner. When it's money time, I made sure to make my jumpers. It was the result of the year I tore my ACL in Golden State and put up thousands of shots, getting my form and rhythm right. When you can sink a shot from the outside, you're more dangerous.

The guy guarding you has to take that into consideration. You become a multi-dimensional scorer. In fact, that helped me in the second game of the season that year, on November 1, 1997. Just three days after *NBA Live '98* came out with me on the cover, we were playing the Bullets in DC, which was always a tight matchup. In the final seconds, Washington's talented guard Rod Strickland, who continues to be underrated today, took the ball down and made a twisting scoop layup with about five seconds left to put his team up, 108–107. When Mashburn inbounded the ball to me under the basket, I drove the length of the court with my left hand—but I hesitated for a split second at the three-point line and then bolted ahead. My defender Strickland froze momentarily. I leapt from two feet inside the line, double-pumped in the air, floated to the rim, and let the ball go just before the buzzer. The shot was GOOD! We celebrated the victory, our second in a row to begin the season. That's what preparation can do for you. As the year continued, we managed to play solid ball without Zo, going 15–7 during that time. In fact, it wasn't until the middle of December that we lost two straight games. Then in mid-February we lost Mashburn to a thumb injury. It was tough, but we stuck together as we'd done without Zo.

Our team was built on Riley's toughness. We were tough-minded individuals, each one of us. But you couldn't be on the Miami Heat and not understand the influence of our coach and president. Because Riley left New York how he did—wanting to be the team's president but getting denied and then resigning via fax to join Miami—there was always going to be tension between our two franchises. And our squad was always going to be defined by Pat's demeanor. There would always be that lingering sense of hatred between New York and Miami, and it would touch every part of our season. Yet, we thrived off it. And let me say this: I don't begrudge Pat one bit. Get your money! He had confidence in himself and it worked out great for him. Just as I had confidence in myself and it paid off that season with another All-Star appearance.

Since Pat had left New York, the Knicks had undergone some changes of their own. In came Don Nelson briefly as coach and then, when he left, Jeff Van Gundy took over. Jeff's first full season was 1996–97, and with him came new players on the roster, including the aforementioned guard Chris Childs. New York also acquired the veteran frontcourt player Buck Williams and two big stars: sharp-shooter Allan Houston from the Detroit Pistons (on a record contract) and All-Star power forward Larry Johnson from the Charlotte Hornets (which was also Zo's former team). LJ was a bit diminished due to a back injury, but was still a potent scorer and badass.

We stood atop the Atlantic Division at the All-Star break with a 30–17 record. I was also voted to my fifth All-Star Game. The 1998 All-Star team was my favorite to play on—and, even though I didn't know it at the time, would also be my last. It was thought to be Michael Jordan's final All-Star team, too, and his last year both in Chicago and the NBA. I remember sitting next to Mike prior to the game, thanking him and expressing my appreciation for all he'd done for basketball. In the game, he would go on to score 23 points, matching his famous jersey number, and win MVP honors. Mike's a great guy. People get on him for being too cutthroat, but that's only if you aren't willing to do what it takes to win.

The East won the game, 135–114, which meant that my teams had won in four of my five appearances. It also marked Kobe's first All-Star appearance, and he and MJ went at it some on the court, as anyone who has seen the documentary *The Last Dance* knows. Also playing were stars like Grant Hill, Shawn Kemp, Penny Hardaway, Reggie Miller, Glen Rice, Gary Payton, Kevin Garnett, Shaq, Karl Malone, David Robinson, Mitch Richmond, and Tim Duncan.

While it felt good to give Mike his props, he and I didn't often interact when we were on the court during the season. Even though we'd played them in 1996 and 1997, it was all business. Mike is a lot like me that way. You don't need to give either of us something to get our fires going. Don't need to give us something to think about. Because once you fuel that fire, you're looking for hurt. You're basically asking us to take it to the next level, and Mike was good enough as it was. That's why I knew not to talk to Mike and he knew not to talk to me. We had that mutual understanding. We left each other alone while on the court. We didn't want to rile the other up and then have to answer to our teammates on the bus about it after, even though we both knew what buttons to push when it came to the other one. Spike Lee, too. He never talked trash to me when I played the Knicks. He knew better. He knew I got my trash talk game from the streets of Chicago.

Some guys, though, I did like to talk with. Gary Payton comes to mind. We had our little back and forths, though I think Gary had those with just about everyone. We kept it to a minimum most of the time, but we both had such big mouths that we mixed it up and a few words got exchanged in the heat of battle. Kevin Johnson could talk a little trash here and there as well, but the great John Stockton *never* talked. He just went out and played. He was the kind of guy to hit you twice in a row on picks and, on the third time when you hit him back, he'd fall and the ref would call you for a foul. Mark Price never talked, either. A lot of guys didn't say anything. But we knew the ones around the league who would give it that much more if you talked smack. Payton, Jordan, Larry Bird, Charles Barkley, and me to name a few.

Even though I was almost a decade into my career by now, I felt at the top of my game. I was healthy and feeling good, with no restraints or restrictions. I was motivating my team and feeling sharp. My knees felt great, my body felt great. I attribute it all to what we did as a team in practice and how we took care of ourselves. We'd get regular massages and make sure to rest between games. While I started all 81 games I played in during the 1997–98 season, I still felt fresh. I averaged 18.9 points and 8.3 assists, finishing sixth in MVP voting. One person that helped me stay ready was our great head trainer, Ron Culp. So was our strength and conditioning coach, Bill Foran. The only thing you couldn't do when it came to them was be late!

* * *

Another thing for certain back then was that I still had the best crossover in the NBA. Even though there was this new kid coming up in Philadelphia by the name of Allen Iverson, I knew I had the best *one-two* dribble in the league. Today, people have tried to put a wedge between me and AI, and I want to be clear once and for all that there is no beef between us. None whatsoever. We never had beef, and will never have beef. I'm fifty-seven and too old for that. But, at the same time, I'm not going to sit up here and let anyone tell me someone has a better crossover than me! If they do, it's a flat-out lie.

Even though the crossover has evolved, coaches are still teaching my crossover to young players to this day. That's how I know mine is the best, and always will be. When it comes to "The Answer," I'm happy for everything that comes his way and I'm happy he's back doing things with the NBA. We were worried about him there for a time; he lived a wild lifestyle for a number of years. But he's back where he belongs, in the arms of the league. He deserves the world. He helped push the game forward and brought it to a whole new level (and also owes his coach in Philly, Larry Brown, a ton for that chance). But when it comes to crossovers, mine is still king! Why? Because mine is the tightest. I don't carry the ball when I make my move. I just come down and shake and bake and get by the guy guarding me.

My dribble is in the box—no extra movement, no wasted time or effort. If you dribble outside the box, you give up ground and waste time. When I do my killer crossover, I keep the ball on a string and go right by your shoulder, and if my shoulder hits yours, I'm knocking you over because that's how low and under control I am.

Still, though, when it comes to the fraternity of the crossover there are some great names, including Iverson's. There's also Jason "White Chocolate" Williams. There's Mahmoud Abdul-Rauf (formerly Chris Jackson when we played against each other in college), there's Jamal Crawford, Chris Paul, and Chauncey Billups. When those guys needed to get somewhere, they *got* somewhere. Today, Kyrie Irving has an excellent handle. James Harden, Stephen Curry, and Donovan Mitchell do as well. Back in the day, Kevin Johnson could handle the rock and had a nice crossover. And of course there's Rod Strickland. Those are some of the guys that come to mind when I think about the brotherhood of the crossover. But we all know who is still No. 1, don't we?

* * *

As I said, the 1997–98 season, despite some bumps in the road, went well for us. We were one of the best teams in the East heading into the second half of the season, but it was two weeks later, on February 19, when we felt our biggest blow. The problem was, unfortunately, self-inflicted. That day, we played the Los Angeles Clippers in Anaheim (for some reason), where the NHL squad, the Mighty Ducks, played. We won the game, 89–80. But before it, Pat made a trade that would haunt us. Making a deal with the Clippers, he sent away our Sixth Man and beastly center, Isaac Austin (along with guard Charles Smith and a first-round pick), and brought back the young guard Brent Barry.

I heard the news as I was headed to the gym to get ready for the game around 4 p.m. The move stunned us all because we thought we already had the team to make a run at a championship. If we were, we shouldn't have dealt our award-winning backup center for an unproven, third-year guard. *What are we doing?* It all came down to money—the NBA is a business, of course. We had several big contracts on our books, and Pat needed to clear money to fit them all in. What sucks is that the decision to make the trade wasn't about making us better. Now, I'm not trying to trash or bad mouth Brent here. But he wasn't going to come in and make us better (he only played 17 games for us that year and we released him over the summer).

But Austin was a key player. Everyone on the team resented the trade. You could see it on our faces. Pat saw it on our faces. He knew. He addressed us before the Clipper game that night, and we talked seemingly for an hour. We just stared blankly back at him. Like, *What the fuck did you do that for?* We talked so much about the move that we almost missed tip-off. Normally a team comes out with about 20 minutes to go before the start of the game, but Pat kept talking and talking about the deal that we only made it out with five minutes to warm up. He was trying to get the point across and tell us the trade would help, but nobody was buying what he was trying to sell.

During the game, Pat didn't coach much. He was mad at us for being mad at him. So he felt that if we thought we knew so much, we should coach ourselves that night. *Let them do it on their own!* When halftime came, he didn't say anything to us in the locker room, so we just went out there and won the game on our own. I scored 16 points and dished five assists while Zo got 28 with 11 boards. P. J. Brown added nine points and a whopping 20 rebounds. We had a great frontcourt, but I knew that, in the playoffs, you need all the depth you could get. We needed Austin, and we'd soon find that out against our rivals.

* * *

Around that same time, we lost Mash for the rest of the regular season (though he'd come back for the playoffs). Still, we finished the season 55–27 after going 13–2 in February, which was good for second in the East behind the Bulls. After splitting our first two games with the Knicks in January, we split our final two in April, with the home team winning all four contests (and a total of four points separating each team's totals).

Heading into the playoffs as the second seed, we would be matched up against the seventh seed in the first round. And do you want to guess which team was the seventh seed? Yep, the New York Knicks. As previously mentioned, Pat had built the Heat in the Knicks mold. We were mirror images of each other. And it seemed like fate that we kept matching up against each other in the playoffs. Even if we tried to get away from one another in the seeding, it was our destiny to go to war. The NBA loved it, and so did the fans.

The Knicks knew we were a force in the East and wanted to inject talent to keep up. Today, I wouldn't change our rivalry for anything. I loved every minute. Each playoff series was nip and tuck, back and forth, with fights and shoving. Each series went the distance. That's what made it so fun. The nail-biting from game to game. There was real pressure. We knew that whenever we went to Madison Square Garden or whenever they came down to play us in Miami, it would be a slugfest.

Patrick Ewing had injured his wrist early in the season and was not expected to be back for the first round of the playoffs. With that edge, we wanted to make quick work of the Knicks to get a breather before the next round, unlike the season before when we'd gone the distance in the first two rounds.

With home-court advantage, no Ewing, and a healthy Zo, we were ready to dominate—which is just what we did in Game One. Up by 20 at the half, we were able to coast to an easy 94–79 victory. I had a game-high 34 points, and only LJ scored at least 20 points (21) for the Knicks. They were just no match for us! Even with Zo wearing a mask and looking like Jason from *Friday the 13th* in the game.

In Game Two, however, they showed their resolve and came back strong. The first half was back and forth. We finished the first quarter with a 10-point lead, but the game was tied by the half. We continued to go back and forth, and I think there were like ten or so lead changes in the third. But they outlasted us and won, 96–86. While Zo had 30 points and 13 boards, we lost Dan Majerle to a groin injury that would keep him out for Game Three. The Knicks, though, had three guys score 20-plus and we couldn't get the win. It was also their first playoff win without Ewing in the lineup in more than a decade. Even so, the series kept going back and forth.

No matter who was playing for either team, the battle, the matchup felt the same. It wasn't two teams or two sets of players facing it, it was two cultures engaging one another. But the funny thing was, we were mirror images of one another. The *same* culture going up against its equal. It didn't matter who was sitting with injury, what new free agent either squad picked up. The evolution was always happening, but nothing about the tension changed. Still hard-nosed, still get-up-in-your-jersey defense. Even as we went deep into the '90s. For me, my biggest rivals were Chris Childs and Charlie Ward. But I didn't care who was on the team, I just wanted to beat the Knicks.

In New York, as the series continued, we won Game Three, 91–85. Voshon Lenard went crazy, scoring 28. I had 27 with seven assists and five rebounds. After stumbling in Game Two, things were now looking good. One more win and we'd take the series and move on. Our rivalry was great for basketball, great for TV, and great for the fans. It was like the old Boston Celtics and Los Angeles Lakers battles—bloody and personal. It was beautiful.

Two days later, on April 30, we prepared ourselves to close out the series, though again without Majerle. However, as had been the case in our matchups with the Knicks, things didn't go as planned.

Throughout the first half things were essentially even, with us exchanging buckets back and forth. We went into halftime tied at 47 apiece, knowing that we'd need to turn things up to get the win and close out the series. New York had a balanced attack all game, and five guys finished in double-figures. I scored 33 points with nine assists, and Zo had 29 points of his own, but we didn't get much out of our bench and they were able to out-muscle and out-rebound us, pulling out a 90–85 victory to tie the series. In fact, Zo and I had 18 of our teams 20 points in the fourth quarter, which is never a good sign (unless you're talking about Jordan and Pippen). But it was what happened in the game's final seconds that doomed us.

Things were still close, and we were down just five with 90 seconds left after I got a steal off Childs and then drained a three, and followed that with another bucket at the top of the key (thanks to my killer crossover) to make it a three-point game, 86–83. Things had already been aggressive under the boards, and with just 10 seconds left LJ had muscled Zo under the boards to draw a foul, hitting both free throws. I had to shoot a long three as time was expiring, and Starks grabbed the rebound and went to dribble the ball out before getting fouled. But it was what happened away from the ball that would make people talk about this game to this day.

It was common knowledge that Zo and Larry Johnson disliked each other. It'd gone back to their Charlotte days and carried over into the Heat-Knicks rivalry. But just before the whistle blew on the foul of Starks, I looked over and saw the two big men start swinging their giant fists at each other like they were in some backyard brawl. The two had been going at it for most of the game, and I guess they couldn't contain themselves at the end—especially with LJ hitting Zo in the neck on a box out. Thankfully their punches didn't connect. Still, the event was ugly. Knicks coach Jeff Van Gundy seemingly lost his mind and tried to break up the fight midway. What's crazy is Oak was one of the first to get in between the two, trying to keep Zo from getting back at LJ.

But after Larry hit Jeff in the ear by accident, the 5-foot-9 coach got swallowed by the swarm and could only cling to Zo's leg for safety like a child. I had been behind Oakley trying to get him off Zo when I saw Van Gundy on the floor and tried to push the guys away to help him up. In the aftermath, Zo and LJ were each suspended, and so we were without one of our best players for the deciding game back in Miami. That's when the trade of Isaac Austin really came back to bite us in the ass. Even without Ewing they'd been out-rebounding us for much of the series, so now without Zo we knew we'd be in trouble under the hoop. It was a huge outcome and much worse for us than for New York.

To this day, people want to know why Zo and LJ started to fight. What was the *real* reason? All I can say is that it was something personal that went way back. It wasn't about basketball. But that's all I can say. If either of them ever wants to talk about what happened, that's up to them. That's their business. But it was more personal than it was basketball. I wish I could say more, but it's not my story to tell. In the end, though, what hurt us more than even Zo getting suspended was what Pat Riley said to us after the game. Pat came into the locker room, saying, "Zo, what did you do? What did you do? God damn, Zo, you don't do shit like that! You just lost the series for us!"

Meanwhile, we still had one more game. Pat saying that lost him the locker room. (He later said his only regret was that none of Zo's punches landed.) It was as if Pat didn't believe in the rest of the guys who would be playing in Game Five. That hurt the team and took our spirit. The rest of us looked around like, *What are we, castoffs? What about us? You don't believe in us?* That's where our minds went. I could see it flash on the faces of all my teammates. We might have been able to win Game Five, but we were deflated. Our leader didn't believe we could do it *and* we were without our All-Star center *and* Sixth Man of the Year backup *and* no Majerle, too.

It was the Knicks game to win, and they got it done. We were down by 17 at the half and could barely make a dent in their lead. P. J. Brown did his best to step into Zo's spot, scoring 18 points with 10 rebounds, and despite my 21 points and eight assists, we just couldn't compete. Allan Houston got 30 for the Knicks, Oakley had 18 points and 13 rebounds, and we got blown out at home, in the series-deciding game, 98–81.

With the disappointment of getting eliminated in the first round of the playoffs after the season we'd had, we knew there'd be some changes to the roster. I'd averaged 26 points in the Knicks series, and while you never know the future, I was confident I'd be back. It was too bad, though, losing how we did. It was a tough pill to swallow. We'd had expectations to go far—to the Eastern Conference Finals, or beyond. In the next series, the Knicks lost in five games to the Indiana Pacers. Maybe we could have done better, but that's life in the NBA. It comes at you fast. Like a fist flying in the air. You have to duck, bob and weave, and counter. Then there was always another thing coming.

11

A LOCKOUT AND THE BOUNCING BUZZER-BEATER

ALLAN Houston was a killer in the playoffs. But before there was any possibility of us facing him and his Knicks again in the postseason, in the hopes of avenging last season's loss, the entire league had to navigate a complete basketball shutdown. Not only had Michael Jordan retired (again), but the NBA had come to a screeching halt due to an argument over money. The owners wanted changes, including a ceiling on player salaries, and the players wanted changes, including higher minimum salaries. I was there in New York for some of the negotiations. As far as the players were concerned, some wanted to cancel the year and some wanted to play. It was a mess, and a difficult time for everybody—players and team employees alike.

In the end, no one was completely happy about the deal between the owners and players, but that was probably how it should have been. It was what it was, but the bottom line was that we needed to get back to playing for the fans. Officially, the lockout began July 1, 1998, and lasted for more than six months. For a while, we weren't sure if the season would even happen. We weren't allowed to practice in team facilities or work with coaches. Guys worked out on their own or in small groups. We also played pickup games. We tried to simulate NBA practices and games as best we could. All the while we wondered what the future of the season would be.

Before it went down, we knew the lockout was coming. The players had started a fund the year before for those who needed help paying the bills or in case the entire season was cancelled. We tried to prepare as best we could. A lockout is hard—there isn't unanimity when it comes to the issues. Our players union had to be united while also being open to new ideas. It's not easy. I wasn't involved in the decision making, but there was always conversation going between players—on the phone or in the gym—trying to figure out the best path forward.

Another thing I remember from that time was the charity game we played for *Showtime*. The exhibition contest took place in Atlantic City. There were two teams of NBA players. The RED team included Charles Barley, Patrick Ewing, Shawn Kemp, Dan Majerle, Karl Malone, Reggie Miller, Mitch Richmond, and me. The WHITE team included Zo, Vin Baker, Allan Houston, Chris Webber, Glen Rice, Penny Hardaway, Gary Payton, and Tom Gugliotta.

We liked the idea of the game; it would give fans a chance to see real hoops again and remind them that we *wanted* to play. In the locker room, we couldn't help but talk about the NBA situation. "Man, what's going to happen? What are we going to do?" Wondering about revenue sharing and all that type of stuff. But once we got onto the court and started balling, we just had fun. I actually won MVP! I just shot the ball well and dished off to my teammates. Reggie Miller and Mitch Richmond were on fire and I just made the right plays. But I tell you what: after the game, we were all dog tired!

It was a nice break from all the NBA issues . . . but it wasn't a fix. Thankfully, things were resolved between the league and the players and we could resume business as usual (or close enough). In the end, the NBA held a 50-game season. David Stern and the NBA Players Association bet on the product itself and eventually things got back to normal. But the 50-game year was tough. The schedule was packed closely together and there were a lot of injuries as a result.

The season began February 5, 1999. There was only about two weeks of training camp and because players weren't sure there would even be a season, many came to camp out of shape. In the off season, the Heat signed All-Star guard Terry Porter and forward Clarence Weatherspoon. The team had moved on from Brent Barry, but we had a good veteran team and believed this could be our year thanks to our star power and balanced roster. Up north, the Knicks also got better. With their already stellar core of Patrick Ewing, Allan Houston, and Larry Johnson, they added shot-blocker Marcus Camby (trading out Charles Oakley) and former Heat big man, Kurt Thomas.

The Knicks also got my former teammate in Latrell Sprewell, trading away team legend John Starks. Sprewell had missed the entire year prior for choking his coach, P. J. Carlesimo. No team wanted to touch him after that debacle, but the Knicks took a chance and he was a huge help coming off the bench as a scorer and defender. It was shaping up to be another grudge match for us in the East. But, as the season began, we started to distance ourselves from the competition. After a 1–3 start (with our victory coming in New York against the Knicks), we won 17 of our next 19 games. It was remarkable since we weren't allowed to practice leading up to the preseason—not formally, anyway.

Even though players were not allowed to use team facilities, several of us had gotten together in the offseason for pickup games at a Miami grammar school, which had a good gym. We'd get there in the late afternoons and play for several hours. It was a mix of locals who had talent and pros like me, Mash, Voshon, and P. J. Brown. Everyone knew they were there for the possible upcoming shortened season, so even though some games got heated, we kept tempers in check. I also worked with a personal trainer to keep in shape. I made sure to work on my game in the offseason, as even though I'd been an All-Star, my numbers had been down from the previous season. I did not expect the NBA would throw the year away, so I wanted to be ready.

But no matter how much we prepared, it was still a grueling season. First off, we lost six months of training, preseason, practice, and early-season games to get our legs under us. Plus, with the season so condensed, there were stretches where we played three games in a row, back-to-back-to-back. In fact, six of our first eight games were back-to-back-to-back! I imagine it felt like the old 1960s and 1970s NBA and ABA. Players were trying to win games, but we were also trying not to get hurt. The only thing I can compare it to now is the 2020 NBA "Bubble" season. Some said those years deserve asterisks, but it was all about who showed up prepared to win. Despite minor weight issues here and there in my career, I always wanted to show up to a new season prepared.

In October, before training camp in my first full year in Miami in 1996–97, Pat Riley told me about the team's Keith Askins Award. A career backup forward, Askins had been with the Heat since signing as a rookie free agent in the summer of 1990—he was also one of the founders of "Heat Culture." The NBA walk-on had earned the respect of the franchise for how hard he worked in practice and, therefore, got a team award named after him. Since then, Pat said, he'd given it out to people who practiced hard, got the best times in the sprints, never took a day off, and participated in every drill. Hearing that, I told our coach, "I'm going to win that!"

But in all my years with the Heat, Pat never gave it out, despite telling me about it soon after I arrived. He never even brought it up again. Pat, if you're reading this, I'm still waiting for my Keith Askins Award! Maybe it was all a joke. Maybe it was a bait-and-switch—after all, a player is *supposed* to do all the drills, never miss a day, and work his butt off. Maybe it was all a mind game from Riley. But, to this day, I always wonder what that was all about. As far as I saw, no one ever received anything—except Keith, who played for the squad through the 1998–99 campaign. He was an unsung hero of the team, the man who earned his place on the roster and worked hard to prove he deserved to be there.

Over the years, people have asked me about my relationship with Pat; whether we were close, or if it was more like a "frenemies" type of situation. People always think there was tension between us, that it was more love-hate. But that wasn't the case. We were all good. (I mean, how good do we look with Zo on the January 1998 cover of *Sports Illustrated* in our tan suits!) I was in Miami to play ball and win. I *love* to win, and so does Riley. I love to go out there and compete, and so does Riley. It was our job to get the team in the right position to win, and we did that year after year, becoming one of the marque franchises of the 1990s. Pat would get on your ass, that was for sure. But I didn't mind that. Coming from Chicago, I was used to it.

As I've said, my thing was to listen to the message—not always how it was delivered. You have to know how to take it in stride. If anything, your job is to go out there and take whatever frustrations or anger you have out on your opponent and the team you're playing against. That's always been my philosophy, even going back to childhood. It's not "hating on you" if it can make you better. That's the thing about greatness: it takes great pain and sacrifice. Pat only wanted me to be better, which was the same for every coach I've ever had. From my father to him. My job was to focus, improve, and get wins while also helping the team stay positive.

And during that shortened 1998–99 season, we *won*. It wasn't easy, though. During the season, you'd have three games in a row. It was crazy. No one was used to that. But that's what we'd all agreed to in order to keep the season. We had to make up games as quickly as possible. Training camp was short and it was an all-out blitz to the finish. If you didn't come to the season in shape, you were screwed.

The Heat finished the year 33–17, which was good for the top seed in the East. I averaged 17.4 points and 7.3 assists per game and made the All-NBA second team. There was no All-Star team that season (due to the lockout), but if there had been, I would have made that, too. Zo earned his first Defensive Player of the Year Award and finished second behind Karl Malone for MVP. In short, we went out there and did what we were supposed to do in the regular season, and once the playoffs came around, we had confidence we were gonna make a deep run. With no Jordan and no Bulls in the way, this was our year.

Until it wasn't.

Going into the playoffs as the top seed in the East, we would be facing off against the eighth-seeded New York Knicks, who had gone 27–23 on the season. In the league's history, an eighth seed had beaten a one seed just *once* (when the Nuggets beat the SuperSonics in 1994). Normally we wouldn't fear such a low-seeded team, but this was the Knicks. Our foe. Our rival.

Wanting to start out hot on our home floor, we did the exact opposite. We were down by 17 at the half and ended up losing by 20 (!), 95–75. We were blown out, at home, as the top seed in the East, with our fans raining us with boos for most of the second half.

Of course, Riley was heated. He was upset. It was up to us to play harder. It wasn't about a different scheme or a new idea. It was about playing harder, plain and simple. It may sound strange, not to come up with adjustments. You just had to make your presence felt—*WE* had to make our presence felt. That's how both teams felt. But for those in our locker room, we had to forget about the embarrassment and push ahead.

One good thing about the shortened schedule was that we were able to get right back onto the court two days later for Game Two. We wouldn't allow the Knicks to have a repeat performance and put the pressure on them from the jump. Zo started us off strong with nine points in the first quarter and had 17 at the half as we took an 11-point lead into the break. We knew that we'd had leads at the half before and lost them, so there was no room for error. Even though we went cold shooting in the third, we were able to hold on and win the game by 10, 83–73.

With the series tied, we headed to New York for what we knew could be a series-defining game. The margin of error in a five-game series is always small, so playing on the road, in front of a hostile crowd, meant we'd need to give everything we had.

But we didn't.

In the first quarter we showed our toughness, pulling down 10 more rebounds than them, with the help of P. J. Brown, who had nine points and five rebounds. That, unfortunately, was the best we could do. Zo was our only starter to score in the second quarter, and after leading by five after the first, the Knicks went on a 12–0 run to end the quarter, and we headed into the locker room down by eight at the half. It wasn't like they surprised us with anything different. They just were playing better than us. Aside from Zo and P. J., none of us could get anything going—especially me, as I had just two points through the first two quarters. It also didn't help that Dan Majerle hurt his already injured collarbone in the first quarter and was barely able to play the rest of the game.

The truth of the matter was I'd hurt my right knee in Detroit on February 26. The Piston's Grant Hill collided with my leg and, as a result, had a small tear in my meniscus. It could have been that combined with long practices (Pat was famous for his rigorous practices) and a brutal schedule. Who knows. No one knew about it but me, Pat, and our doctors. There was just a rumor I was a little hobbled or "wore down" from the season. Still, it's not an excuse. If you're playing, you're playing.

The second half started and we just could not get anything going. It was so frustrating. We'd yet to make a three-pointer, and it felt like every time we missed, they'd get a bucket. Zo also picked up his fourth foul early in the quarter, and as things went on I just kept getting more and more frustrated. I've always tried to keep my composure on the court, but this shit was getting out of hand. We had scored just 12 points in the second quarter, and instead of punching right back, we scored 11 in the third and went into the final quarter down 25, 73–48.

At that point, I'd just had it. Chris Childs kept talking shit to me and I was getting frustrated with the refs. I'd picked up my fifth foul on a bs call and called them out on that nonsense. I obviously went too far, and after two techs was sent to the locker room. When you're playing like shit and the other team is kicking your ass, you get mad—especially when the guy opposite you won't shut up about it. You start talking shit and then the ref comes in and tells you to quit it. Then you tell the ref to shut the fuck up and maybe to kiss your ass and he gives you the boot! You're mad so you just start talking crazy. That's how you get your second tech. I shouldn't have gotten myself kicked out, but it was what it was.

The Knicks won the game (obviously), 97–73, and we just played like shit.

With the next game being do-or-die, there was no way we were gonna go out like that. We knew that Zo needed to stay on the floor and out of foul trouble, and that's exactly what he did for Game Four. He got 16 points and 13 rebounds, on the game, and though we were trailing going into the fourth quarter, we hit our shots while the Knicks went cold, and quieted MSG with an 87–72 victory.

Now the series was tied again, and we'd be on our home court for the series-deciding Game Five. I remember how loud the fans were that we had to wear earplugs! Before the game, Riley told us to remember the pain of the previous year's Game Five. "If you remember that pain, remember that hurt, you will not want to repeat that here." But sometimes even the best motivation goes awry.

While we started out strong in the first, at one point up by 13, the Knicks went on a 15–2 run to finish the quarter. It was pretty much even after that, with us trading baskets, and we went into halftime leading by four, 41–37. Then, after three, we were tied again, with the score 60–60 heading into the fourth. It remained a back-and-forth game, and while we were up by as many as seven with 5:35 left, the game was tied at 69. Riley called time out.

In the huddle, he said, "Would you guys run the ball?! Patrick can't even get up the court!" Pat always wanted us to run, to get easy buckets. But if a team is making their shots, that can be difficult. The game stayed close and with just under two minutes left in regulation we were up by one, 75–74.

After a few free throws by Terry Porter and Ewing, we had the ball with 39.4 seconds left. We could taste victory. After getting a pass from Terry I went to drive in but the ball slipped right out of my hands. I couldn't believe it. I tried to grab the loose ball, but Larry Johnson got it and the Knicks called a time out with 19.9 left on the clock. Everyone was gassed—I think even the fans were tired. You try to find any kind of second to catch your breath. Coming out of the time out, Zo put his arm around me—I can't remember exactly what he said, but it was probably, "God damn, Bigs! You should have got that ball. You know we needed that ball!" That's the competitiveness in him, and with the amount of time we shared the floor I knew he was not only saying what he felt, but what I needed to hear to help me zone in.

When the game began again, we made sure to smother New York once they got the ball in, and Terry put pressure on Sprewell as the clock was running down. Tery's stellar defense knocked the ball out of Spree's hands, and though it was still Knicks' ball they had just 4.5 seconds to score.

With their last chance, Charlie Ward inbounded to Allan Houston at the top of the key, who cut down the lane and threw up a floater from 15 feet that bounced around the rim, like, twelve times, before it finally dropped in. He might as well have taken my heart out and put it in the net, too. We knew what they were going to run. We actually made them adjust on the play, but when Allan got the ball, he knew what to do. The game had been called tight all night—anything could have been a foul. While I was close to him—I even took a step toward Houston when he got the rock—I didn't want to put him on the free-throw line. I didn't want to take that chance.

In the film room later, I could see that I had an opportunity to block him from behind. But, in the moment, the last thing I wanted to do was give the refs the excuse to blow their whistles. The game already wasn't going our way. Pat was mad I didn't make the attempt, but so be it. The thing is, I don't even mind that Allan made that shot. That happens. What made it bad was all the bounces the ball took, which cut seconds off the clock.

On our next possession, Majerle got the ball to Terry right away, who got off a 40-foot shot with 0.8 seconds, but it just missed.

And, just like that, it was all over. It was the second straight time New York had eliminated us on our home floor. *That devastating pain again.* It was also the final playoff game in Miami Arena, only the second time in NBA history that an eighth seed knocked off a one seed. Out of all our playoff losses, this was the hardest to swallow. I mean, the Knicks had needed to win six out of their last eight games to even *make* the playoffs! Now they were moving on, and we weren't. I still believe we had the better team, but the Knicks kept playing and went on to the NBA Finals (thanks to Larry Johnson's famous four-point play against the Indiana Pacers), though lost to the San Antonio Spurs and their twin towers, Tim Duncan and David Robinson.

Even so, I think we would have given the Spurs a better run. We had the size and could have even won our first championship. All I can chalk it up to was that our teams were so familiar with one another that seedings didn't matter. We'd played each other a million times, and it was like two brothers battling it out in the backyard. Everything clicked for them, and we went cold. But, in the end, no explanation matters. We just didn't win and that's what I think about today. We could have beaten San Antonio with Zo and P. J. in the paint, but we never got a chance to find out. Still, you can't take anything away from New York.

They beat us fair and square. But it hurts. I'll always remember the feeling of heartbreak it caused me. The series wasn't my finest either, unfortunately. I was playing through knee pain—the meniscus issue— that was so bad I had to get surgery for it over the summer. But Zo was outstanding for us, scoring 21.6 per game. In the locker room afterward, we were all silent. Finally, Pat said a little something. I don't remember the exact speech—it's hard to remember fine details when your brain is zoning in and out after a crushing loss. But what I am certain of is that we all knew we were getting to the end of our road. We had one more try—maybe—at a ring. Time was running out, and so were guys' contracts.

Of course, Pat was furious. We all were mad. When you're the No. 1 seed and have home-court advantage in the playoffs, it's always frustrating to lose. We thought we had a chance to win. We knew we could have.

It was a dismal feeling. After a big loss, even if we're all upset, Pat would usually talk about the nitty-gritty stuff and how we needed to be better. I liked when he did that. It was helpful to hear. But not this time.

A coach needs to be able to talk to everybody on the team, from the star to the last man on the bench. He needs to have control of his squad. But after this one, there was little to say. We'd let a golden opportunity slip through our fingers, and we knew it. Simple as that. Whenever I close my eyes, I can still see that shot from Houston rattling around and going in. I think if I could take away any one shot that dropped against one of my teams throughout my career, that would be the one. But that's sports. That's basketball. I know I've hit my fair share of game-winners during my career and broken many hearts. It's just that, this time, it happened to us.

* * *

The next year, incredibly, was déjà vu all over again. After our loss to the Knicks, Riley sent Jeff Van Gundy a letter congratulating him. In a way, it was the beginning of a new era between them and our teams.

Later that season, we moved into our new home, American Airlines Arena, on January 2, 2000. Given all our ups and downs the previous seasons, we knew this was the final hurrah for our roster. No matter what happened, next year would have big changes. Our roster was getting older, and our injury report showed it. Despite having knee surgery over the summer, I still battled the pain and only played in 52 games, which was the lowest in my career (not counting the strike-shortened season). Our sharpshooter Voshon Lenard also missed a lot of time.

Still, we thought we had a chance—albeit a fleeting one—to get the championship that had eluded us all these years in Miami. It was hard to push forward knowing Pat would likely shake up the roster the following season, but we were all pros and put our best foot forward.

The highlight of the season came on April 9 against, of all teams, the Knicks. The game was in Miami, and they went up big in the first quarter, 28–21. It went back and forth all game and, by the end of regulation, we were tied at 88. Marv Albert was announcing on TV, so you know it was a big one. In overtime, though, with the final seconds ticking away, we were down two. I got the ball off an inbounds pass and dribbled to the left side of the court. We needed a miracle. With Chris Childs stuck on me, I picked up my dribble and ducked under his left arm and put up a heave . . . and the ball found the bottom of the net! We won the game, 95–94, and everyone went crazy.

As for the season, my scoring dipped to 13.4 points per game, but my assists stayed up and I averaged 7.4 dimes. I shot well from three-point range, though, hitting nearly 37 percent from behind the arc. Zo continued to play strong and got his second Defensive Player of the Year Award. For the season, we finished with a 52–30 record, good for second in the East behind Indiana.

With that, we earned our fourth-straight Atlantic Division title. To change things up this season, we would be facing off against the Detroit Pistons in the first round, instead of the Knicks. Led by five-time All-Star Grant Hill, Detroit was an up-and-coming team, but we dispatched them quickly and easily, despite the fact that I sat out the series due to right knee stiffness. I was hurt—or at least in pain. If we had thought we were in danger of losing the series, I could—and would—have played. But rest was what we all agreed on. Though I couldn't be out there, my boys went out and dominated, sweeping the Pistons. We won the first game by 10, and while we were confident, Detroit was dealt a blow in Game Two when Hill, who had sprained his ankle before the playoffs, had messed it up again and was forced to leave the game. He wouldn't play in Game Three—which we won by 19—and that would be the beginning of his battles with injuries. Grant would never be the same.

Into the second round for the first time since 1997, we would be facing off against . . . you guessed it: the damn New York Knicks. And, *again*, the series went the full amount of games. While I wasn't 100 percent (I remember telling broadcaster Jim Grey that I was 85 percent), there was no way I was going to miss these games, and started each one. When you come back from being out, you either start well or you start sluggish. Thankfully, I came out playing well.

New York had also swept their first-round opponent, the Toronto Raptors, with high-flying forward Vince Carter. Now we were set to square off for the fourth postseason in a row.

So here we were. Home for Game One of another series against the New York Knicks. This was another game of runs, with us up for a bit and them doing the same. We were (to no one's surprise) tied at 81 with 3:24 left in the game. We took the lead after two Zo free throws, and after a foul by Mashburn, Sprewell hit both his free throws to tie the game at 83. Jamal had a great game as well with 21 points, and I think his solid play helped keep us in the game. Zo made a huge bucket with under a minute left to put us up by two, and P. J. came up huge on the next possession, knocking the ball away from Ewing to give us possession. We then got the ball back into Zo's hands, and he drilled another big bucket to put us up for good. He finished the game with 26 points, and we were able to take Game One, 87–83. While I had to leave the game at one point to retape my foot—which felt like it was on fire for most of the game—I finished with a game-high seven assists.

The goal after a big win is to carry your momentum on to the next one. While we prepared and did everything to try and get a second win on our home floor before heading back to New York, it just wasn't in the cards. Though Jamal had a game-high 25 points, Zo had 17 and 17, and I had 13 points, we couldn't get the win. Crazy thing is, if you look at the stat sheet, you'd think we'd won, as we had more rebounds, assists, and shot better from three. But despite all that, including Jamal Mashburn's 25 points, we lost Game Two, 82–76. Again, it's a game of runs. We were down by just one point in the middle of the third quarter, but then they went on a 10–0 run that led into the fourth, and that was that.

Game Three sent us to New York, for yet *another* matchup in which the series was tied. After all the games and series we'd played against the Knicks over the year, there really were no more adjustments to make. We knew them, and they knew us. At the end of the day, it was all about will and execution. Pat knew it, we knew it, New York knew it. The game was physical—the rules incentivized it. That's how we had to play. Whoever won—they just played better that day.

We knew it was an important game, and the worst part for me is that I couldn't play as much or as hard as I would have wanted to. Halfway through the third I took a seat, and that was it for me on the day. When you're having a bad day, you sit. Pat knew that, too. He'd learned from his New York days when he didn't sit John Starks in Game Seven of the Finals against Houston in 1994 (where he missed all 11 of his three-point attempts). You can't *always* ride your stars. That's why you have a *team*. I was never one to want to sabotage a franchise for my own benefit, and it wasn't going to start now. I'm all about my team.

Thankfully our backup rookie guard Anthony Carter was able to step up when we needed him most. We were *again* tied with around 90 seconds left in the game when Zo's two free throws put us ahead by two. Neither team could hit a shot after that, and with 24.9 remaining the Knicks had the ball, and each time they put up a shot, it'd miss and they'd grab the damn rebound. So after the ball went out of bounds, with 6.1 left, Ewing hit a jumper to tie the game. Jamal was able to get a shot on the other end that would have given us the win, but it bounced out and sent the game to overtime.

Just like the rest of the game, overtime just went back and forth, back and forth. With 13 seconds left and the game tied at 75, Dan Majerle "fouled" Ewing, putting him on the line. After missing the first, he hit the second to give them a one-point lead. We knew this was do-or-die . . . again. I remember telling the guys that we just need *one* basket. So with the clock running down, we kept the ball moving until Majerle passed it to Carter on the baseline, who drove right to the hoop and got an Allan Houston–esque bounce . . . that was initially called off for basket interference. Thankfully the refs talked it over and got the call right! (You get different calls with different refs. The refs who've played basketball won't call that one; they know it's a viable shot.) On the next play, we knocked the ball away from New York as time ran out and stole a big win to take the series lead.

Game Four. We knew that it'd be huge for our confidence if we could get two wins in New York. I was still in a lot pain, which sucked. All I wanted was to be out there and help my guys, so the fact that I couldn't put in the same effort I'd always been able to was incredibly frustrating.

In terms of the game, we were down by two at the half, but the third was again our undoing, as the Knicks outscored us by seven in the quarter, and we dropped the game, 91–83. I was unable to go back out after the third quarter, watching my guys fight from the bench.

Now back in Miami for Game Five, with us and the Knicks being so evenly matched, the only difference would be that we'd have our crowd supporting us. The two guys that helped us close out this one were Dan Majerle and Bruce Bowen, as Dan hit two straight threes, followed by one by Bruce—his only basket in the game—that helped us take the series lead with an 87–81 victory. Now we felt like we were in the driver's seat.

Back in the Big Apple, we were once again bit by the third-quarter bug. We pushed them around in the first half, and went to the locker room up 15! We felt good about where we were. Frankly, we thought we were going to win. All we had to do was hold on. But in the second half, all of a sudden, shots weren't falling. We turned the ball over. The crowd got louder and louder. Still, we were right there. We should have closed them out.

We were up big, but we let go of the rope, which cost us. They outscored us by 10 in the third and then seven in the fourth, and we threw away a golden opportunity to close out the series, losing 72–70. We even had a chance to win the game, as Carter—who had a playoff career-high 15 points—missed a three-pointer as time expired.

Though I only played six minutes in both the third and fourth quarters, I didn't feel like I was wearing down. Sometimes your teammates are just playing better or your coach just wants another look.

Adding insult to injury—this still sticks in my mind—was after Game Six, after we left MSG, it took us nearly three hours to get to our damn plane. When we played New York, we flew out of Newark Airport in New Jersey, which is just over the Hudson River. But, for some reason, the tunnel was closed. We didn't get home that night until 6 a.m. Riley had to cancel practice on our off day so guys could rest. Not ideal but, again, no excuses.

Game Seven. Another goddamn Game Seven. We knew this was it. Win and you go on to the Conference Finals. Lose and . . . well, normally you would be going home, but I think we all knew this would probably be the last time we'd all be in the same locker room if we lost. There was a lot of pressure to keep things going, and the last thing we wanted to do was let our home fans down *again*.

Maybe the craziest subplot of this whole Knicks-Heat postseason rivalry was that two brothers were in the middle of it. Jeff Van Gundy coached the Knicks, and his older brother Stan

Van Gundy was an assistant in Miami. They couldn't talk with each other. Couldn't eat dinner or have lunch. It was actually like they weren't brothers. Pat didn't want them fraternizing with each other. He didn't want Zo hanging out with Patrick Ewing, either. But they were boys! You can have dinner with someone and then come back and want to crush them in the next game. But Pat didn't like that. He made it a point for you to know that, "We don't fraternize with the other team during the playoffs." That's the way it was.

Though I'd been sharing a lot of minutes with Anthony Carter in the series, there was no way I wasn't going to have the ball in my hands for most of this one. Whether we won or lost, I wanted to be the one responsible. Zo felt the same way, and made a statement in the first quarter, scoring 14 of our 25 first-quarter points. But as I've said too many times already, this series is just streak after streak. So while we were up nine after the first, they outscored us by 15 in the second to take a 45–39 lead at the half.

If we were up at the break, Pat often said the same thing. He wanted us to extend the lead, say, from nine to 20 before the other team went on their run. "Let's stretch it out," he'd say. That would give us a cushion. He didn't want the other team to come out more aggressive. He wanted us to set the tone. But that didn't always work out.

With the third quarter underway, it was up to us starters to do everything we could. That meant we would not be leaving the court at any point. We wouldn't let another third quarter get away from us. Zo, Dan, Jamal, P. J., and I stepped out on that court and went to work. I was able to dish out five assists, while Zo and P. J. each had seven points. We'd fought back to tie the game at 65 going into the fourth, and scored the first six points to give ourselves the lead. But then both teams went cold, and New York was the first to heat up, scoring eight straight points. We were now down two with 1:40 left to go. With the ball, we faked a pick and roll, and I got a clean three for the top of the key and drilled it to put us up by one. Then when the Knicks got the ball back, the team posted up Ewing on the right block and got him the ball down low.

Zo gambled on a pass but didn't get the steal and Patrick got an easy two. Knicks up by one. Then Mash had a good shot, but the ball bounced out and Ewing grabbed the rebound. We were now under a minute to go. Knowing we needed the ball and couldn't make any mistakes, Jamal got a huge steal that gave us the ball. So with 26.3 left on the clock, we took a time out to discuss what we needed to do to get the win.

We needed to go to the hoop, get a basket, or get fouled. We had to put pressure on the Knicks. That was our mentality in a nutshell. Get into them, be the aggressor.

Once back, I got the ball and tried to drive in for a layup but my shot was off. Zo was able to grab the rebound and ended up getting tied up with Sprewell, forcing a jump ball. We won the toss—Jamal caught the tipped ball, handed it to me, and we called time out. We knew this was our last chance to win the game. The plan was to get the ball to Zo, who led the game with 29 points. On the inbound, Majerle got the rock right to Zo, but he was triple-teamed and he passed it out to Mashburn. Instead of taking the open shot at the free-throw line, he faked driving in and passed it to Weatherspoon, who dribbled and missed a contested jumper in the paint. Sprewell got the rebound and as he was falling out of bounds on the baseline, the ref gave him a time out (one Sprewell later admitted that he never called). Instead of us getting the ball back, the Knicks won and that was it. Another big loss.

After the game, I said that ref, Dick Bavetta, should just change his name to *Knick* Bavetta. Ugh. What made it worse was that I had just a terrible series. A stretch like never before. I was in constant pain and couldn't put the ball in the basket. It wasn't necessarily the Knicks defense, it was me. I was exhausted. Maybe I played too many minutes during the regular season, but I just felt hopeless. I averaged just 7.7 points the whole series and couldn't get my team over the hump. Before, whenever we needed a big shot, I could always deliver. But not this time. Doubts began to creep into my mind more than they ever had before. I just couldn't get out of it.

Now, after four-straight battles in the playoffs, our rivalry with the New York Knicks was officially over. The teams were set for changes, and I knew my life would be changing, too. That's what happens in the NBA. Nothing lasts forever. To this day, when Knicks and Heat players from that era run into one another, we're salty and a bit standoffish. More recently, I haven't taken a lot of joy watching the Knicks go through about two decades of dismal play after that, and I wasn't on the sidelines cheering rah-rah for the Heat as they started to win rings with Shaq and LeBron. I try not to get too high or low with whatever happens as long as I know I've done my best every day. But that summer, I had a new challenge ahead of me: the Sydney Olympics.

12

USA! USA! USA!

TO play for your country is a very meaningful experience—when you get that jersey with "USA" on it, you just smile, like *damn*! Over the course of my career, I'd been offered several opportunities to suit up for Team USA before it actually came to fruition. In 1994, I was asked to be on Dream Team II for the FIBA World Championship with the likes of Kevin Johnson, Shawn Kemp, Shaquille O'Neal, Larry Johnson, Reggie Miller, and Zo. Unfortunately, I couldn't play for the squad—which was coached by my guy, Don Nelson—because of my recovery from my torn ACL. In 1998, I was selected for the FIBA World Championship team, but that group never got to play due to the NBA lockout and we were replaced by CBA and college players.

Finally, in 2000, more than a decade into my career, I signed up for the team set to compete in Sydney. The games were a long way from home, but I was excited to play for my country. Ever since the 1992 Dream Team, when Michael Jordan, Larry Bird, Magic Johnson, Chris Mullin, and company destroyed the rest of the world, the international game has only gotten stronger.

We knew we weren't going to cake walk to the gold. Still, with a team that included the likes of Vince Carter, Gary Payton, Zo, Jason Kidd, Ray Allen, Allan Houston, Antonio McDyess, Kevin Garnett, and myself, we also knew we were definitely favored.

Playing for Team USA is high pressure. When you play for America, you're *supposed* to win. A gold medal is *expected.* So you have to channel that pressure and use it to your advantage. The best example of this was probably Carter's dunk on Frenchman Frédéric Weis. It happened on September 25—a day that will live in infamy. In our game against France, their players were about to run a fast break when one of their guys tried an errant spin move and behind-the-back pass—but Carter plucked it out of the air. In a flash, he was airborne. Vince cocked the ball up behind his head and jumped higher than perhaps any human ever has. The only person between him and the basket was Weis. *BOOM!* A first-round pick by the Knicks in 1999 (the summer prior), the 7-foot-2 center's career was never the same after VC posterized him. The ball might as well have been a grenade, as Carter put it through the net with such an explosion, spreading his legs as he leapt full over Weis in one perfect exhibition of athleticism. *Ouch.*

As a team, our strategy in the games was simple. Our coach, Rudy Tomjanovich, a two-time NBA champion with the Houston Rockets in the mid-1990s, instituted a couple of sets. But mostly, we wanted to play tight defense and get out and run, deal with the physicality, and use our superior athleticism.

Everyone brought something unique to the table, from shooting to shot blocking to trash talking. If we slowed the game down and played half court, we looked to post up our bigs. If they didn't have a scoring option, they got the ball back out to a guard to make something happen on the perimeter.

We didn't want to be the first team in recent memory to lose in the Olympics. We never talked about that, but we all felt it. European teams spend more time together than the US does. While we're more talented, we can lack chemistry. Thankfully, we were a great group that year. We built our bonds in practice. Man, a lot of people think that if you're not starting on Team USA, you're going to be disgruntled. That was not the case. All of us on that team were starters, All-Stars, making millions, and many were future Hall of Famers. But the coach has to make his decision on the best five in the moment.

The only thing that fucking mattered was gold. It wasn't a popularity contest, it wasn't a dick-measuring contest. Gold. We were all on the same page. There were a lot of guys, including myself, who didn't get a ton of minutes on the team. But you know what didn't matter? That. You know what did? That's right, gold.

The practices were fun, but also cutthroat. We had a great time, our families had a great time. But on the court, it was a matter of pride and of pushing the next guy. We often played one-on-one knockout games against each other—full court! I remember seeing Garnett win something like 15 or 16 in a row, he was that talented and in that great of shape. He took that shit very seriously and screamed things like, "Y'all ain't shit! I'm the best!" The competitiveness was at an all-time high. Lots of shit talking. No fisticuffs, but lots of guys in each other's faces. All for the sake of glory. Our gym in Hawaii leading up to the tournament was hot, with no air conditioning. But no one minded. We were there to sweat, to work.

It was also marvelous watching Carter come into his own in real time—especially when he hit that dunk over the Frenchman, it's still legend.

To no surprise, we breezed through all the early-round games. But our toughest matchup of the tournament came in the semifinals against Lithuania. We'd won our first six games handily, defeating the likes of China, Italy, New Zealand, France, and Russia. Yet, when we matched up against Lithuania, it was much more difficult.

The country was without their retired legendary center Arvydas Sabonis and my former Golden State teammate Šarūnas Marčiulionis. Still, though, late in the game, we found ourselves in hot water. To begin the contest, we went up big in the first half but then they fought back in the second. And with a minute left in the game, we found ourselves tied, 80–80. If we lost the matchup, we'd be playing for the bronze medal—not silver, not gold. And no USA team is happy with that. In this country, we have standards—and that standard is always to bring home the gold. It was getting tight out there on the court, to say the least.

Then with just 43 seconds left, our power forward Antonio McDyess, who'd come in for Zo when he fouled out, fouled one of their three-point shooters in the act. A cardinal sin. When Zo exited, I'd yelled to our coaches, "Put McDyess in! We need a big!" That wasn't looking like the best idea, though. Lithuania, thankfully, could only hit a single free throw. On our next possession, Carter scored a floater, putting us up by one with 31.3 seconds left. After a great defensive stop by Garnett, in which Lithuania ended up fouling him, he was put on the line for the chance to make it a three-point game. Uncharacteristically, Garnett missed both. McDyess, however, got the offensive rebound and laid the ball in for the score. After a quick field goal by Lithuania, they fouled Kidd to put him on the line, where he hit the first shot. The second, however, bounced out, and a melee went down for the ball between both teams, ending with McDyess and Lithuanian Ramūnas Šiškauskas on the floor with possession, leading to a jump ball. McDyess was able to win the tip, but the call on the court gave the ball to Lithuania. So with 4.6 seconds remaining, and us up 85–83, it was up to our defense to get us the win. And, thanks to great defense from Kidd and McDyess, Šarūnas Jasikevičius was forced to throw up a running three, which fell short of the hoop. Phew!

That quick, Antonio went from scapegoat to *hero*. If he hadn't gotten that board, it would have been rough for all of us back home. And the coaches deserve a lot of credit for putting him in the game. In the next round, we beat France again for the gold, 85–75. Thank goodness. While it wasn't the most dramatic game of the tournament, the France gold medal game was up there. There was lots of drama in the second half. They played their asses off. They wanted to win it as much as we did. But we prevailed thanks to a bit more talent and a bit more good fortune.

By the final game, you're gassed. You're tired. You're exhausted. But you have to dig for that little bit more. It's just like the later rounds of the playoffs. You don't have anything left, but you have to give it a bit more. I remember we were up just a couple points and France had a chance to go up on a three, but they missed. Then we took the ball down and scored. We'd simultaneously dodged a bullet and took the air out of them. When the buzzer sounded, we'd won.

Let me tell you this: When you win a gold, no one can tell you nothin'. At least, that's how I felt. I was on top of the world. My teammates and I had WON GOLD! In Sydney, Australia! I got gold. We got gold. USA got gold. I was walking around everywhere I could after that with my chest out: *I'm a motherfucking gold medalist. You can't tell me shit! Don't even talk to me at all right now!*

The Olympics made stars of many of our players. In terms of VC, especially, that dunk over Weis was his coming out party on the world stage. After that dunk, KG told VC, "Man I thought I was the best until that shit happened!"

When I got into games, I'd pick up my man full court, fight over screens, make it difficult for him to get his team in rhythm. If I was to play 10–12 minutes, it would be the hardest 10–12 minutes I could. For us, it wasn't about how many points you scored, but about getting the win. However, that can sometimes be lost when you're worried about playing time and paychecks. I only averaged about 5.5 points per game, which was about 20 percent of what I did at my peak in the NBA. But no one was counting stats. There was only one number that mattered: victories. And, thankfully, we achieved gold.

It's rare for teammates like me and Zo to win gold together. Karl Malone and John Stockton did it with the Dream Team. LeBron James and Anthony Davis did it in 2012 and 2024. But it's rare. Zo and I celebrated that fact all summer. It was rewarding to be on a team with such amazing players. Perhaps to the surprise of some, there was no shit talking between us. Me and Allan Houston didn't say a word about the Knicks-Heat rivalry. That was all in the past. For us, it was about Team USA and taking on the world. We'd all been together for several years. Before the 2000 games, we had our work cut out for us, having to play in Puerto Rico just to qualify for 2000.

That summer, we were coached by Larry Brown. He was sitting in for Rudy, who was dealing with some personal issues.

Brown would later lead the 2004 Olympic team, which had its own struggles. Playing under the Team USA microscope, we formed tight bonds. There may have been a little recruiting on the side, too. Some guys were trying to get Vince Carter or Kevin Garnett to switch teams, talking about all the rings that could be won together! Could you imagine VC or KG on the Heat with me and Zo? That would have been unstoppable. It was a pipe dream, of course, but still fun to talk about on the bus or in practice.

When all eyes are on you, a tight-knit feeling is born if you respond to it. Today, Team USA is a brotherhood. That was exemplified again just recently in 2024, when I got together with some of my Olympic teammates at the USA Basketball showcase ahead of the Paris games, and even took a selfie with former President Obama, Gary Payton, Reggie Miller, and others. Being a part of the Olympics creates a brotherhood that lasts a lifetime. In the end, the experience was unforgettable. Everyone knew their roles and everyone succeeded within them. That's what a team is supposed to be about.

* * *

While I was in Sydney, I was also negotiating my next contract with Pat Riley back in the States. For much of my career, I'd either played on contracts that were fair, or I'd taken a discount for the sake of long-term financial security. Now it was time for me to get *paid*, to enjoy some of the rewards of being a five-time All-Star and five-time All-NBA player. I was one of the Heat's all-time leaders in assists and three-point shots, and our team were consistent winners. But what I remember about the negotiations from the other side of the world was that Pat was being a little stingy. I remember our hellacious arguments over the phone. The 12-hour time difference didn't make things any easier.

We'd go back and forth, back and forth about numbers and what I deserved. Since I was away in Australia, we couldn't talk face-to-face, which I would have preferred. I felt the Heat owed me for a long tenure of sterling service. I wanted a two-year deal, but Riley didn't. I said, "Pat, why are you putting me through this?" There was a lot of cussing on the phone, but if we were face-to-face there wouldn't have been. Back and forth, back and forth. I don't remember what he was trying to lowball me with, but I do remember him saying we hadn't won a championship yet—he threw that at me. But I threw back at him that I was the best point guard he'd had since Magic. Back and forth, back and forth. I knew I had value to the team, and I knew that I'd played under that value for several years. When you thought of the Miami Heat, I was one of the first people that came to mind. So it was time to take care of me.

But I also knew that it was the GM and president's job during negotiations to devalue me. Even so, my agent Henry Thomas and I were just not going to accept that. In Sydney, Zo was trying to play the role of mediator. "Hey Bigs," he'd say. "Hey Bigs, why don't you just take this offer?" I was like, "Look, motherfucker, you got YOUR money, how come I can't get mine? They just gave you $120 million, you don't think I'm worth at least $20?" And Zo didn't really have anything to say after that. Pat got him his money and power, how come I couldn't get mine? Still, it was odd negotiating with a guy who was both president and coach.

On the one hand, the coach is supposed to build you up and make you a winner. But the team president was trying to make sure he saved millions off your deal. He makes you second-guess yourself. So I had to stand strong and go in there and make sure Pat at least heard my voice during the entire process. Henry Thomas stuck up for me, but I had to make Pat know there was a human being on the other end of that phone. Only I could say exactly what I wanted. If the other side of the talks doesn't want to hear your voice, then you know they don't respect you. If they want the conversation to be one-sided, then they don't give a damn about you. I had to be heard.

Eventually, we came to a *decent* solution. That summer, I signed a one-year, $12 million deal, which made me the highest paid point guard for the upcoming season. There were bonuses in there for wins and if I kept my weight down and, if I hit all those, I'd get a little more. The deal wasn't long, but it was rich and I was okay with that. I was good with money and knew I wasn't going to blow it on stupid shit. I'd save it, like the NBA told you to do in those rookie seminars where they warned about the perils of being a rich and famous athlete. Predators are everywhere (sometimes even on your own team). Thankfully, I knew what I was doing.

But the strangest part of the Olympics was Zo's crazy traveling schedule and what happened afterward. During the *middle* of the Olympics, his wife gave birth. And, as to be expected, he left the team to fly from Sydney back to the east coast to be there for the birth of his child. Just hours later, he got back on a plane and flew the 10,000 miles back to Sydney to continue playing. He was in the air going up and down for, like, twenty-four hours straight. Later, Zo began to experience some serious, life-threatening health issues. While none of us on Team USA were doctors, we couldn't help but wonder if something happened to him during that extreme schedule. Did he eat something that messed his body up? Did all that flying fuck his up equilibrium? Zo flew for a day straight, and that just can't be good for you. Again, I'm only speculating, but not long after the Olympics he began to feel the effects of very serious kidney issues. I was one of the first people to see Zo in his sick state. After the gold medal game, we were in the locker room and he asked me to look at his lower leg. We pushed the skin in on his leg and instead of it coming right back out, it stayed in and looked like Play-Doh. It didn't come back out right away like it was supposed to. Even the doctor didn't know what was going on or why that was happening. He told Zo to get back to the States for tests.

It wasn't until we got back to America that we were able to figure out what was happening. They ran about a million tests on him, and what came back was kidney failure. Zo thought it might have been all the pain killers he took to stave off injuries, but no one really knew the cause. Maybe it was a combination of several things, from flying to the meds. A chemical imbalance. Either way, it was bad news for him and his family and, to a lesser extent, our team. After the Olympics, Zo consulted with numerous doctors, and the conclusion each came to was that he had to retire immediately.

But that wasn't something he was comfortable with. While he wasn't expected to play moving forward, he ended up coming back for a few games toward the end of the 2000–01 season and was able to play most of the 2001–02 season as well (though had to miss the following year due to his kidney issues). He eventually had to get a kidney transplant from a family member. He met with a team of doctors who worked for years—and continue to today—to keep him healthy. During his career, Zo was one of the league's most physical players. He endured all kinds of injuries and always bounced back. But this? This was something else entirely. He was just thirty years old, and now his life was threatened. It was horrible to watch, and I wouldn't wish it on anybody, let alone my close friend and teammate.

* * *

While it was less important compared to Zo's situation, we still had to figure out our upcoming season. So Pat went to work and, in the offseason, picked up talented shooting guard Eddie Jones and bruising power forward Anthony Mason (another former Knick) from Charlotte, trading away Jamal Mashburn and P. J. Brown. Pat also traded for the young undersized center Brian Grant from Portland and signed his former Showtime power forward, A. C. Green. With those deals, we had almost an entirely new team going into the 2000–01 season. It was crazy, but also something of a fresh start.

With all our losses to New York and now the loss of Zo to this health scare, it was hard not to feel at times like the Miami Heat were snakebitten. It was just one thing after another. But Pat was undeterred. You could just see his mind always turning, the wheels going, and so he remade the roster to improve on our weaknesses and hold our own in the East. We knew he was serious about the season, which set the tone for the rest of the team. Eddie Jones could score. Mason was a beast. And Brian Grant was an up-and-coming star in the league. With our revamped roster, we knew we could win and even contend for a championship.

It would take time to develop chemistry, but that was my department. In training camp, Pat talked us up. He told all of us that we had one goal in mind: to win it all. Now, I don't know if, in his heart of hearts, he believed it—what else was he going to say? That we were going to fail? No. But Pat got the troops hyped—especially the new guys who'd never seen how convincing he could be. Pat instilled confidence like a military man. If you had doubts, he removed them from your mind. That was his job. But no matter what, I knew my job. All I ever tried to do on any given day was win. To take it to the opponents and put a notch in the win column.

One of the new guys who was already familiar with Pat was Mason. He'd played for Riley for years in New York with the Knicks. They'd gone to the NBA Finals together in 1994. Mason, God rest his soul, was a wild man. The stories I'd heard about him in college at Tennessee State and in the pros were outlandish, both on and off the court. He always made sure to intimidate during games, making sure people wouldn't fuck with him or his guys. But in practice, Mason was a great guy. He loved his teammates, was always in shape and ready to play. He just wanted to do it his way. So, sometimes you just had to let him.

Mason couldn't shoot well, but he was a damn good defensive player. He could set picks like a brick wall. He could also handle the ball well for a 6-foot-8 guy weighing 250-plus pounds. But I knew that his shooting would be key for us. So one day early on in practice, I called him over and we got to talking. I got the sense that people didn't really tell Anthony what to do, but I had an idea I wanted to share with him. "Anthony, we're going to shoot today. We're going to take shots from spots around the perimeter and make 50 each. We'll make 50 on the baseline, at the free-throw line, midrange between the free-throw line and the top of the key. Like that."

To his credit, he did it with me. We spent hours on it. I told him, "Mase, I know you can set picks, but if you don't make jump shots, we don't win." I knew we were going to run a ton of pick and rolls together, but if defenses didn't respect his outside game, they'd double-team me and we'd be ineffective. We'd have to make defenses respect his shooting. "You've got to make these jump shots here," I said. "Once you do, we're going to be dangerous." And to Mason's credit, he did just that. We needed him to make those damn jump shots! And you know what he got for it? He made his first and only All-Star team with us that season. Winning is about sacrifice, and Mason worked extra hard that year to help the team.

Eddie Jones was another good player. He'd made three All-Star games by the time he came to Miami, and Pat had wanted to acquire him for a long time. He was a great defender, slasher, and scorer. He made a big difference and gave us a new look that we didn't have before. He was young, too, and helped us replace guys like Voshon Lenard, who we'd traded after the season for Chris Gatling and a pick. We also had Bruce Bowen, another up-and-coming skilled defender. Then, early into the season, Pat picked up the former All-Star Cedric Ceballos to help off the bench.

What hurt us that year, though, was obvious: the absence of Zo. Grant was a great replacement, but at just 6-foot-9, he wasn't as equipped to battle guys like Shaq or Hakeem Olajuwon in the paint. Zo was taller and built more like a center. Brian was closer to a power forward. He still managed 15.2 points and 8.8 rebounds for us that season, but he was never meant to play 30–35 minutes a game in the middle, which is what he had to do with Zo out. If it wasn't for his health issues—which I know is a giant "if"—our rotation would have been perfect. But that's life. More than basketball, we hoped he would get healthy.

Without Mourning, we got off to a slow start. I was healthy and feeling good, but we had a lot of new guys to work into our system. It took time to click. It wasn't so much a talent issue as we hadn't played together as a unit. Though we'd worked together in practice, we still had a lot to learn about one another on the court. We were 6–10 after 16 games, and had already lost our bench spark plug, Ricky Davis, to leg injuries. He would be out for the year, appearing in just seven games for us. But Pat picked up Ceballos from Detroit after a couple weeks, who helped to bring some scoring off the bench. With the help of two five-game winning streaks and learning to play as a unit, we'd recovered and were 30–20 at the All-Star break. In the second half of the season, Zo was trying to make his comeback. Always a Greek God of a guy, Zo refused to believe any diagnosis could keep him from playing. He tried like hell all year to come back.

And by the end of March, with 13 games left in the season, he did. Zo, who made the All-Star game ceremonially that season, came back and even started the last three games of the season, averaging 13.6 points and 7.8 rebounds in those 13 tilts. In his first game when Pat called him to come in off the bench, Zo raced to the scorer's table and ripped off his home white Heat warmups. He went so fast he didn't even know who he was coming in for, and Riley had to tell him again as he was about to check in. Our home crowd went nuts, giving him a standing ovation. Our opponents, the Toronto Raptors, were even happy to see him back.

Zo came in with about 3:37 left in the first quarter and immediately made his presence felt. He forced a turnover down low, and he was so hyped he put his hand up and pointed the other toward our basket like a wide receiver making a first down. *Heat ball!* With him back, though, we were all off our game a bit and ended up losing to Vince Carter and company. But the Raptors were a good team and that didn't matter. We had our big man back. We finished the year 8–5 with Zo, and our record at the end of the season was 50–32, good enough for the third seed. In the first round of the playoffs, who did we match up against? Not the Knicks! Instead, it was the sixth-seeded Charlotte Hornets.

It was Zo's former team and, more importantly, the team we'd traded Jamal Mashburn and P. J. Brown to, and they wanted revenge. In that series, Mash and Brown got the Hornets prepared and they took it to us. They were obviously mad at Pat for dealing them after how hard they'd played for our team. It didn't help that I was injured in the series, too. As soon as we got Zo back, I was sidelined. My left foot was killing me, and I missed the final three games of the year heading into the playoffs. I found out I'd fractured my fifth metatarsal, which I'd been dealing with for a while. The only way to *fix it*, the doctors said, was if it broke. I just had to deal with the pain. We tried different shoe inserts, but nothing was quite right. Eventually, later while I was playing in Denver, it broke.

What sucked was that the injury kept me from being effective or even really playing much in the series against the Hornets. I only played 17 minutes in Game One and we lost by 26 at home, 106–80. Mashburn had 28 in that one and Charlotte's up-and-coming burly point guard Baron Davis scored 23. Game Two was a blowout as well, which we lost by 26, 102–76. I only played 18 minutes, and aside from Eddie Jones we couldn't get anything going. The whole situation was deflating.

By the time the series got back to Charlotte for Game Three, we knew we were cooked. We were down 10 after the first quarter and 27 at the half. Mash and Baron absolutely killed us. Charlotte's record may have been worse than ours, but they were the better team, flat out. We lost the game, 94–79, and were outscored in the three-game series by 68 points. It was a big disappointment, to say the least. My injury wasn't an excuse, but it still sucked and was horrible timing. I had no chance against Baron Davis hobbling like that. He was too good.

It was the most games I'd played in a season in three years, and I'd averaged 14.9 points and 6.3 assists. Even so, I knew it would be my final year in Miami. It was also the last one for a lot of guys on the team. Mason went to Milwaukee, Majerle went back to Phoenix, and Pat traded me to the Dallas Mavericks for a second-round pick. I'd helped take the Heat to six-straight playoffs and was the team's all-time leader in assists. Now it was all over. The deal came down later in the summer on August 22, but I wasn't mad. The NBA is a business, and I liked where I was going. Dallas was coached by my old friend Nellie, and the team boasted skilled guys like Steve Nash and Dirk Nowitzki. Time for a new challenge.

* * *

That summer, a few months before I was dealt to Dallas, our Hardaway family expanded. Yolanda and I were already parents to Nia and Tim Jr., but now we welcomed little Nina Hardaway into the world, on June 2, 2001. We call her our "Sydney Baby" because she was, well, conceived when we were in the Olympics in mid-September. It's funny. A few guys on that team, including

Ray Allen, ended up having kids the following year like me and Yolanda. We got our wives pregnant in those close Olympic quarters! But amid all the turnover in Miami, it felt great to have a growing family at home.

As soon as we got to know little Nina, it felt like she'd been here before, like she'd done all this in another life. She had an old soul and picked up life quickly, having a deep understanding of the world as she grew up. Today, she's often on social media, whereas Nia and Tim Jr. largely grew up without it. Nina knows what she wants and goes out to get it, while her siblings are a bit more considered or reserved. Nina is the aggressive child. Her philosophy is that she'll deal with the repercussions later. She's not like her siblings, who mull things over. But it takes all kinds, and I am just happy we have such a terrific family.

13

OLD FRIENDS, NEW ROLE

WHILE I didn't mind going to Dallas, I didn't totally appreciate how I left Miami. Pat didn't show me a lot of love on the way out. All I've ever wanted in my career was to win, and Pat knew that. But in the summer after our first-round loss to Charlotte, Pat let me know that he thought our backup point guard, Anthony Carter, was better than I was, and he was going to be the team's starting point guard for the upcoming season. Drafted in 1999 out of Hawaii, Carter averaged about six points off the bench in his first two seasons with Miami. But now Pat thought he was the one who should lead the team. Maybe it was my injuries, maybe he didn't want to pay me, I don't know. But the real issue was that Pat didn't tell me he wanted me coming off the bench to help tutor the guy or to give our bench unit more pop or to preserve me or that I could try to win the Sixth Man of the Year Award or that I would have been more effective for the team. He just said Anthony was better, and that was that. "You're going to come off the bench for Carter," Riley told me. And I was like, "Nah, nah, nah." What I wanted to say was, "Pat, you must be out of your fucking mind. Anthony is not better than me on a bad day. Not better than me on three or four bad days! Not better than me on three or four bad months!"

That just wasn't going to work for me. But the thing was, I had an out in my back pocket. Don Nelson, the coach of the Dallas Mavericks, was asking around about me. He liked the idea of me backing up Steve Nash. Thought it would be a good spot for me in my career. He was open and welcoming, while Pat had been harsh and cold. Even at our lowest points, I never told Pat that Phil Jackson or Jeff Van Gundy were *better* than him. That's not how I do things.

A coach needs to know his personnel, and Riley should have known me well enough by then. That's how I took it. I thought he was giving me the wrong message, and hurting all of us in the process. If Pat had done right by me, I would have been like, "Alright, cool, I understand." But to come to me and say Carter was better didn't rub me the right way. Nothing against Anthony. I'm just better than him, that's all. He was a fine player, but over his thirteen-year career, he averaged just 4.8 points per game. He wasn't a five-time All-NBA player. So, I thought, *Cool, I'll go to Dallas and play under Nellie and behind Steve Nash.* And I told Pat, "Trade me."

* * *

From the moment I arrived in Dallas and met with my new team, Nash started picking my brain. The future two-time MVP had been in the league for five years already—two in Phoenix and three in Dallas—and hadn't yet made an All-Star team. But that was all going to change this season. I'd also known Steve from years before, when he was at the University of Santa Clara. He would come to Oakland during the summers and find his way into pickup games with the likes of me, Jason Kidd, and Gary Payton. Steve was a dog, too. He'd come to the gym every day and take all the shit we gave him—and we gave him a lot.

We'd hound him, taking away his shots, not letting him get to his spot. We'd bag him up. At the time, he was too small. Didn't have enough weight on him. But he was there every day asking us questions, talking to us, watching us throughout the summer during those pickup and summer league games. I gained a lot of respect for the guy during those hot summer months. To be clear, we weren't abusing Steve, but giving him all he could handle. He absorbed it all and learned to use it to his advantage. And when I got to Dallas, he'd evolved into a damn near complete player.

There was still a lot to talk about, though. We'd exchange notes on what we saw coming off pick and rolls, what we saw in certain defenders in various games. Normal stuff that point guards always chat about. I hadn't worked with Nellie for six or seven years by then, so Steve would bring me in on what coach wanted and I'd tell him stories of the old Run-TMC days. In Miami, for example, we never switched on defense. It was all about going under the screen, going over it, getting around it however you could. But in Dallas, we switched everything and that was hard for me to grasp at first. Thankfully, Steve helped me through it.

It just goes to show you: what goes around comes around. You never know which skinny kid in a hot Oakland gym might become an eight-time All-Star and your future teammate. Dirk Nowitzki was also on the team, the big German seven-foot shooter. It was fun to get to know him a little bit. Dirk is a great guy. He was always working on his game. Maybe more than anyone else, Dirk paid attention to details. Being around him, Nash and scoring forward Michael Finley reminded me of the old days with me, Mitch, and Mully. These incredible trios who just talked and talked in order to get on the same page with each other.

When you looked into their eyes, you knew they wanted to win. That they would do anything for a victory. You saw determination. We'd trade stories about growing up, talking hoops from Chicago to California to Germany. I met Dirk's famous personal coach, Holger Geschwindner, who was a great guy, too. Dirk always knew what he had to do to get better. He didn't try to be anyone he wasn't. His secret? Balance. He focused more on footwork than almost anyone I've ever seen. Spinning, his famous one-legged fadeaway jump shot. A lot of people don't know, but the key isn't the fadeaway. It's the balance he has on that leg. Dirk wasn't really falling back—he was often going straight up with his other knee out to create space. But he had to learn to be able to do it all with just one leg and foot on the ground. That took hours and hours of concentration. Just as Run-TMC used to talk about it, we all got together to dig into where everyone liked the ball. How to pass it to Finley or Dirk coming off a pick on the right side or left side. Finley used to tell me that if a guy was guarding him with a three-quarter stance, he'd spin and I could just lob it up to him and he'd get it. He'd just give a quick flicker of his eyes or eyebrows upward, and that would be the sign.

Those are the conversations you have to get better as a team. You have to talk and talk and talk and talk. There's no other way. And while I didn't spend a ton of time hanging out with those guys off the court, I loved them nonetheless. A lot of the time they'd be sitting in the back of the plane, and I'd be up front trying to be the veteran setting a good example, which was my job. When you get to the end of your career, a veteran is supposed to show the future stars how to be in it for the long haul and be professional. But I tell you this: Dallas had one of the nicest planes in the entire NBA! Dallas and Portland were leading the pack there. It makes sense, too. Both those teams had young, rich owners. And they took care of their players. Both teams had 747s and both had satellites. That was a luxury, man. I believe they have the same planes today, with all the amenities. I could have stayed in Dallas playing with Steve and Dirk under Nellie for a few more years, but my time was cut short there on February 21, 2002, when I was traded midseason to Denver after playing in only 54 games. I'd averaged just under 10 points and just over four assists in my time coming off the bench for the Mavs, which I thought was solid.

But Dallas wanted to go in another direction, and Denver had a few players they coveted. I was collateral damage, with my $3.3 million contract needed in order to make the salaries work in the deal. The Mavericks were 37–17 when I was traded and on their way to making a pretty deep playoff run. Denver, on the other hand, was 16–35. The full deal included me, Juwan Howard, and a first-round pick to Denver for Avery Johnson, Raef LaFrentz, and Nick Van Exel, who was a former All-Star and wanted out of Denver to get to a contender. Dallas, which also liked the idea of getting the shooting big man LaFrentz in the deal, pulled the trigger. The trade out of Dallas bothered me at first. I know it was a good move for the Mavericks, but I wanted to stay there.

I was at home when I found out about the deal. I was getting ready to go to practice when Nellie called. He said, "Hey man, I just want to call you and say we made a trade." He told me the details of the deal, and I said, "Nellie, I appreciate you calling me. We've always been cool and respectful to each other, and I appreciate that. Thank you and good luck on the season." And that was that. As I've said before, this is a business, and the longer you're in the league the more you understand that and stop taking things personally.

In Denver, I was reunited with my former Heat teammate, Voshon Lenard. While I was glad to see him, the experience was very difficult. I'd gone from a team that was 20 games over .500 to one that was 19 games *under* .500. It was, by far, the worst team I'd been on in my career. I was used to winning, and Denver was in no position to do that. The squad's best player was my former Team USA buddy Antonio McDyess. An All-Star the year prior, he was injured now and out for the year (he'd also miss the following season). The only good thing was that I started in all 14 games I played for the Nuggets.

But I wasn't able to start in every game that season due to a silly suspension. Near the end of the year, I got booted for two games after I, *ahem*, tossed a TV monitor onto the court during a game in Orlando. One of the officials in that game was Marc Davis, the shaved-head overly buff guy who has a tendency to insert himself too much into a game. That was the case in this one, too, on March 15, 2002. I'd already tallied six assists in just 17 minutes when Marc blew his whistle. T-Mac had scored a basket when the Magic's Monty Williams started jawing at me. But I didn't want anything to do with that. I was a veteran and knew to stay out of any altercation.

You're not supposed to get a technical foul called on you when you stay out of it. But Marc, who is also from Chicago, thought I'd stuck my nose into something that I shouldn't have. He said I was instigating. So, he called a tech. I shouted, "Why'd you call a tech on me, Marc?" He said, "You initiated it!" But I told him I'd done no such thing. Marc said, "Yes, you did." Now I was getting angry because Marc was calling me a liar. All I'd done was try to stay out of the issue and not make it anything big after Monty started yapping. Even though I wasn't happy in Denver, I was still just trying to be a good vet and bring some wisdom and professionalism. But now I was heated.

When you're calling me a liar, that makes me want to raise my hands on you. But since that is (obviously) a huge no-no in the NBA, I couldn't do anything. Marc gave me another tech for trying to get at him (some of my teammates held me back). He kicked me out of the game and with that I was just done. As I was walking out, I saw a small boxy TV monitor on the scorer's table, and I picked it up and threw it out onto the court. The Magic's Darrell Armstrong later picked it up, brought it back to the table, and plugged it back in. That was funny. After the game, which we lost, 124–102, Darrell and I actually signed the broken thing to auction it for charity. Then I got fined $10,000.

Occasionally in the summers, I'd see Marc at various events in Chicago. He knew he was wrong for what he'd done but never said sorry like a good referee is supposed to. But I could just tell in his demeanor that he knew he was wrong for tossing me out of the game. To this day, Marc and I don't talk at all. After that incident there's no sense in trying to talk to him if he won't apologize. In the end, I regret throwing the monitor because I shouldn't have let my emotions get the best of me, but when you call me a liar and I can't call you one back, that's frustrating—especially when you kick me out of the game for it.

After my suspension, I came back to play a few more games for Denver, but then broke the fifth metatarsal bone in my left foot and was done for the season. (Strangely, my son later had the same injury when he was in the NBA.) We had about three weeks left in the season, but that was it for me. It was a bad way to end a difficult year. It was actually the first time I was feeling old as an NBA player. Like my body wasn't responding as it should. To heal, I flew to Miami two days after the break and got surgery from a doctor I trusted in the area who I was comfortable with. I wasn't sure if this was going to be the end of my career, but I hoped it wasn't. I didn't exactly want to go out like that in Denver.

I averaged 9.6 points and 5.5 assists in Denver but, after the season, my time was up in the mile high city. Over the following summer and into the next year, I healed and bided my time. I was in no rush to get back to the NBA. I'd done a lot, and enjoyed spending time with my family, including baby Nina. Tim Jr. was coming into his own as a young basketball player and Nia was growing into a terrific and talented young woman. To keep busy, I worked as an analyst for ESPN, doing post-game broadcasts. Even so, I continued to work out and hoop. In March, though, my former idol Isiah Thomas called to see if I wanted to join the Indiana Pacers, where he coached.

Isiah wanted to bring me in to tutor his team's young point guard, Jamaal Tinsley, and I said yes to the idea. A second-year player out of Iowa State, the New York City–born Tinsley was very talented. As a rookie, he scored nearly 10 points per game along with dishing over eight assists. Isiah thought he could benefit from a veteran point guard on the roster to show him the ropes. To this day, a lot of people don't remember how good Jamaal was, what he could do with the basketball, and I was happy to help him grow. So on March 27, 2003, I signed with Indiana to play out the rest of the regular season. In my first game, showing no signs of wear, I dropped 14 points and seven assists against Chicago.

Indiana was solid that year and finished 48–34. The team had a lot of good players and were just beginning to gel—vets like Reggie Miller, Brad Miller, Ron Mercer, Jeff Foster, and Austin Croshere mixed with rising stars like Jermaine O'Neal, Al Harrington, and Ron Artest. What I didn't know was just how good Artest was. He had a great basketball IQ. That guy understood the game and could take one over with his defense. We had a solid team, but just couldn't quite get over the mountain top, losing to Boston in the first round. Though it was a short run, it was great to reunite with Isiah.

By the time all was said and done, I played in 10 games for the Pacers, scoring 4.9 points and dishing 2.4 assists per. It was a fine farewell for me, and with that I was ready to call it a career.

The following season, though, I *almost* came back for one more taste of NBA life. It was a few weeks before the 2003–04 season when the Clippers called me up. One of their rising stars, Duke University product Corey Maggette, said the Clips needed a point guard. "Come help us out, Tim," he said. So I agreed to give it a shot. Me and the Clips were getting a deal together when I got into a car and headed for the airport to fly to LA.

We were halfway there when I tapped the driver on the shoulder and said, "You know what, man? Turn around." He balked and said, "Huh?" I repeated, "Turn us around." I got on my cell phone then and called my agent Henry Thomas. "Hank," I said, "tell them thank you, that I appreciate the offer. But you know what? It's time for me to retire and be around my kids." I was finally ready to be a full-time dad and husband. The decision came to me right then and there in that car. It was what my heart told me. I needed to be with my family. I was done with the NBA, and it was at that moment I officially called it quits. My career was complete.

Memory Lane: Scott Williams

I didn't play with Timmy long—we only overlapped on the Nuggets for about half the season. We were on a really bad Denver squad in 2001–02. Dan Issel was the head coach to start the year, but he was let go after some controversial statements he made to a fan. Mike Evans, who was on staff, took over. We started struggling and Denver started to trade away pieces. They shipped guys like Raef LaFrentz to Dallas, and we got back Hardaway and his "UTEP Two-Step."

My memories of Tim are of a guy who had a fiery personality and wanted to win. He loved to compete, and I thought that type of energy was right up my alley because that was how I played, too. I wasn't a star on any team I played for, except maybe in high school! But Timmy's and my personality were the same from that competitive standpoint. We really meshed well.

The story that I remember—we were in a heated game, and it was close down the stretch, and Timmy got so upset that he took one of those old school TV monitors and smashed it on the court. That was one of those moments from a sports perspective that you always take away because it was something unusual. It was both serious and funny at the same time. I don't remember the aftermath of exactly what happened, but I'm sure the league issued a fine.

But that was Timmy. That was his fiery personality. He could get explosive with his emotions, go from zero-to-sixty. I don't think there was anybody quicker. But he was a great teammate and a good dude to be around. At that time in my career, I was just trying to enjoy what I thought might be my last year in the league. I knew we wouldn't make the playoffs, but I enjoyed my teammates as an extension of my family. That was my philosophy.

And he was one of those guys. We would get on a plane or a bus and have conversations after the game. I always loved to talk basketball, but I also enjoyed getting to know guys outside of what we did between the lines—their personalities, behaviors, and mannerisms. Timmy and I were only in Denver a short period of time together, but we made a friendship that has lasted to this day. Now, his boy is playing in the league and that's just great.

14

MY BOY'S A BALLER

DURING my playing days, it was fun to have Tim Jr. around. When I was with Miami, the team's assistant coach Stan Van Gundy used to allow him to hang out under the basket while we shot before games. Tim could rebound and pass the balls back out to the coaches, but wasn't allowed to shoot himself. That was the rule. Stan was strict about that. So, one day Tim came to me to complain about it. "He doesn't let me shoot, Dad!" Tim was mad about it. Mind you, he was maybe seven years old at the time, so I had to set him straight. "Coach Stan is right. This is the team's time to shoot, and he's letting you be a part of it. But it's not your time, Tim." I explained that Coach Van Gundy could've not let him participate at all, but instead was being nice. If Tim didn't like the arrangement or didn't want to abide by the rules, he could go in the back and play with the other kids. "So what do you want to do?" I asked. Tim paused, "Okay, I'll do what he asks me to do." I said, "Well, that's a good answer!" So, he kept rebounding and bounce-passing the ball out to the coaches, who then passed to the players to shoot.

The deal was that if no one on our team was out there, he could shoot a little, but never if a player was getting his shots up. "Do you understand? I asked. "Yes," he said.

That, in a nutshell, is parenting. Kids want to do what they want to do, but it takes boundaries and relatively strict rules to help them understand the world doesn't revolve around them. I was glad for Stan's direction and help, and that he wasn't giving my son special treatment other than letting him be out there in the first place. Tim wasn't on the team, and it wasn't time for him to play. But Coach still let him be around the guys and soak up what it meant to be in proximity to NBA players. That was more than other children in his position had, and that either needed to be good enough for him or he could leave the gym.

At some point in shootaround, someone saw Tim had a ball and said, "Take a shot, Tim!" But my son responded, "No, my dad told me not to." I was so proud! He understood and kept with the right approach. And we never had a problem with him at practice again. Of course, being a parent is tough. In a way, all you ever want is to give your kids what they want. But you also know life is a long game and it's not about instant gratification. I learned that every day when I was growing up. I heard the word *no* more often than I could count. There has to be rules. But Tim got to be around basketball ever since he was six months old when I was in Golden State.

He loved the game, and I was glad I could give him that. When he started playing as he got older, it was only natural. As a teenager, he played AAU on a team in Miami. He would travel around the city on the squad and then later around cities in Florida (like Orlando), then outside the state to cities like Memphis. I was excited for him and wanted the best for him and his game, so I started to teach him how I learned it. But I came on too strong. I acted like a drill sergeant—so much so that one time he looked like he wanted to clock me. As a kid, I put so much pressure on myself to get better, but I had to realize that my son and I are different people.

I watched him, but it was as if my eyes were closed to *his* game. Sometimes I would say, "If you're not going to play the right way, we're not going to come back to these tournaments. I'm not going to spend my money on them anymore." Now I just shake my head, knowing that was the wrong thing to say. I was frustrated, but for all the wrong reasons. When I hear parents say those things now, I want to tell them how I used to be like that. It took me a while to realize that I'd never really praised my son. I'd never told him, "Good game." It wasn't as if I got that from my dad, really. He was rough, but he was always encouraging about my game.

It took me a long time to realize Tim and I are different people. He and I grew up different—he had more than I did as a kid. Of course we would have different mentalities! I realized my error when, as a sophomore in high school, I asked him if he wanted to watch a playoff game on TV, and he said no. He wanted to watch it over at his friend's house, and kind of just ignored me. I knew something was wrong. First it was Tim's high school Athletic Director who told me I was messing up. Then my wife Yolanda had to set me straight. "You're tearing this house up," she said. "He's getting tired of all your *shit*." I said, "I just want him to learn!" But she said, "He *is* learning!" So I decided to back off. I decided I would go up to the bleachers and watch him play and not say a word. I told myself, *You better check yourself. That kid out there is playing ball, and you have to be quiet.* I was making him hate the game. *Even if he doesn't play his best, you be positive.* Afterward in the car, I gave him the praise he deserved. "You played a really good game," I said. "Man, you was hoopin'!" He thanked me and I apologized. "I'm sorry that I've been on you and been hard with you about this game. And you're doing the right things out there. Helping your teammates, getting to the right spots."

Right then and there, everything changed between us. I'd been tearing him down, taking his joy and, in a way, causing a big rift in our family. I had to learn to be better. He had almost quit playing because of me. I'm so glad I stopped trying to be his coach and decided to be his father. It was a big change for me and, looking back, one that took longer than I would have liked. But I'm grateful that I was able to make it. Able to grow. Able to adapt. Basketball is about adapting to what the game needs—so is being a parent. You have to set general rules, but enforcing them requires a little ad-libbing. Life is too short to be so rigid that you hurt people.

Tim started enjoying the game again. He looked forward to basketball. It was no longer a burden on him. He was no longer trying to satisfy me. Instead, he was working to satisfy himself. That was great to see. Only if he asked would I offer advice. Growing up, he'd always been in the gym, but I almost took that from him by how I was acting.

Though his name is Tim Hardaway Jr., he was never going to be Tim Hardaway 2.0. We are different and have different skill sets. Besides, he's a whole six inches taller than me! A fact he would not let me forget as it was unfolding. As Tim began to shoot up and eventually got taller than me, he'd start calling me "Shorty." He'd do that thing where you stand close to someone and look over the top of their head, as if pretending he couldn't see me. "Where'd you go, dad?" He'd laugh his butt off at that one. "I don't see you!" What really got under my skin was when he just started leaning on me like I was some kind of fence post. "Yeah, Shorty," he'd say, "let me lean on you." I just told him, "Okay, okay, I see what you're doing." It's a rite of passage, in a way, for a son to do that to his old man, and Tim soon got to be significantly taller than I ever was. He shot up to about 6-foot-5. When that happened, I knew he had a real chance for the next level.

As he grew, so did our relationship. And his game. When he saw I was serious about supporting him, things changed.

My advice to all parents, as a result, is keep your mouth closed—just be cool! Let your child figure themselves out. If you stay on them, there is a good chance they're only going to resent you and the thing you keep pushing them toward. If you're criticizing your child, it means you want it more than they do, and then what are you *really* doing? They have to want it more than you. And if it takes them a little longer to get there, just enjoy the ride. Let them grow at their pace. Besides, they already have a coach and teammates to listen to!

* * *

It was about six years after I retired from the NBA when the Miami Heat decided to retire my jersey. That was a fantastic ceremony where my family, my agent, and many of my teammates and Heat friends came to celebrate my career. The team played a special video for me, complete with announcers calling some of my famous buzzer-beaters. In the video, Riley called me one of the most "courageous" players he's ever coached, and Zo reminded fans that I helped build the championship foundation for the franchise. I may not have won a ring, but others might not have won theirs had I not done what I'd done.

The event took place on Wednesday, October 28, 2009, and it was overwhelming. To see the highlight clips, to walk down memory lane. Pat Riley talked often about the honor I brought to the team. To be surrounded by the people you love and mean the most to you—it's an experience I wish every player and every person could feel at least once in their lives. And in my life, I've been lucky enough to experience it three times. Once in Miami, once at UTEP, and once at Carver High School. I've been fortunate to have a trio of places hang my No. 10 jersey from the rafters. Now I'm just waiting for Golden State to call me up!

* * *

The end of the 2000s and heading into the 2010s was a great time for me and my family. In 2009, I played for the NBA Generations team in the 2009 NBA Asia Challenge, which was a string of exhibition games against the Korean Basketball League and the Philippine Basketball Association. The NBA has always been great about growing the game overseas, and I was happy to be a part of that, to give back to the league and to show off my killer crossover in a few new countries. And just a few months after that, my son was making some travel plans for himself. But just where he would go was still up in the air. It was college recruitment time.

Tim and I worked out together in the summers. I found a gym and got players to help him work on his game. He played on my team and I'd get him open, directing him to come off screens, get to his spots. I put him through an NBA regimen, knowing he had to be ready. John Beilein at the University of Michigan was one of the first people to come down and watch him work out. "How does it feel to have a dad just throw you the ball all the time?" he'd ask Tim. "You're the focal point." John said he'd never seen a dad work so hard for his kid before. Tim knew I was doing everything I could to prepare him, and he took to it like a duck in water.

Those were some of the best times we had together. Making the NBA is near impossible. Fewer than five thousand people in the history of the sport have ever done so. And to have two people from the same family is like seeing lightning strike the same spot twice. A lot has to go right, and making the correct choice for college is at the top of the list. My son made a name for himself at Miami Palmetto High School. Like me, he enjoyed playing multiple sports. He thought about playing football before he focused on basketball exclusively. And it was the University of Michigan that continued to show interest in him as his high school career unfolded.

But they weren't the only one. Along with Beilein at Michigan, Frank Martin, the often red-faced coach at Kansas State, also reached out. But I talked with Frank, letting him know that Tim wouldn't be an especially great candidate for his program. Not because Tim wasn't great or that Frank was a bad coach, but I knew Tim wouldn't respond to his in-your-face style. Tim never liked when my wife or I yelled at him, so I knew he wasn't going to take to Frank's mode. Frank said he appreciated my candid talk and, as time passed, it seemed more and more like Michigan was the spot. Tim visited the school as a junior and saw Michigan beat Duke in a big upset on campus.

But despite Michigan's interest, he thought about other schools closer to home. I liked coach Beilein because he gets the most out of his team, and in a reasonable and respectful manner. He likes guys who can play multiple positions and who can switch on defense. You have to know how to fit in. I encouraged Tim to go there, but he also held out hope for the University of Miami, Florida, or Florida State. Miami, though, was recruiting guard Brandon Knight hard and passed over my son (Knight later went to Kentucky). Their coach, Frank Haith, said Tim couldn't hang in the ACC (that made us stop attending their games). At the eleventh hour, Billy Donovan at Florida called. But at that point it was too late.

* * *

Tim had made his decision. He was first-team All-City in 2009 and 2010, and for his senior year averaged 31.7 points per game. In the state championship, he scored 42 points against Brandon Knight. With that performance, ESPN ranked him the 93rd overall prospect. And he picked Michigan. As a freshman, Tim had an up and down season, but that was to be expected. But toward the end of the year, he picked it up, winning several Freshman of the Week awards and averaging 20-plus points in his final seven games. That allowed him to earn honorable mention All-Big Ten that season. And in the NCAA Tournament, Michigan beat Tennessee before losing to Duke.

As a sophomore, Tim was named to the preseason to the watchlist for Player of the Year, and during the season his scoring increased from 13.9 points per game to 14.6. But his Wolverines team wasn't quite as strong. They made the NCAA Tournament, but lost to Ohio in the first round. After the year, he told me he wanted to declare for the NBA Draft, but I knew it wasn't the right time. It pained me to have to tell him that. No parent wants to defer their kids' dreams. But I had to tell him that he wasn't ready to come out. "Look, son," I said, "I know the NBA like I know you. If you come out, you won't make the NBA like you want to." I knew he needed to work on his ball-handling and defense. His shot, while solid, needed to get better, too. "I'd be doing you a disservice if I didn't tell you that." Like I said, it's important to encourage your kids, but if they ask you your opinion, you have to be honest with them. "No matter how bad it hurts me to see you disappointed now, I know this will help you in the long run." Oh boy, was he mad at me after that! He cried. That's how bad he wanted it. He called me every name in the book. But I said, "Son, if I let you go to the NBA, it won't be what you want. And you don't want to go to the G-League and play yourself out."

He needed another year, I was sure about that. I didn't know why he was so eager to leave. It wasn't like we needed the money. He had everything he needed at school. But I also know that young people always want to get their life started. I wasn't *hating* on him. I was just trying to be honest, given what I knew. So I told him we should compromise. "Go to sleep tonight," I said, "and just think about it. Think about what I'm saying to you. And you know what? The next day he said, "I understand." He agreed to stay one more year. The following season, he had a great year and so did his team. His rebounds and assists went up. So did his three-point percentage. Plus Michigan made the NCAA Finals, putting him on the big stage. He and his teammate Trey Burke were called the best backcourt in college. Michigan won five straight NCAA Tournament games, beating bluebloods like Kansas, Florida, and Syracuse. But in the Finals, I believe, they got robbed, losing 82–76. I believe the refs cheated them out of the game, calling early fouls on Burke, including a questionable call on a blocked shot. Playing against Louisville and coach Rick Pitino, I thought the officials were biased. Pitino had them in his pocket! Maybe it evens out because Michigan beat Kansas in a two-point game that could have gone either way.

In the end, what matters is Tim did everything he needed to get the attention of NBA scouts. I was so proud. What was incredible—and you couldn't script this—was that he was selected 24th in 2013 by . . . the New York Knicks! The team that I'd battled against in four straight playoffs. The team that caused me more nightmares than Freddy Krueger was my son's new home! Wow. As a rookie in the Big Apple, Tim stood out. He made the All-Rookie team and finished fifth in Rookie of the Year voting, averaging double-digit points for a solid Knicks squad. My son was in the NBA and beginning to flourish! Now it was my turn to make it back to the league.

* * *

As a point guard, I was an extension of the coach on the floor. When I got a chance to prove that fact in the NBA as an assistant after I'd retired, I jumped at the chance. I'd heard that my former coach, Stan Van Gundy, had been recently hired by the Detroit Pistons. So I called Stan up and asked him if his coaching staff had been completed. He said it hadn't, so I pitched myself to be one of his assistants. Stan flew down to Miami to talk with Pat Riley about it. At the time, I was working as a scout for the Heat, so if Stan was going to take me on, he'd have to ask them for permission to interview me.

Pat granted him permission, and Stan and I talked about what my responsibilities would be. He offered me a series of tests, if you will, like putting together a scouting report and a practice plan. To draw plays up and explain how other teams ran theirs. In the end, I passed the tests and he hired me on August 7, 2014. It was actually my second coaching gig after I'd hung up my sneakers. In 2006, I took a brief job with the now-defunct ABA. Back then, investors were trying to revive the brand that had meant high-flying dunks and red, white, and blue basketballs in the 1970s, and hired me on for the new iteration.

I was the short-lived head coach for the Florida Pit Bulls, playing our games at BankAtlantic Center in Sunrise, Florida. I even played in them a little like a player-coach. Sometimes I'd start, sometimes I'd come off the bench (but I never played in back-to-backs). Our players were from the Fort Lauderdale and Miami areas. It was good experience for them to be in a professional environment, and it was fun for me to get back on the court and get some run in. I'd done a little volunteer coaching with my son's high school squad, but now I was getting paid for the responsibility. With the Pit Bulls, we had a good record, finishing 19–8 and first in our division.

We had to fight Florida hurricanes, too, which forced us to cancel a number of games. But the league folded, and we didn't even play in the playoffs. With that minor league stint over, I was glad to be back in the NBA to share my knowledge with a new generation, just like guys had done for me when I was coming up. Coaching the guys was a lot like coaching my son—shoot, they were the same age as him! Part of me had hoped I'd be coaching at home in Miami, though. I'd worked for the Heat as a team ambassador and scout after I retired, but the Heat never extended a formal offer. I'd hoped I might join Erik Spoelstra's staff like several other of Riley's players had, but it never materialized. (I love Spo, he's an educator and a very personable guy.)

Riley told the newspapers after I went over to Detroit, "We were coming very close to making a decision with Tim to have him work with our point guards. Look, he's one of the greatest players that I ever coached, one of the greatest point guards that I ever coached. He's a great competitor. He knows the position. He's very smart. But we always had a plethora of coaches, a lot of 'em. He did a great job for the organization in being an ambassador with Zo, and then he went out and scouted. I think he learned a lot when he went to summer leagues and stuff with our guys. But it just wasn't happening right now." Alright, so be it!

It was okay. I didn't really mind. Even though I'd been inducted into the Florida Sports Hall of Fame just prior to getting the gig in Detroit, it turned out that moving my family up from Miami to Michigan was a great decision for us all. We still live in the area today, and we love it. I'm a hoops junkie and was grateful to get back in the game. I'd have worked wherever would have me. But to be with my former coach in SVG was terrific. I loved picking the brains of the other assistant coaches, too, including Bob Beyer. A longtime NBA assistant, Beyer knew how to connect with players and coaches. He's with the Lakers now, but he even worked under Bob Knight at Texas Tech. I learned a lot from him in Detroit. Beyer reminded me of a young Stan Van Gundy—always prepared and always pushing to get better.

But part of me struggled working with the twenty-somethings on the roster. At times, though I was a five-time All-Star, I felt a bit like a dinosaur.

When I was in Detroit, we were a young team. Stan, who had success as an assistant and head coach in Miami and then as the head man in Orlando, was hired to turn the team around. Detroit had won an NBA title a decade prior, but the franchise was in one of its lower states in a while. We had fresh faces to go along with vets—that's the kind of balance you want when rebuilding a team. Promise, potential, and experience. My job role included coaching in practices, as well as conducting a lot of scouting from film, writing reports on teams we'd be playing in the coming days.

For example, if we were about to play the Lakers, I'd write about what I thought their strengths and weaknesses were, what plays they ran, how they trigger their offense, how we should run plays against them, what our practice plan should be in shootaround before the game, etc. I learned quickly what the team needed from me. But what Stan—who was both head coach and head exec in Detroit—taught me most was how to understand personalities on a team. Putting together a roster is as much about meshing personalities as it is meshing talent. That's something I'd made a priority on when playing, but this was the big-picture vision before players even got onto the court. One guy I kept trying to pump up was our big center. He was a lively player who was solid down low. I knew that, if he'd have set his mind to it, he could've been a regular 20/20 guy. Shoot, he was *already* a double-double guy. He was a Moses Malone–like player. Maybe he didn't have Malone's overall skillset, but he could get to the ball quicker than anybody. He moved his feet, he was agile. He could jump three times before you got off the floor. Another guy I tried to inspire was our point guard. He was a dynamic guy who I thought could have been unstoppable if he put his mind to it. I don't know what he was worried about or where his mind was at the time, but I felt that, if he concentrated, he could have been an All-Star instead of just a starter.

The roster just wasn't clicking. If you want to have a good team, you can't have players with individual agendas. But when you have guys worried about what other people think, worried about social media and what people are saying about them, you get into trouble. Players need to worry about what's happening on the court and let the rest take care of itself. You have to pay attention to detail—that's the top priority. It's hard work to win. Everyone thinks they're *almost* there, but when you see a winning franchise then you really know how much further most other teams are. Everyone has to be pulling in the same direction.

It's a different thing to be a coach who's a former player. I played the game at a high level and loved every minute of it. But when you see someone just going through the motions on the court, just waiting to get their next check, it's frustrating. I couldn't say much at the time, since I was only an assistant (and a young one at that). But I *wanted* to say something, to address the young guys who were slacking. You want your players to play like you did and you can't understand it when they don't make the same effort. You also have to realize you grew up differently than they did.

You might even talk to someone on the team and he'll nod his head, "Yeah, yeah, Coach, I got you." But then he'll do the same damn stupid thing on the court. The same stuff you went over in film and showed him *directly* was hurting the team. That's the difficult part of the job. The wisdom going in one ear and out the other. That was never me. Even as a young player all I wanted to do was learn more and get better.

Being the head coach, you have to lay down the law. You have to make sure everybody knows how we are going to run things, how we are going to approach winning, and what they need to accept to get playing time. We're playing a game, but it's also all business. The year before we arrived, Detroit was 29–53. In our first year in 2014–15, we were 32–50. In our second, after adding Tobias Harris, we jumped up to 44–38 and made the playoffs (losing in a competitive sweep to LeBron James and the Cleveland Cavaliers). We went 37–46 in our third year, and were 39–43 in our last season in 2017–18. Then Detroit's ownership fired the entire staff.

I don't think Stan got enough time to turn the team around. But I also know that he may have been more of an old school coach than the new era could handle. Sometimes I think the new generation of players—especially those who are young and aren't as hungry to win—need more of a babysitter than they do a signal caller. We had a chance to do something in Detroit, but there wasn't always the attention to detail that the team required of its players. It wasn't there for 48 minutes. Stan is a superb coach and had won wherever he was prior to Detroit. But even though we didn't get the results we set out for, I learned a lot on the job.

With my time in Detroit over, the family and I were in no rush to head back to Miami. Nina still had two years of high school left and we didn't want to uproot her, so we stayed in the Detroit area (where we've been ever since). My wife and I love the area, and Detroit has an incredible basketball tradition, from Isiah Thomas to George Gervin to Spencer Haywood. I even went to India in the summer of 2018 to hold camps and teach kids the game. These days, other than camps like that, I have no desire to get back to coaching. Shoot, I'm almost sixty! I don't want to say the new players are knuckleheads, but they don't seem as hungry as the guys from my era. It's okay—I'll just hang out with the other stegosauruses!

* * *

The blessing of not coaching anymore was that I could watch my son with a father's eye and not have to scout or root against him when we played his Knicks team or the new squad he'd been traded to after his second season, the Atlanta Hawks. It's very weird scouting, rooting, and coaching against your own son. I couldn't even call him my son in the coach's rooms, I just called him, "Tim Jr." But I had to do my job and so I said things to our guys about running him off the three-point line to get him out of his shooting rhythm. I had to devise defenses against him despite watching him play my whole life!

After my coaching stint was over in Detroit, Tim was back with the Knicks and then traded again to Dallas in a deal that also sent the big Latvian center Kristaps Porziņģis to the Mavericks to pair with the up-and-coming All-Star Slovenian point guard Luka Dončić. In his fifth season now, Tim was really coming into his own as an impact player. In 2017–18, he averaged 17.5 points, 3.9 rebounds, and 2.7 assists. He'd also signed a massive four-year, $71 million contract in 2017. I was very proud of him. Proud of the man he'd become. And I was equally glad I didn't have work to hamper his game when he played the Pistons.

Because of that, I made sure to discuss money with him. Growing up, I talked to all three of my children about the subject. My parents had told me no so many times and I'd learned the benefit of patience and being frugal that I knew I had to instill that in them, too. They learned to work for what they got, how to rely on themselves when they were old enough. These days, I've seen how Tim handles his money, and I think he's done a hell of a job. It can be a lot of pressure to make that much money (he's since signed *another* four-year, $75 million contract in 2021). People want handouts, or you think you have cash burning a hole in your pocket.

He's smart with it, though. He invests and saves what he needs to save. His money is growing, and that's all you can hope for. He and his agent have been smart. Sometimes people ask me if I'm upset at the bloated contracts young players get these days. I say, "Why be upset?" It is what it is. When I was in the league, we got paid well. Now that's just grown for the new generation. I just hope they know that their success came on our backs and that they should be respectful about that fact. Many are. But don't get me wrong, just because their bank accounts are bigger doesn't mean I wouldn't whoop their ass on the court. That's for sure!

Kidding aside, I'm so happy for Tim. And so is his mother. In his five seasons in Dallas, he's averaged 15.1 points, 3.4 rebounds, and 1.9 assists. He's a scorer, a slasher. He's started and he's come off the bench. He's done whatever the team has asked him. He's even shot 37.5 percent from three-point range, which is crucial in today's game. To me, he reminds me of another former Maverick, Michael Finley. "Fin Dog" may have scored a bit more than Tim, but they have the same body type and move the same way on the court. They're similar one- or two-dribble guys who can shoot, get to the rim, make good plays, and play strong defense.

But don't try to watch one of Tim's games with his mom. Oh boy! She'll talk your ear off. Like any mother, she wants him to succeed. She feels his pain when he's struggling and is over the moon when he's on top of the world. But sit next to her on the couch during one of her games and she'll ask you question after question. She talks up a storm! It's very loving—she'll wonder why a certain thing happened, what's wrong with this player, why did that player do that, what is the coach thinking here. But sometimes I can't take it. That's why she's upstairs and I'm downstairs when one of Tim's games is on TV.

I like to watch Tim, too, of course. I'm glued to the screen. I want to see how he's doing and be able to offer critiques (if I'm asked). But I like to do it in silence. That's just me. I went so far in 2024 during the NBA Finals as to go watch him play. His Dallas Mavericks squad was in the Finals against the Boston Celtics, and while Boston was favored, it began as anybody's series. The difficult part for me, though, was that Tim wasn't getting as many minutes as I thought he should. And when he did, his team didn't work to get him the ball. He's always been a scorer, whether starting or coming off the bench. But in the Finals, it was all about Luka.

During the summer of 2024, I was covering the playoffs for FOX Sports, but would fly to games to watch my son and do my broadcasts via Zoom for the radio. I'd be going all over the country, but the best part about it was that I could see Tim during one of the most pressure-packed times of his career. I played in college, but never made the NCAA Finals. I played in the NBA, but never made the NBA Finals. So being able to watch him in both over the course of his life was a father's dream. Maybe I would have made the NBA Finals one year if it wasn't for that fucker Michael Jordan, but that's neither here nor there.

Yolanda wasn't able to travel during the summer. Unfortunately, she was recovering from foot surgery, so she couldn't see him play live. But she and Tim would talk on the phone every day. That just made me want to be with him more on the road, going from series to series. His big 2024 playoff moment came in the second round against the Oklahoma City Thunder. Except for the opening game, which OKC won, every matchup in the series was close. But Tim, wearing No. 10, was a big spark in Game Two. Coming off the bench, he scored 17 points, shooting 6–10 from the floor and 2–4 from three. He was a plus-15 in just 18 minutes, and Dallas won, 119–110. Without him, they might have gone down 0–2 to Shai Gilgeous-Alexander and OKC. In Game Three, he scored eight points in a 105–101 win for the Mavs, but his coach Jason Kidd, who I knew well from my NBA days and winning gold in Sydney, stopped playing him after that. It wasn't until a Dallas blowout in Game Four of the Finals that he got significant time. In that one, he shot 5–7 from three for 15 points. Doris Burke called him an "igniter" on the TV broadcast, and they even put my mug on the screen from my seat in the stands.

But that was all the action Tim got. As a father, that was tough to watch. Jason and GM Nico Harrison weren't communicating. I could see on Tim's face that he was hurting, and there were commentators making him the butt of jokes. I told him to just keep doing what he was supposed to be doing in practice. The team just never ran any offensive plays for him. In Dallas, Luka ran the whole show (until he was traded to the Lakers). But I just told Tim there would be new and better days to come. Parenting is not something that ever stops, and I was glad I could be there for him. To console him during a tough time in his career.

After the Finals, once Dallas lost 4–1 in the series, the team cancelled Tim's scheduled exit meeting, which we knew was fishy. Then, eleven days later, they traded him to the rebuilding Detroit Pistons. At least he was now close to home. I believe Tim will continue to have a bright future in the NBA (maybe one day he'll even play for the Heat!). My son has a brilliant basketball IQ and has helped every squad he's been on throughout his time in the league. Shoot, he averaged 17.8 points per game for Dallas during the 2019–20 postseason, and 17 a game in 2020–21. But that's okay. You got to get in where you fit in.

I'm just glad Tim is living his dream and glad he can do what he loves to do. That's all that matters to me as his dad. That's all that's ever mattered. I learned my lesson years ago not to impose what I want on him or on Nia and Nina. Today, Nina is a successful real estate agent in Atlanta, and Nia is working with animals at a veterinary hospital, which she loves. She also has a three-year-old daughter, Reza, who just melts my heart. Reza brightens up a room and puts giant smiles on her grandparents' faces. I love spending time with her. Family is so important, and I know that today better than ever.

Memory Lane: Tim Hardaway Jr.

When I think of growing up with my dad, a lot comes to mind. First off, it was hard-nosed. He always kept me humble. He never let me have the perks, the glam, or anything that resembled something flashy as a kid back then. He always kept me in my lane, appreciative of everything we had. I think that's because that's the way he grew up in Chicago. That was the only way he knew. He wanted to make sure I never got too high or cocky or spoiled, given the lifestyle that my siblings and I had growing up. It was a way of him making sure that we were always grounded.

As a dad, there were lots of phases. He loved us dearly as kids. He was a great father. Knowing what I know now as an adult, I know that it's hard to juggle your job and your life and your family and coming back home, getting the proper rest to go out there and perform. So now I can see why he was the way he was when my sisters and I were younger. He was great, but it also got to a point where he was tough on me. Not toward my sisters, but to me. Now I understand why but, back then, I didn't really get it. I'm pretty sure he was like that because his dad was the same way.

I later realized he had to understand that I wasn't brought up like he was. He didn't live in a big house with a huge backyard that could fit a full basketball court and a swimming pool and a playground and trees to climb on and friends with boats and a beach that you could drive to. He never had that. So, I had more options than he did. He saw basketball as a way out. I never really saw it that way. I didn't have to. I saw basketball as more of a hobby and something that I was good at. But don't get me wrong, to grow up in an NBA environment was incredible. It was cool to be around the guys.

You don't really know what's going on—all you know as a kid is that you're with your pops. You don't know any better, just that you're going to a game and they're rooting for your dad, then you get to go back home. But then you start getting older and when you're in elementary school and middle school you realize, *Oh shit, my dad is a big effing deal*! He's a huge deal. He's an All-Star. He's the guy in the city that all the kids run up to and want autographs. You start to see that. And then you really are excited about it. But then when you get to middle school and high school and you try to follow in your dad's footsteps, it can be tough.

Then it's a lot of people trying to bully you, trying to get under your skin. Some people just don't know how to take it. It's a pros and cons thing. The pros are that you're growing up in a privileged lifestyle with successful parents—because my mom had to take care of us, and she did a hell of a job. So I always give my mom credit for that. You grow up in a big house with everything you need. But the cons are that when you go outside that gate and you're following in your dad's footsteps, and you're performing how you perform, you have kids bullying you. Kids tell you you're not as good as your dad. Your dad sucks. You suck. You'll never be this, you'll never be that, you'll never make it. You're only doing this because your dad did it, but you'll never get anywhere. You're constantly hearing that. It's a gift and a curse. That's something I had to deal with in school. Then you're trying to defend yourself and you get in trouble or detention or suspended from school for a couple of days for fighting. It's hard, but I don't think there's anything I would have changed because you don't get to where I'm at by backing down. You would probably hear the same from any son following in his father's big footsteps in any job.

There are kids that grow up who want to be their father or want to be something and the only way to get through that is sacrifice, determination, and having integrity in yourself. Just having that all-out mindset of *I'm going to make it.* Whether someone is bashing me or not. But when I think of my dad, if there was one picture I would want to get of him, it would be a "before and after" photo. The "before" is where he's sitting down on the court in the front row, yelling at me and bashing me, trying to get me to do things and not see how hard I was trying to make him happy. Then the "after" picture would be where he is sitting high in the stands and keeping his mouth shut and watching me play. And seeing me do all the things that he has taught me and told me to do throughout the years. When he saw the amount of spirit and passion and energy and focus I had to do everything I could do to make him happy that day. The reason why I say all that is because the before picture was when he was, for me, at his worst. It was a dark time for me as a basketball player trying to find myself. And that's why I feel I'm in the position I'm in right now, because I had to try to fight through that. To make him happy.

I get emotional talking about this even today. Sometimes tears come to my eyes. There would be times when he wouldn't understand the amount of fight that I had to go through with everyone in my life. There would be times when he wouldn't understand that I had to fight not only him, but my peers. And I don't think he got that at first. It was like I was fighting him, my friends, and my teammates in order to make everyone happy, and sometimes it just felt like too much. That was the case from middle school until my freshman year of high school. Then the summer going into my sophomore year, everything changed.

It took someone else, my school's athletic director at the time, Miss Yvette McKinney (who sadly passed away several years ago), but it took her to tell him, "You can't be putting that much pressure on your son because it's affecting him and what he's going through in school." It took someone like her to tell him, "Sit up in the stands and see how hard he's trying to play to make you happy." And then when he did that, he finally saw me for me. Right after the game, he apologized and said, "I'm sorry for destroying the family, I'm sorry for putting you through all this bullshit, and I'm sorry for not letting you flourish."

He let me be the player I was always going to be, the one I was trying to be from early on. He told me he was going to be there for me and that he saw everything I was doing, everything that he'd asked of me. And he said, "I love you and I'm happy for you." I was smiling in my head, but I was also like, *What the hell's going on here?* while we were driving home in the car. *Why's he doing this right now?* But I was smiling inside—like, *finally*. And after that, it was just so much weight off my shoulders, so much weight, that it allowed me to flourish on and off the court. And now I'm *here*. I made it.

15

TAKING RESPONSIBILITY

VALENTINE'S Day. February 14, 2007. I'll remember it forever and regret what I said out of ignorance that day for the rest of my life. I'll also be making amends for it just as long. During my career, I talked a lot. I was known for it on the court. But the dumbest thing I said was in an interview with sports journalist and Miami radio host, Dan Le Batard. It wasn't just bad for the result it had on my career, but it was stupid for the impact it had on others—many of whom I'd never even met. It began like this: in February of 2007, the former 6-foot-10 NBA center John Amaechi came out as gay. With that, he became the first former player to make such a public statement.

Not long after that, I was in Las Vegas for the NBA All-Star Game doing camps and other stuff for the league. Someone from the PR department pulled me aside and asked if I wanted to talk to Dan for his radio show. I said sure, no problem. I knew Dan from Miami, and he'd always been a good guy and a fair journalist. Then at the end of our talk, Dan asked me, "Tim Hardaway, last question before we let you go. How do you deal with a gay teammate?" He was asking me, like any journalist would, about the topic because of Amaechi's recent revelation. And I could have said anything, including that I just live and let live.

But instead I said, "Whew. First of all, I wouldn't want him on my team. And second of all, if he was on my team, I would really distance myself from him because I don't think that's right and I don't think he should be in the locker room while we're in the locker room. And just a whole lot of other things. So I wouldn't even be a part of that. But stuff like that is going on and there's a lot of other people I hear like that that are still in the closet and don't want to come out of the closet. So, I just leave that alone." Dan then responded, "You know that what you're saying there, Timmy, is flatly homophobic, right? It's bigotry."

Then I doubled or even tripled down. "Well, you know, I hate gay people. So, I let it be known. I don't like gay people. I don't like to be around gay people. Yeah, I'm homophobic. I don't like it. It shouldn't be in the world or in the United States and I don't like it."

Ugh.

After that, my world came crashing down. The NBA pulled me from all my All-Star Weekend activities. My job with Trinity Sports dismissed me and I endured an avalanche of public ridicule and criticism from news outlets and television shows like ESPN's *Pardon the Interruption*. Now I'm talking about it all here because I'm not afraid to address anything I've done, dumb or not.

Why? Because my story may still be able to help other people. I don't want to leave anything out just because I'm ashamed of it or it's hard to relive. What I said to Dan haunts me every day, and I'm so sorry for it. But I've also grown a great deal. A lot of people since that 2007 interview told me that they thought Dan baited me into the conversation or that it was a trick question. A lot of people said they thought he was doing me wrong. But that's just not the case. *I* was the one who was wrong. It's not an excuse for my behavior, but my beliefs then about gay people had been seared into me as a child. And I spoke to Dan thoughtlessly based on them.

People all around me in Chicago had shitty nicknames for gay people when I was growing up. They said gay people would try to grab you and even pull you into the shadows. People made me scared of them. Growing up in the church didn't help either. The church instilled in me that to be gay was wrong. But the only thing wrong was me and my thinking. In the wake of what I said to Dan, people reached out to me. I heard from friends, my parents, and my wife about it. While they expressed support for me as a person, they told me in no uncertain terms that I had to change my thinking. They rightly suggested I seek counseling.

But the hardest part for me, personally, was seeing how much my actions had upset my kids. You could just see it on their faces. Disappointment. How much I'd hurt them. Not only did they see their dad now on the wrong side of something important, but they had gay friends and knew how upset they would be when they'd have to face them at school or work. I was so sorry to disappoint them. My first public apology came a few hours after my interview in a phone interview with FOX affiliate WSVN in Miami. "I'm sorry," I said. "I shouldn't have said I hate gay people or anything like that." I also released a statement with my agent the next day, on February 15.

I talked more about what I'd said, admitting I had no idea how much I hurt people. A lot of people. I quickly realized my comments were the biggest mistake I'd made in my life—and I admitted that I was going to do anything and everything I could to make it right. To correct what I'd done. I knew I couldn't change what some people thought of me. It's all you can do to change yourself. Even Oprah wanted me to go on her show to talk about that, but I knew I wasn't ready for that kind of public scrutiny. So I just made sure that I said something publicly to clear the air, to let the world know how wrong I was, and that I would get help.

But, at the same time, I knew that just saying I was sorry wasn't enough for me or anyone else. As the saying goes, it's about action not words. It's easy for people in trouble to play "apology bingo" and then hope everything blows over. But I didn't want that. I wanted to use this as a learning experience. To be a better person. So I set out to put one foot in front of the other and do the work needed to make amends. I knew I had to do some soul-searching. And after my conversation with Dan, I began to educate myself. That was the first step for me. I learned that what gay folks go through on a daily basis can be horrible. As a kid, I'd walked through Chicago scared of gangs, but many gay folks have to go through life scared of everyone around them, even people in their own homes. Their own parents may not accept them, let alone let them live under the same roof. I realized that the LGBTQ community often went through hell, and the last thing they were trying to do was harm me. One of the worst parts about the whole experience was that I have gay people in my family and now I was one of those people hurting them. Cousins, nephews, and friends of mine are gay. I knew they were gay, but it had never come up in conversation between us—now I know why. But when I realized what

I'd said, I thought about them, and it made me sick. Not only did I hurt myself, but I hurt people in my family, people I cared about. What I said hurt all of us.

I really don't know why I wasn't thinking about them when Dan asked me his question. I really don't. But I wish I had. I know I'm not the only person who has dealt with unhealthy thoughts about gay folks, too. Even Magic Johnson had to overcome his own issues. That started with his son, EJ, who is gay. For a long time, Magic struggled with that fact. But through education and understanding, he sorted out his issues and now Magic and EJ love one another deeply. For my part, it was about two weeks after the interview with Dan when I went to counseling. It came after a conversation I had with NBA commissioner David Stern.

I'd had a few interactions with Stern before in my career. Shaking hands, talking here and there. I had a lot of respect for him, but we didn't know each other all that well. He was a good man and all the players could talk to him like a friend for the most part. But that wasn't exactly the case on this occasion. My agent and I went to his office a week or two after my conversation with Dan, and Stern . . . well, he ripped me a new one. He cussed me out—and I deserved it. "What the fuck were you thinking?!" "Why did you say some bullshit like that?!" I'd heard about him cussing people out, but now I knew what it was like firsthand.

Stern made me feel really small that day, and I had to go ahead and just take it. I understood what he was talking about, and he was right to do it. But then after he was done, he talked to me and said, "Tim, you're going to do right. And I believe that you're going to do right because I read good things about you."

Stern didn't tell me exactly what to do. He didn't tell me how to go about it. He just said, "I believe that you're going to do right and you're going to be okay from this." I responded, "Okay, Mr. Stern." But I had to pick my face up from the floor. After I left his office, I sought out a proper counseling center so that I could educate myself.

That's when I found myself at The Yes Institute, a South Miami–based suicide prevention group that focuses on LGBTQ youth and offers counseling to people like me. That place helped me a lot and, to this day, I tell people that if they want to be educated about the LGBTQ community, go to The Yes Institute. When I was there, we focused on a lot of empathy techniques. I remember sitting on benches and having conversations with people there. I enjoyed the experience tremendously and was given a new understanding of the gay community. I knew through and through what I said to Dan was not only wrong, but immensely misguided.

And, to their credit, the people at The Yes Institute were so very kind and welcoming. They told me they understood my situation, why I said what I said, how I grew up misinformed. They knew that I had to change my mind, and were there to help me with an understanding perspective. They respected my choice to come in and see them. A lot of people who say hateful things don't do anything past a quick apology. But I knew that wasn't going to be enough for me. I'm so grateful for The Yes Institute's help. The people there could have shunned me. They could have been horrified by me. But they treated me with respect and, in turn, my eyes were opened.

* * *

I want to talk now a little bit about faith. As a kid, I went to a Baptist church with my grandma, Minnie. I remember not exactly being excited to attend, but she dragged me up in the morning and made me go with her. When you're nine years old, church can feel like punishment. But as an adult, there is a lot of good to find. You start going and listening and identifying with things that are helpful. My father's mother, Julia, was also religious. To both, the Word was the Word. They would quote the Bible at least once a day. If you ever talked back about it, they'd say, "Stop sassing me, boy!" So I grew up believing in God and the way of life the Bible espoused.

But while the general lessons of discipline and responsibility are good, the downside of all this religion is that you can take some things too literally—and that's what I did. At times, religious people can be so caught up in adhering to the Word of God that they can forget about people who are just trying to live day to day. It's easy to become close-minded that way. To let your view of the world narrow. I'm not saying that either of my grandmothers were that way. I do know, though, that I didn't let myself question enough of what I heard in church. And that, combined with everything I heard about on the streets about gay folks, colored my opinions.

In the end, it's my fault, though. I was the one who didn't do the work. I was the one who didn't consider the lives and feelings of my family members, gay or not. I was the one who said those things to Dan, and I am the one who has had to deal with the consequences ever since. I accept that. I just want people to know that I'm trying, and have been trying, since that Valentine's Day in 2007. This is something I'll never live down—I know that. I live through it every single day. I think about it every day.

While I've forgiven myself, it's always there. I've tried to move forward, but someone always brings it up. Someone always has something to say about it.

We say we live in a forgiving culture, but what I said is not something the world can easily forget. And I understand it. I wish it was different. What I told Dan has cost me sponsorships and jobs. Companies like Nike distanced themselves. Even if I'm the perfect guy for a gig, a company will say they won't hire me because they say people are still thinking about what I said. It's just not something the world can get past. I dug my own grave. So be it. But at least I know in my own heart that I've grown. I can't demand forgiveness. I can only trust that the people who truly mean something to my life know who I am because I know who I am.

As Pat Riley says, "Adversity introduces a man to himself." I've had to look in the mirror and say to myself often, "Get better. Get better." Along with my own internal growth, a small benefit to my stupid big mouth has been the recognition that those sorts of comments should never be tolerated. It was a reminder to athletes and to the world at large that ideas like that are wrong, plain and simple. Violence of any kind toward the LGBTQ community should never be tolerated. At the same time, I'm not taking credit for any of that awareness. But I know it happened. Others did some self-evaluation because of me. I can take solace in that. It's a silver lining.

* * *

After I'd educated myself on the subject, I began to put my new perspective into action. In 2009, I began to work with the Trevor

Project, a national suicide hotline for gay youth. It's important for me to say here that you aren't your lowest or worst day. If you've made a big mistake in life, you can come back from it. You can be better tomorrow. And I worked to prove that as much as I could. With the Trevor Project, I helped them raise money. It was important for me to put time in and prove to myself that I meant what I said when I made my apologies. This was not anything I wanted political "points" for.

A few years later, in 2011, I went down to El Paso to fight against religious conservatives who were behind a recall effort to remove local government officials who were pro marriage equality, including then-mayor John Cook. As a Black man, I know what unjust discrimination is like and I should have always realized that was the case with gay people, too. But now I was ready to fight for my brothers and sisters in Texas. I told folks in El Paso who were fighting against marriage equality to, "Grow up and catch up with the times." People who love one another should be allowed to marry, plain and simple.

I talked about my former UTEP coach, Don Haskins, who was at the forefront of racial equality in the 1960s. "A lot of people said, 'What is Don Haskins doing?' But El Paso understood." I also said during a press conference, "It's not right to not let the gays and lesbians have equal rights here. If I know El Paso, like they came together when the 1966 team won a championship and Don Haskins started those five [Black] guys, I know the city will grow and understand that gays and lesbians need equal rights." I know that to some, it may have seemed like a PR stunt, but in my heart I knew I was doing the right thing.

A couple years later, in 2013, I was the first person to sign a petition for a ballot initiative to allow same-sex marriage in

Florida. The organization Equal Marriage Florida launched a petition to amend the definition of marriage as described in the state constitution, and I wanted to help the group make a statement. So I went downtown to city hall and added my signature. I wanted to show that change was possible. That it was okay to be open to the rights of the LGBTQ community. I said, "If you're married, you're married—you should see your significant other in the hospital, make choices for your significant other if you need to make those choices."

Listen, I know I've said it already, but what I said to Dan was wrong. It was born of an ignorant, macho place and I learned quickly that I'd added fuel to the fire, allowing people to ridicule and "other" our brothers and sisters in the LBGTQ community. I've never been a bully in my life. I know what it's like to be hit, to be hurt, and to be made fun of for who you are. If I'd stopped to think about that for three seconds when it came to gay folks, I would have never had said what I'd said. Perhaps my homophobia was a way to make myself feel better for all the abuse I'd incurred earlier in my life—I don't know. But what I do know is that if I can change, you can change.

In 2013, another NBA player came out and announced he was gay. Center Jason Collins became the first active player in a major sport to make such an announcement. The former Nets big man who had played with the team in back-to-back NBA Finals made headlines with that. When I heard the news, I called Jason to support him. I congratulated him on his decision to make the public statement and I told him I was happy for him. You can't hold something like that in, I said, because if you do, you're going to be walking on eggshells all day long. And I told Jason that I hoped no one would judge him for his decision. I said he had a friend in me. Today, if I hear young people say dumb crap like I'd said, I straighten them out and make them understand why it's wrong. That's important to me, too.

* * *

A couple years ago, I realized I'd never called John Amaechi to formally apologize to him. Someone had reached out to me to let me know that. I thought I had, but I realized I'd just done so in public, not man to man. So I made it a point to call John and talk to him personally and apologize. I'd heard he was skeptical about my attempt to make amends and to change. I understood that. People see a public person make a mistake and then apologize and it can seem like a stunt. But when I called John, I told him how sorry I was. I told him it was beneath me to say what I did, and I should never have done anything to make him feel less-than.

I also told him that I never should have said anything like that about a former colleague, either. Thankfully, John accepted my apology, hearing the remorse in my voice. He said he appreciated me giving him a call and talking to him about it. We wished each other well and said that if we were ever in the same place, we could sit down and talk (John works as a psychologist today in London, England). Some believe he worked behind the scenes to keep me out of the Basketball Hall of Fame for a number of years, but he did nothing of the sort. I'm just happy the air is clear, and we can both move on with our lives.

As for me and Dan, I still see him all the time. He apologized to me, saying he was sorry that our conversation led to such an outcome. Sorry he asked me that question. But I told him repeatedly he did *nothing* wrong. He has nothing to apologize for—he's just trying to be nice to me because he's a standup guy. He's a reporter and was just doing his job. It was my blunder, my screw up. My head that needed examining, not his. Today, I'm just glad I was able to learn and fix what was wrong in my mind. Life is about change. Change is the only constant. Now I can only hope that other people understand that.

16

FROM THE SOUTH SIDE TO SPRINGFIELD

LIFE is remarkable. Sometimes it can feel like a series of rejections after rejections. But then everything can change in a moment. That was the case for me when it came to the Naismith Memorial Basketball Hall of Fame. It was 12:01 p.m. one afternoon when my phone rang. I was in the gym working out. The Caller ID read, "Hall of Fame." For the past five years leading up to that day, a man named John was on the other end. He calls everybody with *the* news. And each time so far, he'd told me, "Tim, I'm sorry, but I don't have any good news for you today." Knowing it was John on the other end of the line again, my hand started to shake.

I was sweating, scared to even answer it. I thought, *God damn, do I even touch this phone? I have to answer it, right?* I couldn't hear another rejection from John. But when I finally took a deep breath and picked it up, John spoke to me on the other end and said, "My man, I finally got some good news for you!"

Tears streamed from my eyes. They'd already started gathering even before I picked up the phone. But now they were free to fall. When I got to the gym that summer afternoon, I knew my phone might ring, but I didn't want to think about it. Then when I heard the sound, my stomach turned. Finally, though, it was good news.

John continued. "I want to congratulate you on being inducted to the Naismith Hall of Fame class of 2022." I thanked him repeatedly. And then when we hung up, after the five-minute call, I just sat there for two or three more minutes, thanking God, saying, "Thank you, thank you!" It had been a long time coming—likely largely due to my own mistakes—but the day was here. Jubilation ran through my veins. Patience paid off. While no one told me directly that my comments on Dan Le Batard's radio show held up my entry into the Hall of Fame for fifteen years, it was the only conclusion to come to. And if it was, I understood.

Some said I should've never made it because of what I said, while others knew I'd worked hard to earn forgiveness. But however we got here, we were here now. One of the greatest (small) point guards of all time with one of the best handles ever was now part of the Hall of Fame! As far as I'm concerned, all's well that ends well. After I got the call, I had to decide which Hall of Famers I'd ask to help induct me. One of my first calls was to Mully. I told him, "Chris! I'm in!" He was so happy for me. We laughed and he congratulated me. Then I called Mitch, "Mitch! I'm in!" And he said, "In *what*?" Ha! But both guys were there for me on my big day.

They were joined by the great Detroit Pistons point guard Isiah Thomas and the former WNBA MVP and Carver High

School graduate from Chicago, Yolanda Griffith. I'd also wanted Tiny Archibald there, but he was unable to attend due to health reasons. Nevertheless, my Hall of Fame weekend was incredible. Truly, making it is my biggest accomplishment as a basketball player. It was the period—no, the exclamation point—on my entire career. Not everyone can make the Hall of Fame, but I'm grateful that I did. My name is etched forever in stone in Springfield, Massachusetts. No one can take that away from me. Officially one of the greatest players ever.

The best part about the weekend was having my parents there (even if they still don't exactly get along, which I also understand). For me, their presence stood out the most. It was beautiful to have my wife and kids with me and my little brother Donald. But my parents have been with me through everything. From the very beginning. And they've each always had confidence in me and stayed positive even when few others would. When I was going through the worst stretch of my life after my conversation with Dan, my parents were very supportive. They both let me know I was wrong in what I said, of course. Like good parents are supposed to do. They talked to me and made me understand what I did was bad, what I said was wrong, and that I shouldn't be talking about other people that way. They didn't curse me out or distance themselves, but they expressed disappointment. They also told me I was going to make it right. That they knew my heart was good and that I'd be okay. My parents know me well, and to have them at the Hall of Fame ceremony in 2022 meant the world. The only sad note was that my agent, Henry Thomas, wasn't there to experience it. He'd passed away five years earlier from Lou Gehrig's Disease. I wish he could have been there since we'd made the NBA together.

* * *

As professional basketball players, we owe so much to the fans. So I was glad to spend the HOF weekend meeting lines of them, signing tons of autographs and doing interviews. Afterward, though, it was time to accept my place in Springfield. It was humbling to be inducted with the rest of the class of 2022, including people like Manu Ginóbili, George Karl, Swin Cash, Lindsay Whalen, Del Harris, and Bob Huggins. When it came to my moment, the great NBA broadcaster Ahmad Rashad gave me a terrific introduction. He began, "It's often said that a journey of 1,000 miles begins with a single step . . ."

Then it was time for the punchline. He continued, "But in the case of Tim Hardaway and his journey into basketball immortality, it might be more accurate to suggest that it all began with two steps—or more precisely, the UTEP Two-Step!" Ahmad always did have a way with words! The Hall played video snippets of guys like Nellie, Zo, Riley, and Mully saying nice things about me and my game. Then it was time for me to talk. I thanked all the people there supporting me, from my wife and kids to Isiah, Yolanda, Mully, and Mitch. I thanked Donald Pittman, Nellie, Don Haskins, Micky Arison, Pat Riley, and all my Heat teammates.

Lastly, I took a moment to thank all the people in the NBA offices who stuck by me. I'm sure it wasn't easy. People like Jerry Colangelo and Adam Silver and the late David Stern. "Men who never wavered in their belief in me, even when it wasn't always popular." And I concluded the speech saying this victory was bigger than just me. It was for the entire south side of Chicago.

"I can't name all y'all, but y'all know who you are and I love you to death. Thank you from the bottom of my heart." When it was all over, my spirit was full. I'd done what I'd always hoped: I sent love to the people who made me who I am. What could be better?

After the speech, I got my gold Hall of Fame jacket—it fit like a glove. When I put it on, I pantomimed a killer crossover with a giant smile on my face. Then someone asked me who in today's NBA has a crossover like Tim Hardaway. I laughed and said, "Nobody!" When the NBA started up its next season, the Miami Heat honored me with a Tim Hardaway Night. And I got to thank the city, the fans, and everyone in the organization. When people come out to honor you like that, it makes you know that you did your job right. That you brought joy to people's lives every night. That same year, the Warriors threw a Run-TMC Night, too. I was on cloud-nine.

Today, I'm the same Tim Hardaway. Making the Hall of Fame was the cherry on my basketball sundae. But, at the same time, it didn't *change* me. I'm still a Chicago guy who cares about the next generation, personal growth, the game of basketball, and representing my values the best I can. I tell young people all the time: get an education, stay out of the streets, if you don't want to do something then don't do it, and be the best you can be. The Hall didn't make me a guy who walked with his chest puffed out, because I've always been confident in who I am. Coming from where I come from and doing what I did, you have to be that way.

I'd have to imagine it's the same for most pro players as well. It takes a lot to make it to the top of your craft in any field, which is why I have so much respect for past generations and those still achieving greatness today. Some of the former legends that used to get me geeked were Jerry West and Julius Erving. One time when I was in maybe sixth grade, Dr. J signed a napkin for me after a game in Chicago. I didn't have a piece of paper, but I wanted his signature so bad that I found a napkin. Then I lost it 20 minutes later! But what I remember most was seeing Doc dunk in the Chicago Arena. I was in heaven! That's why I stood outside in the cold waiting for him.

Guys I enjoy watching today include LeBron James (I remember seeing him when he was sixteen years old playing pickup in Chicago, he jumped from the free-throw line in a game and it was like a cartoon), James Harden (who uses my crossover every game), Kawhi Leonard, Paul George, Ja Morant, Stephen Curry, and Draymond Green. It's players like that who make me think the NBA will be full of talent and stars for years to come. But people have short memories. And that's why I wanted to do this book. To tell my story in full, to show how I grew up and what I had to do to achieve greatness and deal with the ups and downs of life, all my bumps and bruises. I feel good today, though I know there is always room for improvement. If there's one thing for sure about me it's that I'm not ashamed to admit where I need to get better.

Life doesn't stop. I'm grateful for every morning I wake up and can greet the day. I'm a grandpa now, which I adore. It's all about family for me these days. I know that I've done enough in my life. I'm just trying to stay healthy, work out, stay away from too much beer, enjoy a cigar here and there, and be there for my kids and granddaughter. My parents are still alive and in their eighties, which is a blessing. My father is doing well today. We have a good relationship, thank God. He knows that I don't forget those early years, but I can and do forgive them. Alcoholism is a disease and, sadly, it's taken some great people. He's worked hard to overcome it.

During the NBA season, I do radio for FOX Sports 1, as well as some speaking engagements around the country, along with summer camps and traveling for the league. I just went to Singapore to teach the game of basketball to kids, which was great fun. I never turn down a chance to see the world, meet young fans, and show them the fundamentals. The best players in the world have their fundamentals down, so that tells you how important they are. In life—just as in ball—they're key, which is why I'm glad my parents instilled in me a sense of street smarts and frugality. I'm also the vice president of Banneker watches, if you're looking for a timepiece!

Truly, all things considered, I can't complain. When I look back on my time in the NBA, what I loved most was the camaraderie, the competition, crossing people over, making big buckets, and recovering from the failures that are part of any career. Growth is more important than success. I was a five-time All-Star and All-NBA player, an MVP finalist in 1997, an Olympic gold medalist, and now a Hall of Famer. My number is retired in high school, college, and the pros. I made the fourth most threes in the entire 1990s and dished the fourth most assists as well. On top of that, I was the 1989 WAC Player of the Year at UTEP, and invented a signature move.

There were other achievements along the way, but my head's plenty big at the moment! What I'll remember most when I'm a hundred years old and in a nursing home is the Run-TMC days and all those victories with my Miami Heat brothers. But the most important part of my life has been the ability to go from one side to the other. From the gangs of Chicago to the solace of El Paso. From an abusive home to the NBA. From west coast to east. From expressing hate toward the LGBTQ community to being a big proponent of human rights. From a pushy dad to a supportive one. From zero scholarships to a lottery pick. From injured to the NBA's best point guard.

* * *

Every summer these days, I make a trip out to Cincinnati, Ohio. A few years ago, one of my brother's friends asked if I would hold a basketball camp in the city, which I was happy to do. Cincy used to have the Royals, an NBA team with greats like Oscar Robertson and Tiny Archibald. But now, the only basketball presence they have are universities like Cincinnati and Xavier. Today, we get so many kids signing up that it's almost overwhelming. But we have a lot of fun. We have some great counselors, too. I love talking to the campers about how they work on their game. At times, though, some will tell me they aren't able to work on their game on their own.

I know they don't mean anything negative by it, but it always hurts my heart to hear somebody say that. If you really, truly want to improve, get better, be your best, you will find a way to do the work on your own. I worked on my game on my own tirelessly as a youngin. I rode my bike—which was always missing its seat—to basketball courts. Climbed up the pole and put my own net on the rims and worked the entire court with dribbling drills, shooting drills, sprints, and everything else, inventing imaginary defenders and last-second scenarios. Basketball is a sport—maybe the only sport—that you can get better at on your own like that.

In the Chicago elements, I worked on layups, floaters, stop and pops, coming off pretend screen and rolls, in and out moves, free throws, half-court shots, sprints from sideline to sideline—all on concrete. During the day, when the summer sun was burning or the winter winds were frigid! All of those are things *you* can do, too. You don't need a fancy gym, hardwood court, new nets, pristine leather basketballs. You just need yourself and the will to improve. It's because of this work that, when people ask me today about my career, I can tell them I'm satisfied. There are always ways to criticize a guy like me who never won a championship, but a ring doesn't make you.

If Charles Barkley was on the 1997 Bulls instead of Dennis Rodman, would that make him any different? Same with Patrick Ewing, Chris Mullin, Reggie Miller, Allen Iverson, John Stockton, or Karl Malone. What you can't take away from someone is the hard work they put in every day. The willingness to get better and stay great. The fortitude and confidence to put in the effort. Everything else? Let the chips fall where they may. I made headlines in the NBA at 5-foot-11-and-three-quarters. I gave people something to cheer for every night. That's my win. Home or away, the audience wanted to see that shake and bake. That killer crossover.

INDEX